W9-DEE-470

Representing the Republic

PICTURING HISTORY

Series Editors
Peter Burke, Sander L. Gilman, Ludmilla Jordanova,
Roy Porter, †Bob Scribner (1995–8)

In the same series

Representing the Republic

Mapping the United States 1600–1900

John Rennie Short

REAKTION BOOKS

GA
405
.S466
2001

For Lisa
for everything

Published by Reaktion Books Ltd
79 Farringdon Road, London EC1M 3JU, UK

www.reaktionbooks.co.uk

First published 2001

Copyright © John Rennie Short 2001

All rights reserved

No part of this publication may be reproduced,
stored in a retrieval system, or transmitted, in any
form or by any means, electronic, mechanical,
photocopying, recording or otherwise,
without the prior permission of the publisher.

Series design by Humphrey Stone
Printed and bound in Great Britain by Biddles Ltd,
Guildford and King's Lynn

British Library Cataloguing in Publication Data

Short, John R. (John Rennie), 1951–
    Representing the Republic: mapping the United States,
    1600–1900. – (Picturing history)
    1. Cartography – United States – History 2. United States –
    Maps
    I. Title
    912.7´3´09

ISBN 1 86189 086 9

4433367I

Contents

Acknowledgements

Books may have individual authors, but their production is deeply bound up in wider social connections. The research and writing of this book would have been impossible without the generosity and support of a number of institutions and individuals. The work in the first section grew out of my visits to the New York State Library in Albany. I was awarded the New York State Library Research Residency for 1995, which allowed me great access to the map collection, free photocopying, and special assistance. During my many visits, Paul Mercer and his colleagues introduced me to the collections and responded to my questions. In Albany, I met Dr Leslie Mano, who very graciously allowed me access to her work, her insights, and her knowledge.

In March 1996, I took up an Andrew Mellon Visiting Fellowship at the American Philosophical Society in Philadelphia. During my one-month stay, the director and staff were extremely gracious. Roy Goodman, in particular, was very generous with his time and support. I was also invited by the society and Professor Edward C. Carter II to make a presentation at a conference they held in 1997. This provided me with an opportunity to collect my random thoughts and scattered notes.

In the summer of 1996 I was a participant at the National Endowment for the Humanities Summer School in the History of Cartography held at the Newberry Library in Chicago. The summer school allowed me to learn from Barbara Belyea, David Buisseret, Michael Conzen, Bob Karrow and David Woodward as well as from all the other nineteen participants.

At Syracuse I have made constant use of the map library and special collections in the university's Bird Library. Staff in the Geography Department were most helpful: Kate Steinmetz proof-read a wild and woolly manuscript; Marcia Harrington scanned a large number of illustrations and Mike Kirchoff drew a number of maps.

Syracuse University awarded me a sabbatical leave in the spring semester of 1996, which gave me time to think and write, and an Appleby-Mosher award which covered some of the photographic costs.

I photographed all of the maps myself, but would have been unable to do so without the help of staff at the libraries in Albany and Philadelphia and at the library of Congress in Washington, DC.

The book is dedicated to Lisa. She has lived with this project, nurturing my obsessions, soothing my fears. She has encouraged, consoled, and loved me during the entire period from vague idea to completed text. This book is a small token of my enduring love and affection.

Introduction

Not only is it easy to lie with maps, it's essential.[1]

Geographic Representation

The world is imagined and represented in a variety of ways. I will focus on the geographic representations and cartographic imaginings of one particular part of the world: the area now known as the United States in the period from 1600 to 1900.

This book is a continuation of ideas on the relationship between nation-states and the spatial environment that I first mapped out in my book *Imagined Country*.[2] There I developed the idea of national environmental ideologies and their representation in cinema, novels and landscape painting. Here I focus on national geographic representations and their expression in maps.

Geographic representation involves books, paintings, music, rituals, festivals and maps. Here I am primarily concerned with maps, though I use a wider definition than most: texts which include both maps and the discourses that enframe these maps. In subsequent pages the term 'map' will be used to cover this enframing. This book will provide a detailed study of the practice and politics of imperial and national representation by examining geography texts and associated maps and mapmaking.

The geographic representation of the USA, as in other countries, has been concerned not only with the depiction of place but also the mapping of encounters with the physical world and the social other. The mappings of the encounters not only reflect but also embody conceptions of the physical world and the social other. Maps not only reflect physical space, they embody social order. Geographic representations 'inscribe not only the physical space across which the men and women of the past lived their lives but also the changing social orders within which they were constrained to act'.[3]

Maps are not neutral transmitters of universal truths, they are not bearers of neutral knowledge. Maps are social constructions, fictions if you like, narratives with a purpose, stories with an agenda. They are not mirrors of nature. Their reflective power is rather more subtle and more complex. They indicate the degree of technical progress; they suggest the limits of knowledge and embody the knowledges and ignorances, articulations and silences, of the wider social world. They bear the imprint of bias, selectivity and partiality.

Maps are a form of communication, a language with a chequered history, different genres, many authors, different readers, and multiple interpretations.[4] The project of the traditional history of cartography was to note the improving relationship between reality and the map. It was a story of cartographic improvement that held the existence of a solid singular reality as a basic assumption. It was an uplifting tale of how we have moved from the darkness of misinformation and ignorance of the past to a better, fuller, sounder view of the world. Books like Leo Bagrow's *History of Cartography*, Gerald Crone's *Maps and their Makers*, and Lloyd Brown's *The Story of Maps*[5] all present the story in the traditional history of science perspective: as an uncomplicated picture of greater precision and increasing knowledge all in a broad forward movement toward a more exact picture, an upward trajectory toward the glow of greater enlightenment. In the introduction to *Maps and Their Makers*, Gerald Crone writes: 'The history of cartography is largely that of the increase in the accuracy with which these elements of distance and direction are determined and in the comprehensiveness of the map content.'[6]

In his book, *The Mapmakers*, John Noble Wilford treats the history of cartography as 'the expanding reach and growing precision of cartography'.[7] There is some measure of truth to this assertion but demonstrating it is not my aim. Rather, I want to take the selectivity and partiality of maps as the very basis of this book to show how maps can tell us something about changing perceptions of the world.

Deconstructing the Map

In recent years, the history of mapmaking has been enlivened and enlarged by scholars making the connections between maps and wider issues of representation, the sociology of power and the political economy of knowledge. The postmodern perspective focuses less on 'reality' than on 'realities', less on improvement than on changing constructions. This view sees maps as constructions not reflections, as sources not illustrations, as texts full of silences and secrecies as much as utterances and enlightenment. This emerging school can be termed the new history of cartography, the social history of cartography, or the postmodern history of cartography. These names are used because they suggest an increased awareness of the cultural and social context of map production and consumption, and an engagement with wider debates about power and knowledge. Maps are no longer seen as a value-free, socially neutral depiction of the earth but rather as a social construction, a selective representation with biases and silences. As one of the most prolific cartographic commentators notes, 'Not only is it easy to lie with maps, it's essential.'[8] In this angle of vision, mapmaking is a selective process bearing the imprint of wider debates and the history of cartography is enmeshed in a net of wider social concerns and broader political concern. Scholars such as Brian Harley, Geoff King, David Turnbull, Denis Wood and David Woodward have all added to this new perspective. The work of the late Brian Harley, for example, shows the shift in the course of a lifetime's cartographic interest from the enlightenment story to the deconstruction school. Harley's early work looked at the rise of mapping in Britain from a traditional perspective. In his later work he was opening up an enormously interesting and productive field of inquiry that developed the notion of deconstructing the map, the hidden agendas of maps and the relationship between maps and power.[9]

The postmodern history of cartography has also been enlivened by historians who look at maps and mapping as important themes in their own right and as powerful metaphors for the exercise of power, resistance and contestation.[10] The postmodern turn that has emerged in many academic disciplines has raised issues of representation to new heights of importance. Maps and mapping are now important topics because they condense central issues of language, representation and power. Although this renewed interest in cartography is to be applauded, there is a danger of it remaining at the metaphorical level, for rhetorical use only, with the terms mapping, maps and cartography being used as general figures of speech, rather than as foci of renewed interest. In this book I seek to use maps as both metaphors and artifacts. The actual production and consumption of maps are key elements in my analysis.

Maps are complex constructions. A map is not just a text in the passive sense, an inscription to be decoded. It is also a theory, a story, a claim, a hope, a scientific document, an emotional statement, an act of imagination, a technical document, a lie, a truth, an artifact, an image, an itinerary, a mode, an inscription and a description. A map, like a speech act or musical event, is performative.

Maps are physical objects. They have a size, a shape, a look, a feel, a smell. In an age of mechanical reproduction, maps are often reduced to a reproducible image that gives us the image but not the feel of the text. Maps, whose meaning is found in their size and shape and smell, touch and wider textual context, can be distorted by being reduced to a standardized reproducible form. Walter Benjamin once queried the meaning of art in an age of mechanical reproduction. A similar question can be posed for the history of cartography. As we look at images of images, as old maps are standardized to fit the page of text, we perhaps lose as much as we gain. The images are easily reproduced but we no longer have their tactile meaning, their physical presence, their 'thereness' as things in the world.

The deconstruction of the map is not an easy task. The map is consumed as well as produced, and its consumption takes place across space and through time. While we may be sure of the production methods we can be less certain of the multiplicities of how the different messages of the map are consumed. The messages people take from a map cannot be read off from the intentions and techniques of the producers. A map produced over 300 years ago has been consumed in a variety of ways since its original production. The meaning of it is never fixed: even if the makers of the map had a simple message, creative readers can produce complex readings. Maps are open texts, perhaps some of the most open of texts because they do not have the linear discipline of written texts or the rigid conventions of some genres of painting. Maps are capable of multiple readings.

Three broad stories are told in this book. In the first, *Representing the State*, I look at geographic representation and its connection with colonial and imperial discourses of discovery and appropriation. Theoretical arguments are developed while original material is drawn from an analysis of the geographic representation of New York State from the early Dutch explorers to the American Revolution. By holding the area constant, by looking at different maps of the same state, we can focus more clearly on the more subtle shifts in representation. There are other stories to be told of the mapping and appropriation of the south and west, cartographic histories of the French, Spaniards, English and Germans, and explanations of the delineation of 'longlots' and ranchos. This is too big a story to tell in this book. I therefore concentrate on New York and do little justice to California,

Texas and Louisiana. However, although attention is focused on New York, on the Dutch and English in the north-east, it should be borne in mind that this is only a small part of the overall story of mapping in the territory of what became the United States.[11]

Attention is also paid to the cartographic encounters between the Europeans and the Native Americans. Beginning with the Block map of 1614 and ending with the state atlas of 1830, the emphasis will be on the changing depictions of landownership, Native Americans and civil boundaries in order to highlight the extension of European control over the landscape. I concentrate on the representations of the country by Europeans. This representation was never innocent of wider economic and political objectives. The New World was mapped and appropriated; the two went hand in hand. The connection is hinted at in Chinese, where the term for map, *tu*, when used as a noun, means chart, drawing, plan, or illustration, but as a verb it means to covet, to plan, to scheme. The New World was coveted and desired as well as mapped and traversed. I begin with a Dutch map that was part description, mostly claim. I then look at subsequent Dutch maps and later English, French and US maps of the region from the early seventeenth century to the early nineteenth century. This cartographic transect reveals much about the social meaning as well as the historical geography of the state. In this section, maps are primarily seen as claims to territory. The New World was appropriated and claimed by European powers, and these claims were represented in maps. These maps were an integral part of European rivalry for they contained imperial claims and challenges. The colonial maps are not so much simple descriptions of territory as claims to ownership, acts of domination, a cartographic legitimation of control.

The second, and largest part of the book, *Representing the Republic*, examines the development of a national geography that grew from the 1780s.

At the dawn of the American Republic, national identity was not a given. The revolutionary rupture created a radical break with the past. New identities had to be forged. Attempts were made at the creation of a distinctly American viewpoint in a range of areas from writing and language to politics and art. The search for national identity in the new republic also involved experiments in fine arts, architecture, fiction, science and philosophy, and linguistics. Shortly after the Revolution, Noah Webster wrote, 'Every engine should be employed to render the people of the country national, to call their attachment home to their country; and to inspire them with the pride of national character.' Some of the experiments are better known than others and their legacy continues. Webster himself published his *American Spelling Book* in 1783 and distinguished distinct American forms of spelling(e.g. the 'u' was dropped from 'colour' and 'labour', and the 're' was reversed 'theatre' and 'centre') and introduced such words as 'tomahawk' and 'prairies' – words not used by the English lexicographers.[12]

An important discourse was of geographical writing and map production. The need to write a national geography was part of the broader attempt at cultural independence and the deeper search for a national identity. To become independent a country needs to present and represent itself. It has to paint its own picture. Geographical representation was an important element in the presentation of the country. Jefferson's *Notes on Virginia* (1784–1785) was both a geographic description of his state and a counterblast to those Old World writers and scientists who derided the New World. A national geography was a portrait in words and maps, a collection of narratives that gave a picture and told the story of an emerging nation.

Two genres of geographical writing can be identified: informal and formal. Informal geographies, such as the *New Travels in the United States of America* by Jacques Brissot de Warville, translated from the French and published in New York in 1792, were part travel accounts and part geographical accounts. They were concerned with describing natural resources, providing hints on agriculture and suggesting further improvement. A strong boosterist rhetoric runs through these early accounts. Joseph Scott's *A Geographical Description of the States of Maryland and Delaware*, published in 1807 in Philadelphia, has the subtitle *Includes observations on internal improvements and manufactures*. The subtitle of Thomas Ashe's *Travels in America*, published in London and reprinted in Newburyport, MA in 1808, is *Offers data on the navigability of the rivers, also on salt springs, lead deposits, and manufacture enterprises*; while James Mease's 1811 *The Picture of Philadelphia* is subtitled *Giving an account of its origin, increase and improvements in arts, sciences, manufactures, commerce and revenue*, and Thaddeus Masin Harris's 1805 *The Journal of a Tour into the Territory Northwest of the Allegheny Mountains* has as subtitle *Includes observations on mineral resources and industrial enterprises*.

The more formal geography texts were also important. They constitute most of the body of schoolbooks in the eighteenth and early nineteenth century in the United States. Texts on history, for example, did not appear until the 1880s. These early geography texts were compendiums of knowledge, widely used in schools and the more literate homes. The early geography texts were the encyclopaedias of their day.

In the geographical writings and cartographic representations an emphasis was placed on the construction of a national geography, a description and representation of the territory of the fledgling nation. In the last two decades of the eighteenth century and the first two decades of the nineteenth century, some of the most important and best-selling books were geography texts and maps that created, advanced and codified a national geography. This project had a number of elements. We can identify four.

First, nationalist concerns were wrapped around more purely 'scientific' endeavours, such as accurate location and description of unknown territory. Geography was part of science and the more universal truths sought by the Enlightenment. Geography was considered a science and science is about universals, the search for laws that hold up across space and time. But there was a particular American concern to create and describe a particular American geography. The tension was between the search for scientific universals but also the perceived need to create a national geographic discourse. There was an ambiguity between the depiction of space and the construction of a national place: space and place, global debates and local concerns, an international language of science and the vernacular concerns of a particular nation. While geographical matters had a connection with the general language of science they also had a direct connection with national identity. This ambiguity was at the centre of geographic representation in the new republic, and the resultant tension between the two connections was most obvious in the use of a prime meridian. There is no natural starting point establishing the $0°$ of longitude, the prime meridian. Before the end of the nineteenth century it was an arbitrary designation that varied from country to country. The British established theirs at Greenwich. As we will see, the early American geographies used Greenwich, then Philadelphia and, later, Washington – some maps even had a dual system.

Second, the mapping of the national territory, especially at a time of geopolitical flux in the Far West, was also loaded with political significance as well as geographical science. There were a variety of strands to this discourse. Early forms of American exceptionalism and Manifest Destiny can be discerned. The geographies and maps both described and celebrated the extension of the national territory toward the Pacific, the intensification of settlement and the westward movement of the frontier.

Third, the geographies not only described and mapped national space, but they also sought to promote spatial unification. This unification was concerned with economic and political unity. The early atlases, for example, by bringing the individual states under one cover promoted national cohesion and national consciousness and the many geography texts that listed all the states helped create the construction of a national market and a national polity.

Fourth, moral geographies played a part in the national geographies. The national geographies were full of moral injunctions, social criticism and policy directives. With their implicit – and often explicit – dichotomy of nation/non-nation, these geographies also had an 'otherizing' quality that at times filtered into notions of moral purity, political correctness and consequent images of moral cleansing and political enemies. The 'others' identified by a variety of writers included Native Americans, foreigners, the French and Southerners. The discourse of national geography/identity was racialized, gendered and moralized. The Native Americans rarely figured as little more than blocks to westward progress. Women were rarely discussed.

There was no unitary national geography. The differences are exemplified by two of the most important writers of the time. Jedidiah Morse was the Protestant zealot, disdainful of the South and able to see conspiracy everywhere. His nationalism differed from that of John Melish, who emphasized promotion of immigration and the fostering of economic independence. Criticisms of slavery were raised by some of Morse's descriptions of the South, but this was lacking in writing by Melish, whose audience of emigrants was assumed to be all male. Because of his religious convictions, Morse also moralized the debate; his writings were theologically value laden and highly critical of moral backsliding, the South and liberal interpretations of Biblical injunctions. Whereas Morse saw a moral geography, Melish was more concerned with an economic geography.

The first section looks at maps that had limited circulation. Many of them are manuscript maps. In this second section — *Representing the Republic* – we move into a time when maps and geographical writings were reaching a wider audience through book and map publishing. A truly mass market did not appear until the 1840s. In the initial period of 1780 to 1840 there were limitations to mass production and consumption. Books and maps were expensive items; an important part of the material culture of the political and economic élites, they still were not cheap enough for mass consumption. There were also limitations on the use of illustrations and especially of maps in books. Most printed maps came from engravings on individual sheets which were often added to printed books by hand, an expensive and cumbersome method that restricted the wide use of maps in books. Of 49 geography texts published before 1840, 24 had no maps. In contrast, in the period from 1840 to 1890, when map production became much cheaper and easier, only ten of 97 geography texts had no maps.

The second section examines the contribution of some of the most important writers, geographers and mapmakers: Jedidiah Morse, John Melish, Henry Schenck Tanner and Samuel Augustus Mitchell. Attention will also be paid to the network of connections that made Philadelphia the nation's mapmaking centre from the 1790s to the 1860s. Close study of a range of writers and mapmakers shows that the discourse was varied and often conflicting. It is more accurate to think of national geographies as opposed to one geography and national identities rather than a single identity, because, even at this early stage in the life of the Republic, there were differences in the production and consumption of images and texts.

These writers and mapmakers contributed to the formation of an American identity. This is a point easier to assert than to prove. Although their texts were produced with a distinct aim in mind, the extent and way that they entered the national discourse is impossible to prove. Their works were selectively and creatively read by a small minority of the population – by the literate more than by the non-literate, the wealthy more than the poor, those in the north and central states more than the southern and western, the political and economic élites rather than the masses, the urban dwellers rather than the rural residents. There was no unitary national geography, national audience or national identity. A national identity was undercut by regional differences and along the fracture lines of race, class, religion and gender.

The project of a national geography was one of the major intellectual discourses of the new Republic. This national geography – like the nation itself – was paradoxical, ambiguous, richly varied, argumentative, full of conflict, unfinished.

The third and final part of the book – *Representing the Nation* – considers the mapping exercises involved in inscribing a national landscape, creating a national community and constructing a national economy.

A distinction can be made between a nation and a state. A nation is a community with a territorial affinity, a group of people with a shared identity and common allegiance. A state is the formal institution of power and coercion that has a monopoly of sovereignty over a particular territory. The relationship between nation and state can be problematic. Some states (such as Britain) have more than one nation and certain nations (the Kurds, for example) are not represented by a state. The United States is one of the more interesting examples because, apart from the Native-American population, there is a high degree of congruence between nation and state. Since the Civil War, there have been no separatist movements of note and even groups who consider themselves a distinct nation (such as the Nation of Islam) had, and have, no territorial affinity that can be considered separate. National identity and state formation thus play an important parallel role in the United States. Identity is bound up with state formation and the rituals of the state have become acts of national commemoration. The geographical construction of the state is intimately bound up with the territorial imagination of the nation. This imagining takes many forms. There are national histories, national characteristics and national claims to greatness in the course of world and regional history. 'National' events are enacted and re-enacted, 'national' stories are told and retold. National identity has become one of those basic assumptions that, in the words of Pierre Bourdieu, 'structure what is thought'.

The construction of national identity has been an important subject of recent writings. In an argument of great subtlety, Benedict Anderson argued that nations were not so much facts of race or ethnicity.[13] Rather, they were imagined communities. Anderson paid particular attention to the role of print capitalism in creating a national discourse. In a later elaboration, Anderson identified three institutions of power: the *census*, the *map* and the *museum* that together allowed the state to imagine the people under its dominance, the geographic territory under control and the nature of historical legitimacy.[14] In this book I want to concentrate on the *map*.

I want to look at the connections between the elaboration of a national geography and the construction of national identity. Attention has focused on the narrative of the nation and the connection with gender and race.[15] More focused studies have looked at ideas and practices of contested national landscapes, national environmental ideologies and competing sites of historical memory.[16] To take just one example: in an interesting study, Lyn Spillman examines how national identities are created through commemorative activities. Exhibitions, fairs and sites of historical memory and commemoration are common vehicles for celebrations and claims of national identity. In particular, she looks at the centennial and bicentennial celebrations in Australia and the United States. Her basic argument is that these 'big, dense, inclusive, but transient, rituals were mobilized by cultural centers to invite the participation of cultural peripheries'.[17] In the centennial celebrations (1876 for the United States, 1888 for

Australia) both countries were celebrating a century of sovereignty but an uneven and contested cultural unity. In both countries, the indigenous peoples were excluded. In the United States, however, women were making larger claims for cultural inclusion whereas in Australia organized labour was an important voice claiming a place in the national celebration. Both events practised a cultural exclusion. In the United States, Native Americans and African Americans were conspicuous by their absence in the nation that was celebrated; in Australia, women and Aborigines had a similar role on the far edge. The identity that was being celebrated differed markedly. The United States had been a sovereign nation for almost a century. Australia was still a fiction; federation would not occur for another twelve years and in 1888, it was still a series of states that took Britain as a pivotal source of identity, meaning and place in the world. In Australia, identity was bound up with ties to Britain and a national holiday was plausible but still struggling to emerge from state rivalries.

In both countries, the claims to nationhood involved founding moments, visions of progress, the international gaze, the glorious future, shared political values, national prosperity and images of the land. Although sharing this broad range, they differed in the relative weight. In the United States, more emphasis was placed on a political culture of freedom, especially the importance of the founding moment in 1776. In Australia, the founding moment was less significant. The year 1788 marked the beginning of an Antipodean Gulag, not the creation of an experiment in political freedom. In Australia the land was more central; images of landscape were more pivotal to identity than they were in the United States.[18]

In this part of the book, I am more concerned with the construction of a national geography and, in particular, in developing an understanding of the role of geographic representation in the formation of the state and the creation of national identity. The cartographic representation of territory is full of political significance and social meaning. By mapping a territory, the state reinforces its claim to power and dominance. Its claim to sovereignty is partly vindicated by its ability to map and represent the territory. The cartographic representation reinforces its claim to legitimacy. Maps of the state's territory suggest a permanence, the unfolding on paper of a 'natural' organism, the picturing of a 'natural' object beyond the winds of arbitrary adjustment or historical contingency. Maps embody space and make concrete particular places. Maps reinforce state dominance and also help in the creation of a national community. A national identity is fostered, encouraged and created by a shared cartographic depiction, a common cartographic understanding of the nation, its outline and its boundaries. A national community can even be defined by the widespread usage of the same cartographic convention. The saturation of cartographic images has created a widely accepted semiotics of states. Outline maps of the United States or Italy or the United Kingdom, for example, are easily recognizable; they are used as symbols of these nation-states with a quick and easy understanding. Maps of a nation-state are not just depictions of surface area or even representations; they also embody the nation-state.[19] Maps do not simply reflect or represent: they are.

In this third section, I look at the cartographic representation of the nation-state in the United States, paying particular attention to the period from 1865 to 1900. From the end of the Civil War to the close of the nineteenth century, the United States went through enormous changes: the expansion of the railway system, the industrialization of the economy, massive immigration from overseas, enormous urban growth, the creation of a national market, the growth of big business, the closing of the frontier, the increased settlement of the West, the enlargement of federal government and the creation of an overseas empire. In the last third of the nineteenth century, the United States became a more industrial-urban society, a more densely settled nation and a more important power in world politics. These changes were recorded, embodied and reflected in maps.

After the Civil War, there was a cartographic explosion as many more maps were produced and available to a wider, broader audience. The decreasing cost of cartographic images meant that their purchase percolated down the income scale, becoming part of the national debate, the national image, and an integral part of the way the country was represented. These cartographic representations gave shape, form and embodiment to the expanding and evolving nation. A rich variety of maps were produced and consumed: county maps, state maps, survey maps, maps of the country and of the city, maps produced by public and private agencies, maps made by small firms, maps made by big companies, maps made by local, state and central governments. These maps were sold, read, displayed, presented, distributed and consumed throughout the country.

Maps are important texts that provide an invaluable and innovative way of illuminating wider social processes. In the following chapters, I examine a range of maps/mappings and their relationship to the history of the late nineteenth-century United States. In particular I focus on the inscribing of the national landscape, the mapping of the national territory, the describing of the national community and the locating of the national economy.

Together the three sections provide a narrative of geographic representation, which, on the one hand, develops the general theory of geographic representation, while, on the other, also highlights the particular connection between geographic representation and national identity in the USA, with special attention paid to the pivotal period after independence when a 'new mode of thinking' was introduced.

The three main sections also give an indication of the variety of geographic representations of the United States. The first section looks at geographic representations as claims to territory; the second section analyzes them as important elements in the construction of the new republic; the third section examines them in relation to the creation of national identity in the mature republic. Imperial claims, state definitions and national ideologies merge one into another, eliding and shifting as claims become taken-for-granted facts of state territorialization that in turn are constantly (re)interpreted into national narratives.

The context of geographic representations differs in the three sections. In the first section, they are documents, often rare manuscripts, circulating within a narrow range of users. In the second section, they have a wider circulation, appearing in books and articles and as independent artifacts. They have become part of the embodied discourse of a literate élite. In the third section they are part of an even wider discourse –they are readily and cheaply available to a range of readers. Atlases, maps and formal geographic texts have joined the more public discourse of mass literate society. Through the years the consumption of geographic representations shifts from political élites to encompass mass society. Maps not only reflect the nation-state; they condense the national community.

PART I

Representing the New State

1 'The Seeking Out and Discovery of Courses, Havens, Countries, and Places'

> We understand it would be honorable, serviceable, and profitable to this country, and for the promotion of its prosperity, as well as for the maintenance of seafaring people, that the good Inhabitants should be excited and encouraged to employ and occupy themselves in the seeking out and discovery of Courses, Havens, Countries, and Places which have not, before now, been discovered or frequented.[1]

At their heart and origin all creation myths have a basic mystery. It is fitting therefore that this crafted tale begin with an uncertainty.

In the chronological card index of the map collection of New York State Library, kept on the eleventh floor of the Cultural Education Center building in Albany, one of the very first entries in the section dealing with maps of the state of New York is dated 1616. The title on the card is *Map of New Netherlands.*

This would seem a definite beginning? A good place to begin? Not so. The intellectual security is illusory. The map is not quite as it appears in the index. The date of the 'original' is a mistake. It should be 1614. The map was 'missing' for years and was discovered in the Royal Archives in The Hague in 1841. A copy was made in that year and the New York State Library text is a facsimile of that copy. There may even be no original. It could even be a forgery. The uncertainty is a humbling reminder of the instability and speculative nature of all intellectual endeavours.

A map shrouded in mystery, with an uncertain past, a hazy origin, subsequent and multiple copies. This is a good place to begin.

The map first appears in historical records at a meeting in 1614 of the States General of the United Provinces. They liked to call themselves Their High Mightinesses, and they constituted the federal assembly of the seven provinces of the Dutch Republic: Gelderland, Holland, Zeeland, Utrecht, Friesland, Overijssel and Groningen.[2] This was a loose federation; sovereignty resided in the estates of each of the provinces, and these estates were dominated by wealthy merchants.

Each estate had one vote in the States General, which acted as the official representative of the republic and was responsible for foreign affairs and the regulation of international trade. The republic and the States General were dominated by Holland, which was the wealthiest province with the largest navy. In recognition of Holland's centrality, the States General met in The Hague. The meeting in question took place in The Hague on 11 October 1614.

Imperial Decline and Ascendancy

The early seventeenth century marked a transition in European and world affairs that involved a shift in global power northward away from Spain towards France, England and the Netherlands. The sixteenth century had belonged to Spain; it had carved out a huge overseas empire in the Americas and amassed a considerable fortune, which allowed the Spanish Crown to pursue its role as defender of the Catholic faith in Europe. The very success of its imperial position was to provide the basis of its subsequent decline. Spain illustrates an early example of what historian Paul Kennedy describes as 'imperial overstretch'.[3] Superpowers arise on the basis of their military and economic strength. Challenges, however, are made to their dominance, and to maintain their position more of the resources are devoted to shoring up their geopolitical position and defending the frontiers of insecurity. Imperial commitments undercut the economic strength of the state. Spain was committed to ensuring its continued dominance in the Americas, safeguarding its commercial trade, and fighting numerous wars in Europe, especially against the Protestant English and the Moslem Turks. Imperial overstretch was heightened by the massive increase in the costs of war, the failure of the Spanish Government to raise enough taxes, and the existence for Spain of 'too many enemies to fight, too many frontiers to defend'.[4] There were recurring state fiscal crises caused by increasing royal expenditure yet declining income as the mines in Spain's American empire began to run dry. By 1600, interest payments totalled two-thirds of all state revenues and by the 1650s, Spain was no longer a superpower.

If Spain was on a downward slide at the beginning of the seventeenth century, the Netherlands was on an upward swing. The Netherlands achieved wealth and power through the creation of a worldwide trading system. Trade and commerce were the lifeblood of the new republic. By 1600, the northern provinces had almost 10,000 ships sailing around the coasts of Europe and across the oceans. Trade was conducted in grain, tobacco, barley, herring, timber, sugar and spices. The tentacles of Dutch trade stretched around the Baltic and Mediterranean, across the Atlantic, south to Africa and across the Indian Ocean to India and Southeast Asia. At home, a vigorous merchant community was successful in establishing a commercial society. The East India Company was established in 1602; the Bank of Amsterdam was founded in 1609 and soon achieved a prominent world position. At this time, there was a wide variety of coins and currency. The Bank of Amsterdam took them all, assessed the gold and silver content, and allowed depositors to withdraw the equivalent in gold florins minted by the Bank of Amsterdam. The bank became a depository of huge holdings and a central exchange of global financing. The new-found wealth was filtered through the moral membrane of a Calvinist theology. The dilemma of how to be wealthy and moral at the same time helped give shape and substance to a distinctively Dutch culture.[5]

The Dutch Republic – and Amsterdam in particular – became a shipping centre, commodity market and capital market for the world economy. Daniel Defoe summed it up thus:

The Dutch must be understood as they really are, the Middle Persons in Trade, the Factors and Brokers of Europe ... they buy to sell again, take in to send out, and the greatest part of their vast Commerce consists in being supply'd from All Parts of the World, that they may supply All the World again.[6]

To ensure a monopoly over trade, the Dutch (like their European competitors) needed to have control over local commerce. The prevailing ideology of the time was mercantilism, a belief that foreign trade was the chief method of increasing national wealth. The mercantilists believed that the world's wealth was like a giant cake, fixed in size: any increase for one nation was at the expense of the others. The most favourable conditions of trade thus depended on monopoly control. Successful commerce implied a commercial empire where prices could be fixed, markets protected and competitors kept out. The overseas expansion of European countries in the seventeenth and eighteenth centuries was a commercial undertaking driven by mercantile capitalism.

The growth of the commercial empire involved the search for trading areas and territory in Africa, Asia and the New World. There was intense rivalry between the European powers for overseas trade and territory. North America was just one more commercial opportunity on the surface of the globe: most of South and Central America was under the control of the Spanish and Portuguese; in the far north, France had already staked substantial claims. But between New Spain in the south and New France in the north the other European countries, including the Dutch Republic, sought trade openings and commercial opportunities.

Appropriating the New World: Creating New Netherland

The big prize for the Dutch merchants was Asia and the East Indies, which contained spices, timber, jewels and all the exotic things that enabled merchants to make big profits. Trading companies were formed to pool resources and share the risk. In 1602, the Dutch East India Company was formed, becoming hugely successful and paying annual dividends of never less than 20 per cent and often 50 per cent.

A common belief held at the time was that it was possible to find a way to the East Indies around the north coast of Europe. The Dutch already knew the way south around the Cape of Good Hope on the southern tip of Africa. A northeast passage would open up another and perhaps shorter route. There was intense and growing interest in the northeast passage. In 1609, the East India Company signed a contract with the English sailor, Henry Hudson, who had experience in searching for a northeast passage. Two years earlier he had sailed as far as Spitzbergen in search of the 'islands of spicery' for the Muscovy Company of London. The possibility that Flemish traders were considering an expedition hastened the contract between Hudson and the Dutch East India Company, which agreed to furnish him with a vessel, the *Half Moon*. He was to sail north and east to find a passage to the East Indies. After his return Hudson was to make a report to the directors. In return he was to receive 800 guilders, and, in an intimation of the dangerous and uncertain task ahead, his wife was to receive 200 guilders if he did not return in a year.

On 25 March 1609, the *Half Moon* set sail, accompanied by the *Good Hope*, heading north. Progress was slow. After a month the *Half Moon* came upon fog and ice. It was too much for the scurvy crew, who mutinied and forced Hudson to return home. Sailing down the coast of Norway, Hudson must have thought about the frosty reception awaiting him in Amsterdam. It was still early in the year, enough time to try the passage west suggested by George Weymouth and John Smith. He turned the ship westward and reached the Faroes by the end of May. The *Good Hope* returned to Holland, while the *Half Moon* pressed on, eventually reaching the Maine coast. Hudson sailed south, looking for the passage to the Indies. Unsuccessful, he returned northward, anchoring in Chesapeake Bay. He continued north and on the second day in September the ship cast anchor off Sandy Hook. The next morning, members of the crew went out in boats and made contact with the local people. The *Half Moon* spent ten days in the area before sailing up the river that we now call the Hudson. The ship reached as far as present-day Albany before the water became too shallow to permit further progress. Hudson sailed back down the river, trading with the local people and making surveys and soundings. On 4 October, the *Half Moon* set sail for home.

On the return journey, the ship put into Dartmouth in southern England. Hudson was seized by the authorities and charged with entering foreign service without permission of the English king. He was held captive by the English, and his maps and reports were confiscated. In the era of mercantile capitalism, trade routes were vitally important; they were national secrets to be guarded, protected, and – given the opportunity – stolen. Hudson did not make it back to the Dutch Republic,[7] but the information about the discovery certainly did. Here was a land where no other European power had a presence and where there was a plentiful supply of beaver, an extremely valuable commodity at the time. The officials of the Dutch East India Company were unimpressed, but a group of Dutch fur merchants, excluded from the rich fur grounds in New France by the king of France, were excited at the prospect of monopoly control over such a territory. In 1613, a group of these merchants sent five ships to rediscover the Hudson River and establish trade with the indigenous people. To secure their interests, the merchants also lobbied the States General.

Unlike Spain or France, the commercial imperialism of the English and the Dutch in the early seventeenth century was more a function of private interest than a concern of the state. The States General, however, did have a regulatory role. They could grant commercial privileges and ensure the monopoly of trade to groups of merchants. Although these pronouncements had little power over foreign merchants, they could stimulate the commercial undertakings of the merchants of the republic and regulate competition among them. The merchants lobbied the States General throughout 1613 and early 1614, indicating their intention to send ships to the New World and wanting the States General to promise some kind of government security. The States General wanted to encourage this kind of enterprise, and on 27 March 1614 it made a proclamation.

We understand it would be honorable, serviceable, and profitable to this country, and for the promotion of its prosperity, as well as for the maintenance of seafaring people, that the good Inhabitants should be excited and encouraged to employ and occupy themselves in the seeking out and discovery of Courses, Havens, Countries, and Places which have not, before now, been discovered or frequented.[8]

The proclamation went on to promise that these merchants be permitted to make four voyages provided that they submit a report within fourteen days after their return from the first voyage. This report would then allow the States General to set a timetable for the remaining voyages because it did not want to grant perpetual rights. The proclamation noted that those breaking this agreement, by sailing to these lands before the first 'discoverer' had finished the four voyages, were to have their ships confiscated and fined 50,000 Netherland Ducats.

In July 1614, four of the five ships had returned and the merchants made their report to the States General. This report was considered by the States General at their meeting in October 1614, at which they made the following proclamation, beginning with a list of the ships, merchants, and captains involved in the commercial undertaking:

WHEREAS, Gerrit Jacobz Witssen, ancient Burgomaster of the City of Amsterdam, Jonas Witssen, Simon Morrissen, owners of the ship named the 'Little Fox', whereof Jan de With has been Skipper; Hans Hongers, Paulus Pelgrom, Lambrecht van Tweehuyzen, owners of the two ships named the 'Tiger' and 'Fortune', whereof Adriaen Block and Hendrick Christiaenssen were Skippers; Arnolt van Lydergen, Wewssel Schenck, Hans Claessen and Berent Sweertssen, owners of the Ship named the 'Nightingale', whereof Thys Volckertssen were Skipper, merchants of the aforesaid city of Amsterdam; and Peter Clementssen Brouwer, Jan Clementssen Kies and Cornelius Volckertssen, Merchant of the city of Hoorn, owners of the Ship called the 'Fortuyn', whereof Cornelis Jacobssen May was Skipper, all now associated in one Company, have respectfully represented to us that they, the petitioners, after great expense and damages by loss of ship and other danger, had during the present year, discovered and found with the above named five ships certain New Lands in America, between New France and Virginia, the Seacoasts whereof between forty and forty-five degrees of Latitude, and now called New Netherland.[9]

They reiterated the March proclamation, eventually coming to their central concern:

… having heard the pertinent Report of the Petitioners . . . do consent and grant, to the said petitioners now united into one Company, that they shall be privileged exclusively to frequent, or cause to be visited, the above newly discovered lands, situated in America, between New France and Virginia, whereof the Seacoasts lie between the fortieth and forty-fifth degree of Latitude, now named New Netherland, as can be seen by a Figurative Map hereunto annexed.[10]

1 The Figurative Map or Block Map, 1614, pen and ink and watercolour on vellum.
Algameen Rijksarchief, The Hague.

The States General's decision to grant the trading monopoly was based on what they termed 'a Figurative Map hereunto annexed'.

Illustration 1 represents a copy of the map that the States General sat around considering at their October meeting in 1614. It is sometimes called the Figurative Map or the Block Map, after Captain Adriaen Block who presented the map to the merchants. The map is pen and ink and watercolour on vellum, 66 x 47 cm.[11] It is the first map to contain the words 'New Netherlands'. It is also the first map to show Manhattan as a separate island. It is thus a map of some significance and worthy of careful consideration. But before looking at it in some detail, it is important to place it in a wider cartographic setting.

The map is a portolan type of chart. The name comes from *portolano*, the Italian name for the pilot book that contained written sailing directions and information about courses, anchorages and ports. These charts first appeared in the thirteenth century; one of the earliest remaining examples is the Pisan Chart, made some time around 1300. In the early part of the fourteenth century, portolan chartmaking was found in Genoa and Venice and associated with such names as Petrus Vesconte, Johannes de Carignano and Francesco Pizigani. By the latter half of the century, a centre of portolan charts production developed in Majorca and Barcelona and later in Portugal and the Low Countries.[12]

Portolan charts mark a significant development in the representation of the world. They mark a break with the medieval maps, the Mappae Mundi, which were as much theological texts as cartographic representations.[13] Portolan maps, in contrast, were based more on direct observation – and thus signal the emergence of a scientific discourse and the development of empirical observation – than on religious belief for cartographic representation.

The portolan charts developed out of the invention and refinement of the compass. Identifying north by compass made direction finding much more accurate. The maps were oriented toward the north because it was much easier to align the compass reading that way. And so began the convention of maps having north at the top. It is now such a taken-for-granted convention that we find it difficult to imagine any other orientation.[14] The Mappa Mundi has east at the top, the map's orientation being guided by the direction of the Holy Land. The legacy of the practice continues, however, in the English language. To orient a map means quite literally to point it toward the east.

The portolan maps aided sea travel. They were covered with a network of lines corresponding to the principal points of the compass. Seafarers could use the lines on the chart to set a course.

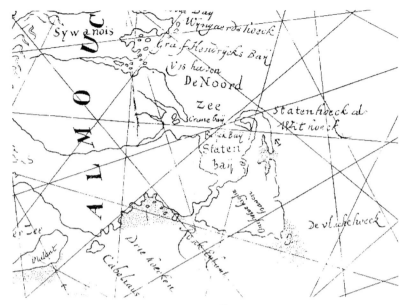

2 Detail showing Cape Cod, from the Block Map (illus. 1).

The lines emanated from compass diagrams, which were called compass roses, divided not by degrees but by wind direction. The more precise were divided into: eight primary winds, eight half-winds, and eight quarter-winds. The directions were coloured in red and blue sequence so that the correct line could be more easily identified and distinguished from its neighbours.[15] In the Block Map, two compass roses can be found.

The portolans were prone to error. The charts used a simple projection that did not take into account the curvature of the earth, thus distorting the east–west direction at higher latitudes. This was not a major problem in the earliest years when their use was restricted to the Mediterranean and the Black Sea. With the voyages of discovery, however, ships began to sail in higher latitudes, where the error became magnified.[16]

Portolan charts were working tools for seamen. They allowed courses to be set and followed. They were more accurate along the coastlines; inland they were less precise, often hazy. The Block Map is no exception: the coastline is drawn with care and some precision (note the elegant delineation of the curve of Cape Cod in illus. 2) while the interior is hazy and uncertain, as in the positioning of Meer Vand Irocoisen (Lake Champlain) in the centre of New England. The northern interior is taken up with an elaborate scale. Portolan charts were produced by those at sea looking landward; they represent the early seaman's view of the world. The Block Map is an early European sailor's view of the New World. But it is not the gaze of a single individual.

Multiple Authors, Cartographic Encounters

There are two misconceptions of early maps of the Americas. The first is what I call the illusion of single authorship. Maps are often treated like a novel or a work of art; the product of a singular mind. In the history of cartography the illusion is fostered by the naming of maps, as in this case; the Block Map sounds like the product of a single person. In fact this map, like many others, has a collective authorship. It is the product of a wider community.

The Block Map did not arise from a lone sailor mapping the coast as he went along. The map was a composite. There were many antecedents to the Block Map. Throughout the sixteenth century the Americas were represented in a series of maps. The discoveries of John Cabot, Verrazano, Cartier, Frobisher and John Davies had all increased the geographical knowledge of the northeastern coastal and riverine areas of North America. In the latter half of the century and the first decade of the next, the cartographic story of the eastern seaboard of North America was recounted in the maps of John White, Samuel Champlain and Alonso de Velasco. The Block Map did not arise out of a cartographic vacuum. It draws upon two sets of maps in the delineation of the New England coast. The first was the maps of Samuel Champlain initially published in 1613. The second was the maps made on Jan Cornelisz May's 1611 voyages by pilot Pieter Fransz. Block used these maps to depict the area from present-day Nantucket through Cape Cod northward.[17] The Block Map distinguishes the areas used from other maps from the areas mapped by Block.

The image of the sailor mapping as he went then presenting the finished product misses an important stage, one played by chartmakers who turned notes and sketches into a more formal map. A likely candidate is Cornelis Doetsz, a chartmaker from Edam. His name was variously given as Doaetz, Doetz and Doedtszaan, and he worked on charts of the coasts of Asia and Europe from 1598 up until his death in 1612. Chartmakers did not produce maps but produced copies of existing documents for outward-bound navigators. There was a flourishing centre of chartmaking at Edam which included Hamen and Marten Jansz. One authority suggests that Block sailed in 1613 with the still-incomplete chart drawn by Doetsz, who had died a year earlier, but had drawn the chart from the material presented to him from voyages made by Dutch seamen in 1611 and 1612.[18] According to this view, and the one accepted here, the Block Map is a composite map sketched in before Block left in 1613, taken over the ocean, and then amended in ink after the return voyage.

The second misconception of early maps of the Americas is that the maps resulted solely from the gaze of the Western observer. In fact, the maps of early North America bear witness to a major native contribution. Despite the traditional view that Europeans created maps of the continent on their own, Native Americans helped in the mapping of North America. It is more accurate to consider the notion of cartographic encounters involving Europeans and Native Americans, rather than a simple cartographic appropriation by only Europeans. The mapping of the continent was underpinned by native knowledge. There is a hidden strata of Native-American geographical knowledge that is only now being uncovered.[19] In the Block Map much of the information was gleaned from native informants, who gave names of tribes and physical configurations. We have some evidence of the Native-American involvement even in the earliest Dutch voyages. Robert Juet, an officer on the *Half Moon*, wrote a journal, which was subsequently reprinted. Juet notes the contact between the ship and the indigenous inhabitants. At a number of points he acknowledges the sharing of local knowledge:

So at three of the clocke in the after-noone they [Native Americans] came aboord, and brought Tobacco, and more Beades, and gave them to our Master, and made an Oration, and shewed him all the Countrey round about.

The phrase 'shewed him all the Countrey' was used often by Juet and represents the exchange of information from the locals to the explorers. Four days after the cited encounter, Juet notes:

This morning two Canoes came up the River where we first found loving people, and in one of them was an old man. . . . He brought another old man with him, which brought more stropes of Beades, and gave them to our Master, and shewed him all the Countrey.[20]

The European maps of the New World resulted from this exchange of information. The European depiction of the lie of the land was the product of a cartographic encounter between two peoples: one with detailed spatial knowledge and the other seeking to obtain and represent this knowledge to claim and entice.

The Block Map is a large-scale map of the entire New England coast from Maine to Virginia at a scale of one-and-a-half inches to one degree of latitude. Names were given to coastal features: for example, Cape Cod is known as Statenhock al Withoek, Nantucket is Texel. These names were taken directly either from the maps of May or, after translation, from Champlain. Much of the coastline is relatively accurate in portrayal. The map has detailed information at a smaller scale but does not have the big picture; the relationship between the coast and the St Lawrence and the position of Lake Champlain, well to the east and south of its 'true' position, shows how the map is more of a composite of small-scale maps than an accurate rendering of how the parts fit together. In this regard it is like many early European maps of North America, revealing detailed knowledge of particular places but not enough information to piece it all together into an accurate portrayal of the whole space.

Most of the inland detail is around the mouth of the Hudson. Tribal names are given, and there is a crude depiction of forests and settlements. In illustration 3 Long Island is clearly visible and Manhattan is shown as a tiny island with the name Manhates. The Block Map does not show an empty wilderness waiting for the European settler. This is a human landscape with rich evidence of settlement: houses are marked as well as the dense patchwork of varied tribal names and affiliations. The map for all its crude outlines and hazy geography is a reminder that people lived here. A human presence is noted in some detail. The information was obtained from communication with the indigenous inhabitants, for whom human settlements were an important part of their geographical knowledge. It was important for the Dutch to know who lived where. The map depicts a populated landscape because the Dutch were looking to trade, and the map provided a spatial ordering of potential trading partners. But it was not an innocent ordering. The territory is crisscrossed with lines emanating from the compass roses in a metaphor of the net that was about to envelop this land and these peoples. And across the map, in block capital letters, New Netherland was inscribed in an act of naming that was also a gesture of appropriation.

When Block returned from his voyage to Amsterdam in 1614 a chartmaker was engaged to draw up the Figurative Map. It must have been a rushed job. Some simple mistakes were made and not corrected. For example, in Long Island the tribal group is referred to as Nahicans, but yet all other reports and subsequent Dutch maps had the more correct designation of Matouwacs. Despite the errors – speed was now of more importance than accuracy – the Block Map served its purpose. It was presented to the October 1614 meeting of the States General. The report that accompanied the map is lost. The Block Map is the only record of the application for the first Dutch

3 Detail showing Long Island and Manhattan ('Manhates'), from the Block Map (illus. 1).

territorial annexation in North America. The application came from the thirteen merchants who had underwritten the expeditions and in the fall of 1614 had combined to establish the United New Netherland Company. At their meeting on 11 October 1614, the States General issued a declaration that gave this company the exclusive right to trade in the land between New France and Virginia 'now named New Netherland'.

2 Representing the New Netherlands

In 1602, the Dutch East India Company appointed an official carto-grapher responsible for collecting information and producing maps. The first was Petrus Pancius, who in 1592 had produced a large-scale world map. Throughout the seventeenth century pilots returning from overseas trips would submit their charts with the latest amend-ments and updates to the official cartographer, who was then respon-sible for collating and improving them. In this way a tremendous data bank was set up; an early geographical information system, constantly updated by the explorations and discoveries of the Dutch commercial fleet, which was scouring the world for new commercial opportuni-ties. Amsterdam became the centre of knowledge about the world and the prime place of the representation of this world.

Around the port area of Amsterdam, especially in the Kalverstraat, a large variety of mapmakers plied their trade; Hondius, Jansson, Blaeu and Visscher were all active in the booming market for maps, charts and atlases. It was a period of intense rivalry. A succession of lawsuits were filed between the Hondius and Blaeu family businesses, for example, accusing each other of plagiarism. The plates of maps were very valuable items and, like all commercial secrets with tremen-dous marketing opportunities, were guarded, stolen, and plagiarized.

In this chapter I will look at the background to three 'Dutch' maps of the New Netherlands: the Blaeu Atlas Map, the Visscher series of maps and the Donck Map.

Maps and mapmaking were an integral part of Dutch commercial success and cultural expression. Maps were embodiments of Dutch culture and there was a cartographic dimension to Dutch culture. Dutch maps were not only instruments of commercial success; they were decorative items that adorned the rooms and walls of the bour-geoisie. We have a beautiful record of cartography as domestic deco-ration in the paintings of Johannes Vermeer (1632–75). A number of his canvasses depict large maps. In *Officer and Laughing Girl* (*c.* 1658) a young girl is flirting with an officer (see illus. 4). On the back wall of

4 Johannes Vermeer, *Officer and Laughing Girl*, *c.* 1658, oil on canvas. Photo: © The Frick Collection, New York. Balthasar van Berckenrode and Willem Blaeu's 1620 map of Holland and Friesland appears in the background.

the room where they sit is a large-scale map of Holland and Friesland published by Willem Janszoon Blaeu. In *Woman in Blue Reading A Letter* (*c.* 1662) the back wall is again framed by a large-scale map. A map of Europe forms the backdrop to *Woman with a Lute* (*c.* 1664), and large wall maps of the Netherlands also appear in *Young Woman with a Water Jug* (*c.* 1664) and *The Allegory of Painting* (*c.* 1666). For the Dutch of the seventeenth century, maps were an important part of material culture and cultural expression.[1]

The maps contained the latest geographical knowledge, but they were more than just neutral transmitters of new data. They were statements of European dominance in the world and of Dutch authority and superiority. Europe was regularly placed in the centre of world map projections; the world was named frequently according to the European names but rarely to the indigenous names; native peoples were often symbolically represented in an inferior position, often holding the cartouches.[2] The maps were icons of cultural power and commercial success, expressing the realities as well as the ambitions of the commercial expansion of the Dutch overseas trading empire and increasing European hegemony. Neither mere commercial tools nor simple items of decoration, the maps embodied and reflected a Dutch sense of world order, European dominance and cultural superiority. It was fitting, therefore, that Amsterdam's Town Hall, built in 1655, contained an inlaid, double-hemispheric map of the world set into the marble floor of

Citizens' Hall. The burghers of Amsterdam could walk across a world that they had codified, named, possessed, represented.

The Blaeu Atlas Map

Atlases were an important part of cartographic production. They were very popular, somewhat akin to encyclopedias of the present period. Atlases collected and represented the sum of contemporary geographical information; they were systematic compendiums of a rapidly increasing and changing knowledge. A variety of atlases were produced by the best-known mapmakers of the day, including Hondius, Jansson, Blaeu and Visscher. One of the most important mapmaking firms was the Blaeus.

Willem Janszoon Blaeu (1571–1638) was a mathematician, astronomer and instrument maker. Around 1599 he set up business in Amsterdam as a globe and instrument maker. Six years later he established a printing press near the centre of Amsterdam, now part of the west side of the Damrak where he published various works on navigation, astronomy and theology. He worked with his son Joan Blaeu (1596–1673), and together they published a magnificent series of atlases. The first was published in 1630 consisting of 60 plates; some original, some copied (a year earlier Willem had bought several copperplates from Jodocus Hondius). In 1631, an expanded version was printed. And in 1635, a massive atlas was produced consisting of 208 maps in two volumes entitled *Novus Atlas*, with an alternative title of *Theatrum*. This atlas was enormously successful, and the Blaeus built upon their success and their business grew. They were both official cartographers to the East India Company, although they did not print 'classified' information. In 1637, they had to move to larger premises in the Bloemgracht, where they had nine presses for letterpress printing, six presses for copperplates and a type foundry, where type for numerous languages was produced. It was the largest establishment of its type in the whole of Europe. Willem Blaeu died in 1638, but his son Joan carried on the business as well as taking over his father's appointment as official cartographer to the East India Company. The *Novus Atlas* was expanded to three volumes in 1640, continually enlarged in successive printings until six volumes were produced in 1655. Between 1662 and 1664, the 600-map *Atlas Major* was produced. This marks the magnificent zenith of seventeenth-century Dutch cartography. It is still the largest atlas ever produced. The atlas quite literally represented the world to the literate public. It portrays the world in the middle of the seventeenth century in a beautiful style, without the overblown excesses of baroque ornamentation.[3]

In both the *Novus Atlas* and the *Atlas Major*, the Blaeus printed a map of New Netherland. Volume 8 of the *Atlas Major* is devoted to maps of Spain, Africa, the West Indies and America. The 46th map in the Dutch edition (the third map in vol. 12 of the French version) is entitled *Nova Belgica et Anglia Nova* (illus. 5). This map was first published in the 1635 *Novus Atlas* and subsequently reprinted without changes in all subsequent Blaeu atlases. The map, whose precise date is uncertain, draws upon the Block Map and the 1630 map of Johannes de Laet.[4] Unlike many other Blaeu maps in their atlases, it is oriented with west at the top of the page. Most of the other maps used the more usual north orientation. The map still has elements of its portolan origin: a compass rose radiates lines from the top left-hand corner and another from the lower centre; the land shown is a long sliver of coastline; and the interior is hazily constructed and full of decoration and the setting of the cartouche. It is still a view from the sea, a perspective reinforced by the image of Dutch ships ploughing through the waves. The map builds upon the Block representation but corrects the mistake of the Native-American name in Long

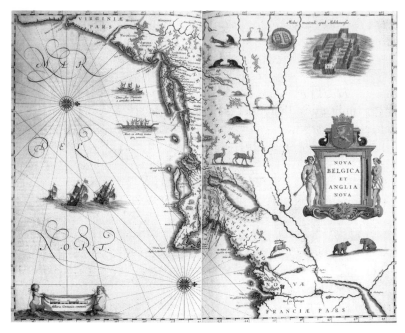

5 Willem and Joan Blaeu's map of New Netherland, *Nova Belgica et Anglia Nova*, from *Novus Atlas* (Amsterdam, 1635).

Island, correctly referred to in the Blaeu Map as Matouwacs, whereas the Block Map incorrectly stated Nahicans. Other changes include the use of the term 'Nieu Amsterdam', and 'Noord River' for the Hudson. The map in the Blaeu atlas is more than just a rehash of other maps. It uses information but presents its own look. This is the first printed map to show native canoes, turkey and beaver. The map is richly illustrated; there are small pictures of turkey, deer, polecats, otters, elk, bear, birds and beaver. There was intense interest in the flora and fauna of the New World, reinforced for the Dutch by their participation in the fur trade. The fauna indicate nature's bounty, the distinctiveness of the New World, and the opportunity for trade.

The indigenous people figure very largely in the Blaeu Map – they are shown in a long canoe and two smaller canoes. Powered by human muscle, they are contrasted with the larger, more technologically advanced Dutch ships driven by wind and sail. The landscape is filled with tribal names, including Manatthans, Mahikans, Sanhikans, Makimanes and Quirepeys. In the top right-hand corner, two villages are shown, both of them palisaded. Indigenous people also appear either side of the cartouches containing the appropriating title of *Nova Belgica et Anglia Nova* – a male with bow and arrow and a modest maiden.. They are in a supporting role, like human bookends located beside and below the European heraldry.

We can see the beginnings of a toponymic colonialism in this map; east of Long Island, the process of Dutch naming has begun: there are two islands now called 'Adriaen Blocx' and 'Hendrick Christiaes'. The early traders left their mark and their name. At the tip of Manhattan, the name 'Nieu Amsterdam' is indicative of the Dutch presence. Even the name of the map, *Nova Belgica et Anglia Nova*, indicates the imperial appropriation of the New World. This is New Netherland, sandwiched between the named lands of Virginia, New England and New France. These capitalized names are in larger print than that used for the tribes; this is a land being divided up among the European powers. There is a sensitivity in this map to a native presence, but it is the anthropological and commercial sensitivity of knowing one's territory – of recording the natural and human resources of the land – that one has appropriated.

The Visscher Map

The Dutch represented their territory in a number of ways and there were many maps made of the New Netherland. In their appropriation, the Dutch surveyed, measured and represented their possession using a variety of scales and represented the new territory in a series of maps, beginning with a 1651 map by Dutch mapmaker Johannes Jansson (1588–1664).[5] This map became a template for the series of maps, referred to as the Jansson-Visscher maps of New England. Tony Campbell has identified 24 versions and states of the Jansson-Visscher series over the period 1651–1730.[6] In 1655, Nicholas Jansz Visscher (1618–79) printed another version, with the title (translated from Latin) of *Map of New Netherland New England as well as parts of Virginia corrected in many places by Nicholas Visscher* (illus. 6). This map was published in an atlas produced by Visscher.

The map is interesting, especially when we compare it with the one in the Blaeu atlases, as it reflects an earlier period of Dutch presence. The map, unlike the Blaeu, is oriented with north at the top. It has the same decorative features of the village and native fauna that appear in the Blaeu atlases. At the bottom of the map is a large cartouche, depicting the settlement of New Amsterdam and Manhattan Island.

A comparison between the Blaeu and Visscher Maps indicates the extent and nature of continuing Dutch appropriation. The space of

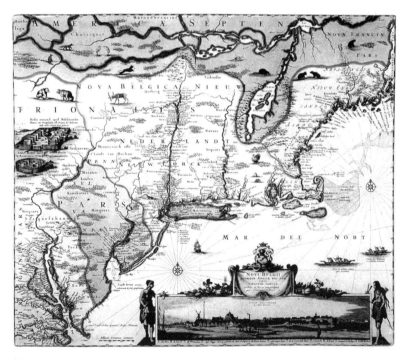

6 Nicholas Visscher's map of New Netherland, *Novi Belgii Novæque Angliæ partiis Virginiæ tabula* (Amsterdam, 1655).

the Visscher Map is inscribed with a growing Dutch presence, which is seen in a variety of ways. First, there are the names. The Dutch word for river, *kill,* can now be found; thus Kats Kill and Wappinges Kill are recorded; some of them are lost to time, such as Marquaa Kill, while others, such as Kats Kill (albeit transformed into Catskill), still remain as toponymic testimony, not so much to the presence of the Dutch on the land but to their ability to name the land. There is also a Dutch urban presence: at the south and north end of the Hudson River, Nieuw Amsterdam and Fort Orange, respectively, are recorded. The bottom of the map contains an illustration of New Amsterdam including houses, churches, public buildings, ships' masts and, in a comforting allusion to Dutch sensibilities, a windmill. In the foreground, a gibbet is shown. This is not arcadia, but a troubled, factious colony. The map is full of visible signs of European urban presence: in the western tip of Long Island (Lange Eylandt) the English settlements of Greenwycjk and Gravesant are shown, and along the Hudson the symbol for buildings is recorded.

The map also records major acts of appropriation: two colonies are shown in bold type – *Colonie van Heer neder Horst* just west of the mouth of the Hudson and *Colonye Renselaers Wyck* in the north around present-day Albany. Let us look at these in some detail.

The charter given by the States General to the New Netherland Company was for four voyages to be made in the three years beginning the first day of January 1615. The company sent ships and traded with the local tribes, especially the Minquas, for sables and beaver skins. On 1 January 1618, the charter expired and an unsuccessful petition was made for an extension. There then followed a confused history of claim, counterclaim and unsuccessful charter applications to the States General from diverse groups of merchants.

In 1619, the Calvinists took control of the republic and were intent on a more aggressive policy of trade war against the Spaniards in the New World. The merchants of Amsterdam were also keen to open up new commercial possibilities in the New World. To secure commercial trade interests, the States General in 1620 established the Dutch West India Company. In this charter, to take effect in 1621, all trade from the Cape of Good Hope all the way west to New Guinea was in the hands of the Dutch West India Company. The company was given a commercial monopoly; private traders caught breaking this monopoly were to have their ships and cargo impounded. By September 1623, the Dutch West India Company attracted over 7 million guilders of investment – a huge amount of money. It was also given immense power, including the right to wage war, sign treaties, construct fortifications and encourage settlement to increase commerce and profit. The company was divided into five chambers established in different towns, but the Chamber of Amsterdam was the wealthiest and took special concern with the New Netherland. The central authority was vested in nineteen directors; they included Johannes de Laet and Kiliaen van Rensselaer, an Amsterdam jeweller.

Colonization of free people was not the goal of the Dutch West India Company; the goal to all decisions was increased profits. And in New Netherland that came from the fur trade. It was no accident that the seal of the New Netherlands depicted a beaver. But the trade had to be established, controlled, monitored. To that end, the company sent out 30 families in 1624. They established trading posts in its new territory: a commercial station on Governor's Island, just off Manhattan, and a trading post further upstream on the west bank of the Hudson, which they called Fort Orange. Here the fur trade was conducted with the Mohicans and Mohawks and, through them, with more distant tribes in the northern and western interior.

To promote permanent settlement and to encourage further immigration, land was obtained from the indigenous people. In 1626, the Governor, Peter Minuit, decided that the main colonial metropolis, fittingly called New Amsterdam, was to be located on the tip of Manhattan. He purchased the island from the Canarsee Indians for $24. On the Visscher Map these purchases are reflected in the growing number of Dutch settlements in Manhattan, Long Island and around the mouth of the Hudson. The symbols for buildings and Dutch names dot the map. Compare this map with the Block Map and see the growing appropriation of the land. The numbers were small. By the 1650s, the time of the map, there were still only a hundred Europeans in New York, less than a few hundred in and around Fort Orange. However, the map's highly symbolic representation is more indicative of the impact and future direction. Although the map exaggerates the Dutch presence on the ground, it is very representative of the actual and future impacts of European contact with the indigenous people and the natural environment.

The map indicates two *Colonyes*. These were established as a result of lobbying by Amsterdam merchants. In the mid-1620s, returns on investment from New Netherland were dismal. Kiliaen van Rensselaer, a dominant figure in the Amsterdam chamber, wanted to colonize New Netherland with private capital. He argued that the company's monopoly power had not stimulated enough profit. To encourage more investment, it was necessary – he argued – to open up the colony to private traders and to promote settlement. In a 1628 plan, entitled

Freedoms and Exemptions for Patroons and masters or private Persons who would plant a colony and cattle in New Netherland, private individuals were allowed to ferry colonists and pay costs in return for tracts of land. This, in essence, was the patroon system. Patroons were given three years to settle 60 people. To encourage the settlement of Manhattan the figure was only 30. The fur trade, however, was still held as a company monopoly. A fierce struggle ensued, and a revised plan of 1629 allowed better access to the fur trade. The plan gave the patroons tremendous power over their landholdings and colonists. They still had to pay taxes to the company and use company ships, but they were given power to discipline their colonists. In effect, it was an attempt to establish a feudal system in the New World. Van Rensselaer successfully won a patroonship on the Hudson covering 700,000 acres with extensive river frontage. This is the *Colonye Renselaers Wyck* that appears on the map in the same position as present-day Albany.

Van Rensselaer never visited his colony, but he actively followed and monitored his business interests. He employed a variety of agents whom he corresponded with, chiding and criticizing them in an endless stream of invective and encouragement. His agents began to buy land from the Mohawks and the Mohicans. From August 1630 onward, a series of land sales are recorded as van Rensselaer, through his agents, amassed a substantial landholding. In April–May 1649, for example, land at the intersection of Catskill Creek and Kaaterskill Falls, west of present-day Catskill village, was sold by Pewasck and her son Supahhot for woollen cloth, a coat of beaver and a knife to Arent van Slictenhorst for the Patroon of Rennselaerswyck.[7] The land was sold for woollen goods, axes, knives, wampum and musket powder. On 13 March 1650, Wanemenheet sold the north point of Schodack Island for four and half pieces of cloth, two handfuls of powder and one axe. Land sales in and around Rennselaerswyck were often used in inter-tribal rivalry, with the Mohicans selling land close to the dangerous Mohawk border and Mohawks selling land they had appropriated from the Mohicans. Conflict between these two tribes was an important context to the sale of land to the Dutch.

While there were examples of cheating and fraud, the Dutch paid for most of the land in a whole series of individual transactions involving agents on each side and hard negotiations. The Native Americans gained consumer goods but lost the very basis of their identity. It was a Faustian pact. The two sides held different views of the land purchase. The Dutch believed they were buying total control. The Native Americans were dismayed to find that the land sales were permanent and not just conveyances of residence and subsistence for as long as both parties were satisfied. They believed that they could still use the land, especially when there were no Dutch farmers in residence. For the Dutch, land sales were permanent and implied further settlement and fencing. Hunting access and eventual return of the land to the Native Americans were denied. The two groups, with their very different worldviews and cosmologies, were dealing in the same commodity but with different long-term perspectives.

On the Visscher Map, Dutch names intermingle with the names of local tribes. Comparing this map to the Block Map, we can see the increasing Dutch presence but the Native Americans continuing to exist. The Visscher Map indicates a shared space. This coexistence lay in the nature of the economic basis of the new colony.

The Native Americans and Dutch shared the same space, and interaction was common. There was the hidden exchange of viruses as the people of the New World succumbed to the diseases of the Old. Indigenous populations soon declined. A more visible Dutch–Native American connection was in the trade of furs. The Native Americans traded pelts for knives, muskets, drink and tools such as hooks, kettles, hoes and axes. The trade changed Native-American society: the tools lightened the domestic burden, the woollen goods led to changed clothing habits, while the liquor had a devastating effect. The furs were sent to Europe by the Dutch to be manufactured into hats, coats and other apparel. In 1624, 4,700 beaver and otter skins were sent to Holland, fetching 27,000 guilders. By 1635, 16,304 skins fetched 134,925 guilders. At the time the map was printed, 46,000 skins were sent from Fort Orange alone. The fur trade was a lucrative business – so lucrative that overhunting soon exhausted the supply, first in the seaboard areas and then later even in the Adirondacks. A distinction soon emerged between tribes who controlled fur resources and the seaboard tribes who no longer had fur to supply. They became more expendable. The Visscher Map shows more of a concern with the interior than the Block Map. The economics of the fur trade were increasing contact with the interior. Fort Orange emerged as the main trading post – it is exaggerated on the map with a cluster of buildings clearly marked. If the map were drawn to 'objective' scale, the buildings would not appear. At the time of the map there were scarcely 200 Dutch people. The map exaggerates because it is concerned with highlighting, not empirically recording, the Dutch presence. The fort was initially owned and run by the West India Company but, after the opening up of the fur trade in 1639, private traders dominated. In 1652, the acting director of New Netherland created a space for a town. It was called Beverwijck (sometimes spelled Beverwyck), an appropriate name for a town that traded in beaver furs. Native Americans brought in pelts either directly or through intermediaries, and these were traded for goods. A standard pricing system emerged: two beaver skins were worth eight pounds of gunpowder or 40 pounds of lead, three beaver skins could get you a gun, and six beaver skins allowed you six quarts of rum. Ships sailed the Hudson River from New Amsterdam, taking trading goods up and fur down the river.

The fur trade was valuable. Both sides wanted the best deals; the Native Americans wanted numerous goods for their fur, while the Dutch wanted to keep the cost of peltry down. On both sides, monopoly control was prized. The West India Company tried to hang on to monopoly control of the purchasing of peltry for as long as possible. On the Visscher Map, just to the left of Renselaers Wyck, there is a small notation: *Mr Pinsers handel huys*. This was the trading post of William Pynchon, who was attempting to capture some of the interior fur trade away from the Dutch. To record this tiny settlement in the midst of all that space reflects the concern and interest in beaver trade. There was also intense conflict between the tribes for monopoly control. From 1625 to 1628, a bitter war was fought between the Mohicans and the Mohawks. We have a cartographic record of this; on the Blaeu, Visscher and even some later maps the stockaded Mohican settlement shown in the top left, not a traditional settlement form, is a sure sign that the people were at war.

Good relations with the tribes were vital to the Dutch. The Native Americans provided food and controlled the supply of peltry, land and information. Officials were told to 'by small presents seek to draw the Indians into our service, in order to learn from them the secrets of that region and the condition of the interior'. The greater the control over any or all of these resources, the more they figured in Dutch calculations. The West India Company produced an entire series of rules and regulations governing relations with the indigenous people, and officials were authorized to punish any Dutch who wronged a Native American. The emphasis was on orderly relations. The Dutch West India Company was not in the business of saving souls – it wanted profit, and good relations lubricated the path to higher returns. Friction did occur, however. The sharing of the same space was rarely harmonious: Dutch livestock trampled native corn; native dogs harassed settlers; there were arguments over women; and trading deals could break down into acrimonious dispute. There were arguments, fights and all-out war. One director, Willem Kieft, exacerbated tension by imposing a tax on the tribes around Manhattan in 1639. Passions were aroused and from 1640 until 1645 there was sporadic fighting;

almost a thousand Native Americans were killed. The Dutch lost people and property and immigration from Holland, always slight even in the best years, fell off even more. Kieft was replaced by Peter Stuyvesant. However, Governor Kieft's war showed the continuing resistance of the local native population. A treaty was signed in New Amsterdam in April 1645 in which Native Americans promised not to approach houses in Manhattan while armed and the Dutch pledged not to go near native settlements without warning while armed.

The Donck Map

As his landholdings increased, van Rensselaer needed agents to look out for his business interests on the other side of the Atlantic and in the interior up the Hudson. His kinsman, Arent van Curler, was soon made business manager of the colony. Van Rensselaer needed someone to work with van Curler and administer justice in his colony. In January 1641, he interviewed a young man with a law degree from the prestigious University of Leyden, Adriaen van der Donck.[8]

Van der Donck's story is important as it embodies much of the history and politics of the New Netherland. Van Rensselaer was impressed enough to offer him the job as scout to look after his legal affairs in the New Netherland. Van der Donck sailed for the colony on 17 May 1641. After presenting his letter of introduction to the director general of the colony, Willem Kieft, van der Donck sailed up the Hudson to meet his administrative colleague, van Curler, and take up his duties. He arrived in Rensselaerwyck, with a population of less than one hundred Dutch surrounded by an endless forest and a wild, exotic people. One reaction would have been dismay at having landed on the edge of European civilization. Van der Donck's reaction was the opposite; he revelled in the opportunity and took every occasion to travel, communicate with the local people and make observations of this new world. Van der Donck took an avid interest in his surroundings and the ways of the Native Americans. He did not remain in the settlement but travelled throughout the interior. He spent more time on this than he did on his job. He was bored by prosecuting the petty criminals and scoundrels of the colony. He annoyed his patroon by moving his dwelling place further away from the colony and by ignoring orders from Amsterdam. In 1642, the patroon wrote to him, 'You bring forward many charges and do not show me a single legal procedure ... legal practice does not consist of discourse or words but formal and judicial actions and procedures.'[9]

When van der Donck's contract finished in 1644, it was not renewed. He remained in Rensselaerwyck and proved useful in the peace negotiations of 1645; his knowledge of Native-American ways and customs proved invaluable in the negotiations. As a reward, Kieft gave him permission to buy land, almost 24,000 acres in what is now Westchester County and the Bronx. Now married, van der Donck built a house overlooking the northern tip of Manhattan. He became known as the *Joncker* meaning 'gentleman'. The name lives on in the area known as Yonkers.

Van der Donck, now a major landowner and one of only two lawyers in the entire province of New Netherland, was soon involved in the bitter politics. In 1648, he was elected to a council of advisors: the Board of Nine Men. He soon emerged as the leader and spokesperson for complaints against Peter Stuyvesant who had replaced Kieft as director of the Dutch West India Company. In 1649, van der Donck wrote up a list of grievances as well as a boosterist text about New Netherland. That summer he sailed across the Atlantic and in October presented his case to the States General in the Hague. He then was involved in labyrinthine bureaucratic machinations that made him unable to return to his wife and estate. He passed his time lobbying for his grievance to be heard, seeking permission to return home and writing up his book, *Description of the New Netherlands*. He was allowed back to New Netherland in 1653 only under the proviso that he was not to practise law or plead in courts. Harassed by Stuyvesant on his return, he spent most of his time on his estate. He died in 1655 at the very young age of 35.

Van der Donck's book, *A Description of the New Netherlands*, was published in 1655, the year of his death. Although written while he was stuck in the Netherlands on the losing side of a political dogfight with the director of the West India Company in New Netherland, the book contains no reference to the intense political machinations then occupying van der Donck. Rather, it is a careful observation of the land and people. He begins by placing the colony in its geographical setting:

The country is situated in the New American World, beginning north of the Equinoctial Line, 38 deg. and 53 min., extending northeasterly along the sea coast, to the 42d deg., and is named New Netherlands.

After a brief history of Dutch discovery there then follows a detailed geographical description of the land and the people. A boosterism runs through much of the first half. The province is represented as one of infinite promise: 'the greatness of this province are still unknown,', 'Barrens and sterile heath land are not here . . . wonderfully fertile,' and 'a land full of nature's bounty'. Van der Donck paints a picture of the New World before extensive European settlement. It is a country full of bears, elk and beaver. The book's second part has extensive discourse on the 'manners and peculiar customs of the natives of the New Netherlands'. Van der Donck is aware of the tide of history and begins this section with these remarks:

Having briefly remarked on the situation and advantages of the country, we deem it worth our attention to treat concerning the nature of the original inhabitants of the land; that after the Christians have multiplied and the natives have disappeared and melted away, a memorial of them may be preserved.[10]

Van der Donck notes that, according to the Native Americans, their population was ten times greater before the arrival of the Christians. Smallpox destroyed the population and, while exaggeration is common, the viral holocaust is a historical reality. Van der Donck gives a straightforward, account. He is concerned with noting their manners and customs in a humanistic manner. There is not the moralizing of reports from New England at the same time. Van der Donck, educated in the humanist tradition of Grotius, is concerned with making the Native Americans more understandable and thus more human. He writes of their ecological practices. The burning of vegetation was so common that ships sailing up the Hudson would see both banks ablaze. He writes of their clothes, food and dietary habits, houses and villages, social relations, mourning rituals, religion and language. Van der Donck describes their hunting of beaver:

The beavers are mostly taken far inland, there being few of them near the settlements ... For beaver hunting the Indians go in large parties, and remain out from one or two months, during which time they subsist by hunting and a little corn meal which they carry out with them, and they frequently return home with from forty to eighty beaver skins, and with some otter, fishers, and other skins also, even more than can be correctly stated. We estimate that eighty thousand beavers are killed annually in this quarter of the country, besides elks, bears, otters, deer and other animals. There are some persons who imagine that the animals of the country will be destroyed in time, but this is unnecessary anxiety. It has already continued many years, and the numbers brought in do not diminish.[11]

The book is written from extensive firsthand knowledge by someone who loves the place and has a quiet admiration for the native peoples. Van der Donck writes from the Dutch perspective and in his careful observations gives us a detailed picture of the land and the people soon after European contact. It is an invaluable document as it is clearly written, informative, and less weighed down by bias and prejudice than many other contemporary reports. There is less religious moralizing and more rational scientific observation. It has its own bias but, because it is closer to our own prejudices, the book reads as a more modern and contemporary text than others that have a more evangelical tinge. Van der Donck represents the province from the view of an observer witnessing and celebrating the transformation of the province from a wild place populated by Indians to the settled and civilized outpost of European culture and Dutch commerce.[12]

With van der Donck we have both a written description and a graphical account, for a map was included in the second edition of his book, published in 1656. It draws heavily upon the Visscher Map, with only minor variations. Compared to the Block Map, the Donck Map represents the increasing Dutch presence. The steady encroachment particularly around the mouth of the Hudson is apparent on the map by the increasing number of Dutch names and the presence upriver of the ambitious schemes of van Rensselaer (illus. 7). The Donck Map shows some changes while it is silent about others. The map does not record the more subtle changes: the destruction of the population by the introduction of European diseases, the destruction of traditional Native-American ways as the fur trade transformed indigenous hunting patterns, forms of war, modes of consumption and gave a renewed vigour to traditional tribal rivalries.

As we move from the Block map to the Donck Map, we see a continuing Native-American presence, but one that is increasingly hemmed in by Dutch names and a Dutch presence. We get an intimation of this trend by looking at how Long Island is depicted in both

7 Detail showing Long Island, Manhattan and the Hudson River from Adriaen van der Donck's map of New Netherland, from *A Description of the New Netherlands*, second edn (Amsterdam, 1656).

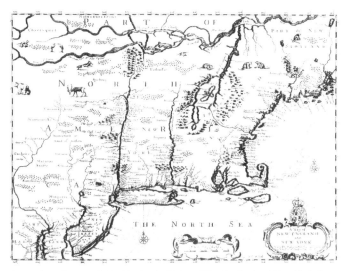

8 John Speed's map of New England, *A Map of New England and New York*, from
A Prospect of The Most Famous Parts of The World (London, 1676).

maps. In the Donck Map, the tribal names are reduced to Matouwacs
while a growing European presence is indicated. Like a giant wave
that would sweep in from the sea and up the rivers as a tidal bore, the
Europeans were coming, changing all before them. The map can be
read as the text of this transformation.

The Donck Map was part of a series of maps – the Jansson-Visscher series that lasted from 1651 to 1730. The very latest map, an
engraving by Matthias, depicts natives paying homage to a king,
probably George ll. The series tells us more about changing iconography than about increased geographical knowledge. By the end of
the seventeenth century, the maps have an anachronistic quality. As
the series progresses, the maps become more suggestive with the
changes more decorative than geographically accurate. In 1676, there
appeared yet another version of the map. It was published in *A
Prospect of The Most Famous Parts of The World* by the English
mapmaker John Speed (illus. 8). Van Rensselaer's colony is still shown
but, instead of a Latin title that begins with *Nova Belgica*, the map is
entitled *A Map of New England and New York*. *Nieuw Amsterdam* and
Lange Eylandt are replaced by *New York* and *Long Island*. With their
takeover in 1664, the English could now enact their own form of
toponymic colonialism and appropriation. Using a Dutch map as
base, the English *re*presented their latest colonial holding.

3 Imperial Claims

> Maps were also inscriptions of political power. Far from the innocent products of disinterested science, they acted in constructing the world they intended to represent . . . Cartographic power was also metaphor. It was expressed as imperial or religious rhetoric, as part of the creation ritual of taking possession of the land, or as a series of erasures by which the Indian geography was partly removed from the map.[1]

The European description and representation of the New World was never innocent of political implications. Geographic representations of the New World were always tied to the claiming of the New World. In this chapter, I will look at four types of representations: as imperial claims in a changing geopolitical order, as acts of military surveillance, as claims to landownership and as representations of the native other.

In the seventeenth century, the three competing European powers in North America were Spain, England and France. For the Spaniards, North America was of peripheral concern, the northern frontier of an empire centred on South and Central America. The most intense rivalry in North America was between the French and the English, both making claims over the same interior land area. The territory of what we now call 'New York State' was a contested area.

Samuel de Champlain (1567–1635) cartographer, explorer and governor of New France, made a number of maps of 'his' territory. De Champlain's activities condense the connection between appropriation and mapping. He first landed in North America in 1603. In 1604, he helped establish a colony in Nova Scotia and, in 1609, established Quebec.[2] He travelled extensively throughout the region, making treaties with friendly tribes, fighting against others, mapping as he went. He also encouraged explorations and collated the findings in a series of descriptions and maps. His maps were not simply the result of European mapmakers. De Champlain was heavily reliant on the information and spatial depiction given to him by Native-American informants. The maps of de Champlain are composite French Native-American maps. In 1609, de Champlain made a manuscript map of the coastline from Cape Sable south to Cape Cod. It contains an accurate depiction of the coastline, while the interior is depicted with trees and native villages. In 1613, his *Carte Géographique de la Nouvelle France* appeared in his book of his travels, *Les Voyages du Sieur de Champlain* published in Paris. This map shows New France from the mouth of the St Lawrence as far upriver as the Great Lakes. The map is richly decorated; the borders contain pictures of Native Americans and botanical specimens. The detailed coastline and river frontage is in contrast with the more speculative treatment of inland territory. The map is a claim to territory. The land has been named in the image of the imperial metropole, surveyed and mapped. It is presented as a land rich in prospect, the decoration bespeaking a land full of nature's bounty. The map is also an enticement: it is presented to a French audience to both record and sell the new colony.

Throughout the seventeenth century, French fur traders, explorers and Jesuit priests looking for converts travelled up the St Lawrence, west to the Great Lakes, and south down the Mississippi. In return for pelts, they traded guns, liquor, metal goods and blankets. There was also a transfer of knowledge as language, customs and geographical information were shared, swapped, compared and exchanged. The French maps reflected this increased knowledge of the interior. In 1656, Nicholas Sanson (1600–1677) produced a map, *Le Canada, ou Nouvelle France*. The name 'Canada' is interesting. Its precise origin is unknown but probably derives from the Huron word *kanata*, meaning cabin, lodge, village. The map, published as a loose map, shows the Grand Bank, the initial attraction for the French, and is richly detailed along the mouth of the St Lawrence. It becomes more speculative further inland. The map is distorted, but its distortion is revealing. The interior is truncated in that Lake Erie is shown as being close to the northern boundary of Florida. This distortion minimizes the English territories along the eastern seaboard and maximizes the French claims to the interior. From the St Lawrence to the Spanish territory of Florida is all French. On the map, Native-American names appear, but the words in the cartouche clearly note that the map is concerned to represent the geographical disposition of the competing European powers. From the mouth of the St Lawrence to Florida the territory is clearly marked as French. The map was produced in Paris by a French cartographer who gave geography courses to Cardinal Richelieu and King Louis XIII. Sanson was paid quite literally to represent French interests.

In North America there was constant friction between Britain and France as they struggled for supremacy. The outright hostilities were called the French and Indian Wars as both sides used Native-American allies in the conflicts. The first, from 1689 to 1713, was only resolved at the Treaty of Utrecht, which stabilized affairs at least for a while. It did not, however, specify exact borders. The treaty called for a commission to settle the boundaries, but that commission could never reconcile the different and competing claims of Britain and France. From 1713 up until the Treaty of Paris in 1763, which established definite spheres of influence, maps of North America were produced in this contested area of geopolitical significance.

A number of French maps were produced that advanced French claims to the interior of North America. In 1718, the same year that a French merchant company founded the city of New Orleans, Guillaume Delisle (sometimes DeL'Isle) (1675–1726) produced his map *Carte de la Louisiane et du Cours du Mississipi*. Delisle was the *Premier Géographe du Roi*[3] – a title which reminds us that cartography was a tool of government.[4] In the map, *La Louisiane* is placed in broad letters across the entire basin. The English colonies are again compressed along the eastern seaboard (illus. 9). One inset on the bottom right-hand corner of the map shows the mouth of the Mississippi, French forts and Native-American villages. The inset is indicative of French interests in this area. Blocked in the east by the English, the great river was the trading outlet of the French inland empire. The new city of New Orleans was founded the same year that the map was published. Both represented French attempts at legitimizing and securing their hold over the interior of North America.

Delisle's map drew upon the observations of French explorers, priests and traders. They had travelled along the rivers of the Mississippi basin, and the compilation of their knowledge led to Delisle's map being the most accurate one of the river system to date. It was immensely influential and was used as a template for almost 50 years. Jefferson had a copy of the map and it was an important source of information for the Lewis and Clark expedition. The map was informed by the maps and writings of a large number of French explorers, including Bourgmont, Marquette, Joliet, La Salle, Sieur Vermale, Father Jacob Le Maire and Louis Hennepin. The map contains an extensive listing of Native-American villages and names. In his key (*explication des marques*), Delisle has only four symbols: one for Native-American villages, one for *nations dérangées*, another for *nations détruites*, and one for the route taken by DeSoto. The middle two are interesting.[5] It is an early use of the term *nation*. A 1690

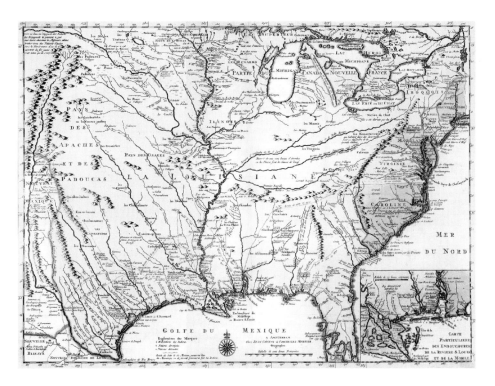

9 Guillaume Delisle's *Carte de la Louisiane et du Cours du Mississipi* (Paris, 1718).

French dictionary by Antoine Furetière indicates that *nation* refers to a large group of people contained within certain limits or under the same domination. *Dérangée* comes from *déranger*, to disarrange, to disturb. I find this term *nations dérangées* fascinating. It has the sense of an order disturbed, a nation misplaced, unbalanced (it is where we get the word 'deranged'). The symbol is used west of the Mississippi in the upper Missouri basin. Was Delisle referring to a nation displaced or a deranged people? It is not clear from the map. The other term, *détruites*, comes from to destroy. One *nation détruite* identified in the Delisle map is the *Nation du Chat*, located on the southern shore of Lake Erie. Delisle notes that they were destroyed by the Iroquois. The terms, rarely employed on the map yet considered important enough to be presented in the key, indicate a world of change, disturbance and destruction. Was there an implication that the French would give order to this chaos?

The explorers were dependent on Native Americans to find their way and survive. Native-American tribal names and the location of their villages were thus of supreme importance. Moreover, French economic interests were primarily in the fur trade. They traded with the Native Americans and thus needed knowledge of the who and where of their trading partners. The Native-American presence is richly detailed on the map.

The map was also guided by French interests against the British. Not only are the British possessions slammed up against the coast by a solid wall of French possessions, Delisle even suggested on the map that Carolina was named in honour of Charles of France. The map is a record of French claims beyond the Appalachians. It presents a picture of a huge river basin in French possession inhabited by a variety of Native-American nations with the British claims sidelined to the eastern coast.

British geographic representations of North America, like those of the French, were part geographic description, part enticement to further settlement and part geopolitical claim to territory.

In direct response to Delisle's map of 1718, Herman Moll (d. 1732) produced a number of maps of North America. Moll was born in Germany and came to England in 1678. Living in London, he found work as an engraver, bookseller and geographer. Moll was the foremost map publisher of the early eighteenth century. He sold maps from a shop in Blackfriars. He published maps, atlases and geographies. Some of his maps were included in Daniel Defoe's *A Tour thro' the Whole Island of Great Britain* (1724–6). He also wrote and published a series of books and atlases, including *A System of Geography* (1701), *Atlas Geographus* (1711–17), *The World Described* (1727), and *Atlas Minor* (1729). On his maps he put the profession of Geographer after his name.

Moll used London as the prime meridian. In all of his maps Moll put British interests first. In 1715, he published a map entitled *A New and Exact Map of the Dominions of the King of Great Britain on ye Continent of North America*. Made soon after the Treaty of Utrecht, it was literally a depiction of the British position. The British colonies are in the centre while the French claims are reduced to a small inset. Another inset shows a view of Niagara with details of beavers, yet another reminder that the fur trade was a major economic motivation for British and French designs on the interior.

Moll's maps of North America were produced in this context of superpower rivalry and competition. In direct response to Delisle's 1718 map, Moll produced a number of maps in 1720. *A New Map of the North Parts of America* was a large sheet map and is included in *The World Described*. It is aimed explicitly at informing a British audience of the latest French claims.

In the same year, Moll also produced *This Map of North America*

According to ye Newest and most Exact Observations and dedicated it to Lord Somers, president of the Privy Council, the body charged in principle with administering the colonies. In Moll's map, the British colonies stretch from the Carolinas to Newfoundland and the Labrador peninsula is marked as New Britain. Off the eastern seaboard, the ocean is marked as *Sea of the British Empire*. Here, New France and Louisiana seem to have shrunk in comparison to the expansive treatment of Delisle. Moll made his map to make the British aware of French encroachments as well to picture a reduced French territory. In the cartouche, the bounty of the New World and deferential Native Americans and Inuits are draped around the dedication to Lord Somers. And below this, there is a vignette of codfish processing in Newfoundland. The economic motive to imperial claims is clearly depicted.

The publication of Delisle's Map also caused an official response. In 1720, Governor Burnet of New York wrote to the Lords Commissioners for Trade and Plantations[6] that the Delisle Map laid claim to Carolina. They responded, albeit slowly. Henry Popple (d. 1743), clerk to the Board of Trade and Cashier to Queen Anne, and with good family connections – his grandfather, father and brother were all secretary of the board at different times – was charged with creating a cartographic response. In 1727, he made a manuscript draft, drawing heavily on Delisle's Map and records made available to him by the board. His huge map, printed in 1733 and entitled *America Septentrionalis. A Map of the British Empire in America with the French and Spanish Settlements adjacent thereto*, is the first large-scale printed map of North America. It is also one of the largest maps of the entire eighteenth century, measuring 93 x 89 inches.[7] The title of the map is indicative of its purpose. Popple produced 20 sheets and one index sheet, all in the form of an atlas published under the aegis of the Lords Commissioners. Popple dedicated the map 'To the QUEEN's most EXCELLENT MAJESTY'. The board ordered the map to be sent to each of the British governors in America.

As the rivalry between Britain and France increased, the Lords Commissioners were not pleased with Popple's map because it did not advance British claims nearly enough for them. And in drawing upon French sources, it could be seen as advancing French claims. An article listing the map's defects, at least in terms of British interests, was published in *The Gentleman's Magazine* in 1746 and in 1755, British commissioners at the conference to delimit British and French claims disowned the map:

. . . he published it upon his own single Authority; the Board of Trade at the Time gave it no extraordinary Sanction. It is inconsistent with the very Records it pretends to have copied; it came into the World as the Performance of a Single Person; it has ever been thought in Great Britain to be a very incorrect Map, and has never in any negociation between the two Crowns been appealed to by Great Britain as being correct, or as a map of any authority.[8]

In 1750, the President of the Board asked John Mitchell to prepare a map of the British colonies in North America. The main objective of the map was to advance British territorial claims. John Mitchell (1711–1768) was a cartographer, physician and botanist. He had experience with North America; he had emigrated to Virginia in 1720. Returning to England in 1746 and well connected – he was a friend of the Earl of Halifax, the President of the Board – Mitchell was able to draw upon the surveys, maps and reports held by the Lords Commissioners. The map was first drawn in 1750 but corrected and improved until it was published in 1755 (see illus. 10). It is the second largest British map of North America up to that time, the largest being Popple's. Mitchell's map has two basic elements. The first is a concern with geographical accuracy. Mitchell makes clear that the geography of North America had been 'grossly misrepresented by others'. He was keen to get the correct latitude and longitude. This was easier for the better-known coastal areas than for the interior. The

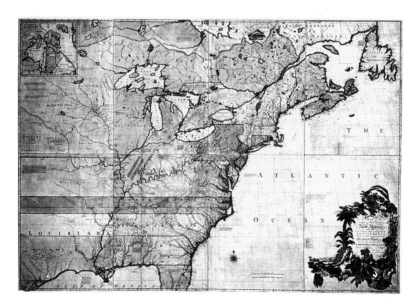

10 John Mitchell's *Map of the British and French Dominions in North America* (London, 1755).

scale of the map is given in minutes of latitude, English miles, English and French sea leagues, common French leagues and Dutch miles. Mitchell was obviously drawing upon a wide source of material and felt the need to provide a comprehensive scale. The locational accuracy of the map was widely accepted as a standard, and the map was used in various editions throughout the rest of the century.

A second concern of the map is with British interests. It is a map of British and French dominions. The map is dedicated jointly to the Earl of Halifax, President of the Lords Commissioners, and Secretary of the Board, John Pownall. A note on the map declares, 'This MAP was Undertaken with the Approbation and at the Request of the Lords Commissionaires for Trade and Plantations.' In the map, Mitchell responded to the Lords Commissioners' complaint of the Popple depiction by extending the boundaries of Virginia, the Carolinas and Georgia across the Mississippi; there is no western limit to British possessions – they stretch towards infinity.

The Native-American presence is richly detailed and well documented. There are three categories of Native-American settlements (towns and forts, villages and deserted villages). There is also a series of notes on the map – 'Nauchees (extirpated by the French in 1730) Conquer'd and expelled by the Iroquois' (see illus. 63). The disposition of military forces and locations is an important topic of this map, with the key containing four categories for military presences: fortifications, forts, habitations fortified, and Native-American towns and forts. The map also has written commentary, especially for the interior and western regions: 'A fine Fertile Country by all Accounts', 'A Fine level and Fertile Country of great Extent, by Accounts of the Indians and our People'. The map is both a geographical description and a mapping of the geopolitics of the continent. French and Native-American settlements and fortifications are studiously mapped and often with a small commentary.

Mitchell produced only one map. He did, however, write a number of books, including *American Husbandry,* which was 'an account of the soil, climate, production and agriculture of the British colonies in North America and West Indies', as well as *The present state of Great Britain and North America*. These are early geography texts that advance the enlightenment project of describing and explaining the physical and social world. In 1757, two years after his map first appeared, he also published *The Contest in America between Great Britain and France* to accompany the map. It is a revealing book because it provides us with a written description of Mitchell's views when he was drawing his map. Although the book's author is described in the title page as an 'IMPARTIAL HAND', it is clearly a partisan text. The subtitle of the book includes the phrase *Giving an Account of the Views and Designs of the French, with the Interests of Great Britain*. In the book, Mitchell wants to draw attention to the 'designs of the French in all parts of America; and of the fatal affects of suffering them to settle on our frontiers'.[9] He begins with a justification for the colonies and pitches his argument against many of his contemporaries who argued that the costs of the colonies outweighed the benefits. It in this context that we can understand the cartouches that accompanied many British maps of the American colonies at this time. By showing trade exchanges and natural resources, the cartouches weighed in on the side of 'the colonies are good for us' argument. These decorations to the maps were more than just fanciful space fillers; they were a powerful political and economic message reinforcing the advantages of the North American possessions.

There were also some who feared that the colonists would eventually overthrow the British, so why spend money and resources defending them. Mitchell argues that the colonies are a source of wealth and power to Britain. His point is reinforced by the cartouche in his map, which shows the colonies as a source of wealth for British merchants, who are pictured sitting on the booty of the colonies. By defending these colonies from French encroachment, Britain would gain economic power and political influence around the world. By resisting French designs, the colonies would grow and flourish in the production of commodities vital to Britain and provide a huge market for British manufacturers.

Mitchell then drew attention to the pervasive claims of the French on the continental interior and cites the maps of Delisle as compelling evidence. He proposes a barrier between the French and British drawn along the line of the St Lawrence through to the Great Lakes. This would have the effect of pinning down the French in the northern regions and make them unable to forge Native-American alliances in the interior.[10] This boundary would then allow British colonies to expand beyond the Appalachians inland, enabling them to grow and prosper, thus opening up resource exploitation for Britain and extending the North American market for British manufactured goods. Economic and political interests were interlaced into a geo-political, geo-economic strategy. Mitchell's clearly written book is one of the most important, yet (today) rarely cited, publications of its time. It covers a range of topics and identifies a number of conflicts and issues that were to surface most dramatically almost 20 years later. The book also provides an important text for understanding both the context and project of Mitchell's Map.

Mitchell's Map became a base point for the subsequent carto-graphic representation of North America. The map was published in French in 1755 and in German in 1775. A total of 21 different editions were published between 1755 and 1791. The map was widely consumed by the political élite in Europe and North America. The map was used to settle boundary disputes in both 1763 and 1783.

In the Treaty of Paris held in 1763, the French lost their hold of the interior. France retained some islands in the West Indies but gave up claim to the continental interior. France ceded all of the land west of the Mississippi to Spain.[11]

The fourth edition of Mitchell's Map (1783) lay across the negoti-ating table at the Treaty of Paris between Britain and the new repub-lic to draw up the boundary between the United States and her neighbours. Later versions of the map were also used by the Lewis and Clark expedition. A map prompted by British interests was used to both map and extend the new US republic.

Military Maps and Mapmakers

The maps of Moll, Popple and Mitchell provided a general picture of geopolitical alignments and claims. They were not detailed enough to provide an adequate basis for political control. More detailed mapping was an important form of social surveillance undertaken by the military. This mapping of the territory provided a vital form of strategic information at a time of intense geopolitical conflict. In this section, I will concentrate on mapping in the New York area, an important outpost of empire.

Military mapping begins in earnest at the outset of – and during – military conflict. Some of the most detailed maps of this region emerged from the French and Indian (Seven Years') War of 1755–63. With the war fought in the northeast of the continent, New York played an important strategic role. Maps were a significant source of information during the war and were crucial to informed military strategy. At the beginning of the war, the need for better maps and surveys resulted in the British sending out to the colonies a large number of surveyors and mapmakers. Military surveyors and engi-neers, such as Samuel Holland, John Montresor and Francis Pfister, became part of a sustained cartographic endeavour. Their knowledge and techniques, sharpened during the war with the French, were later employed in making detailed maps for the war with the American revolutionaries. The British success in the war also led to the gaining of enormous territory in North America. In 1764, the Board of Trade wrote to the king: 'We find ourselves under the greatest difficulties arising from the want of exact surveys of these counties in America ... no time should be lost in obtaining accurate surveys of all your Majesty's North American Dominions.'

Samuel Holland came to Britain in 1754; he had been a lieutenant in the Dutch army. In 1756, he was sent to America as a lieutenant in the 60th Regiment of Foot. He and Montresor were involved in a mapping of the entire region of Quebec and the southern approaches to New York that had been ordered by Lord Amherst in 1759–60. Amherst had been sent out by William Pitt to capture the French fortress of Louisbourg and to defeat the French. When Amherst conquered Montreal in 1759 he ordered major surveys of the region. Under the direction of Brigadier James Murray, the work was completed by 1762. The resulting map measures 45 x 36 feet on a scale of one inch to two thousand feet. It is an enormous map that lists every single building. It is the map as surveillance – a detailed geographical information system that allows accurate military manoeuvres and military intelligence on a scale previously unprecedented. It is a cartographic panopticon.

Samuel Holland undertook many surveys and maps. Hard-working and ambitious, he was promoted to the civilian post of Surveyor General of the Northern District in 1764.[12] His subsequent maps recorded and embodied the constant shifts in colonial boundaries. In 1768, he was appointed to make a map of New York and New Jersey to settle the border differences between the two provinces: the map, *The provinces of New York and New Jersey with Parts of Pensilvania*, was reissued in 1775, 1776 and 1777 and included in several editions of Thomas Jefferys' 1776 *American Atlas*.

Montresor was a military engineer sent out with others at the beginning of the Seven Years' War to provide much-needed surveying and mapmaking skills to a hard-pressed British military. He was wounded at Monongahela in 1756 while building the road to Fort Duquesne (later Fort Pitt and, even later, Pittsburgh). Like Holland, he rose up through the ranks, eventually becoming Chief Engineer.[13] He undertook surveys and continued to make maps. His map of *New York and its environes* in 1766 was published by Jefferys, and his 1775 *Map of the Province of New York* appeared in William Faden's *North American Atlas* (1777). Details from this map shown in illustration 11 reveal the level of detail exhibited in these military maps. On the eve of the revolution Montresor was involved in a survey of the New York and Pennsylvania border.

11 Details showing the upper Hudson River around Kingston and Rhinebeck, and Staten, Long and Coney islands, from John Montresor's *Map of the Province of New York* (1775), from William Faden's *North American Atlas* (London, 1777).

In 1758, Francis Pfister, a lieutenant of the First Battalion of the Royal American Regiment, made a map of New York province. The map was drawn to a scale of sixteen miles to one inch and shows a narrow strip of settlement along the Hudson. The map carries on as far as Montreal with particular reference to settlements and forts. It is a military map in that the focus is on lines of communications, settlements and fortifications. Pfister also drew more detailed plans of Albany and the forts of Oswego, Ontario, Ticonderoga, Crown Point, Edward and Montreal.

Both Holland and Montresor are examples of surveyors and mapmakers whose work was published by commercial publishers. Their surveys and maps were incorporated into the British commercial atlases that flourished in the eighteenth century. The Revolutionary War generated enormous popular attention in Britain, and there was a spate of atlases that appeared at the beginning of the conflict.[14] While we know about Holland and Montresor, they are the survivors; Pfister was less lucky. He lived in Hosack near Albany and, in 1777, he raised a body of Loyalists to fight alongside General Burgoyne. He died at the Battle of Bennington, his wife and children were imprisoned and his estate of 3,000 acres near Fort Stanwix and effects were confiscated. We have a good idea of his estate and effects because his father-in-law, John Macomb, drew up a detailed list when he appealed to the commissioners appointed by the British House of Parliament to compensate those Loyalists who had lost land and effects during the

Revolution. Among the schedule of losses were fifteen acres of Indian corn in good condition, two horses, 77 sheep, a library of books and mathematical instruments, two male slaves (Tuba and Paulus) and two indentured servants (John Stanwith and Richard Webber).

Mapping/Claiming the Land

An important stimulus to mapping was to make legal claim over land. Maps justified, reflected and embodied deeds to land. Maps thus were essential for acquiring and selling land. The commodification of land involved its accurate representation.

Governor Dongan was the first Royal Governor able to dispose of land. He granted the 160,000-acre Livingstone Manor in 1685. Land transfers took off with Governor Fletcher (1692–8) who, in return for bribes, awarded huge tracts of land. Three-quarters of the province was placed in the hands of a dozen men. Governor Bellomont (1698–1702) attempted to clean up the process. He annulled some of the more outrageous grants, persuaded the Board of Trade to limit individual holdings to 2000 acres and demanded improvements on land. Successive governors reversed this stringent policy. Governor Conbury (1702–8), for example, allocated the million-acre Hardenbergh Patent. Government officials and land jobbers worked hand-in-glove. Bribes and kickbacks lubricated the transfer of huge amounts of land into the hands of the rich and powerful. Throughout the eighteenth century, much of the Hudson Valley was privatized into large estates and, by the 1730s, land grabbers looked at the 'empty' land of the Six Nations. The governors themselves, such as Cosby and Clinton, amassed tidy estates, and certain individuals built up huge estates. Sir William Johnson amassed over half a million acres on the boundary zone with the Mohawks. Awkward provisions were overcome through dummy purchases, and Native Americans were cheated in land frauds. Landholdings were stretched to cover as much land as possible, land was sold more than once, and Native-American names were used as a ruse. Much of the acreage was clothed in doubt, confusion and subsequent legal wrangling. The resultant litigation kept the courts busy for years. Illus. 12 shows a detail from a 1746 land claim map; notice how the boundary markings are vague, 'a dry chestnut stake at a white oak'. Such a crude system was open to abuse and deception.

Some land transfers were based on careful surveys, others were quick and dirty jobs. We have a relatively good idea of the land dealings through the correspondence of Cadwallader Colden (1688–1776). He

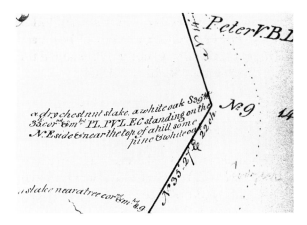

12 Detail from a 1746 land-patent map. New York State Archives (New York State manuscripts).

was born in Scotland, came to New York in 1718 and remained there until his death. He was one of those eighteenth-century enlightenment figures who carried on a large correspondence about both scientific and political matters with the savants of the day, including Benjamin Franklin. He was made the colony's Surveyor General in 1720, a position he held until 1775. In his survey of 1732, *The State of the Lands in the Province of New York*, Colden referred to 'ambulatory grants' whereby the patentees would claim land for the same grant in different parts of the province as they were driven around the province. There were few decent surveys, often with good reason because landowners tended to exaggerate their legal holdings. Colden came across a case of two men in Albany who had been given a tract of 200 acres by Governor Andros but who years later claimed 60,000 acres. In another case, some enterprising souls were claiming 70,000 acres when their initial grant mentioned only 400 acres. Colden set about surveying the land and trying to avoid the worst excesses. Although he tried to clean up land dealings in the state, Colden was embroiled in various incidents as claimants sought to exaggerate their holdings and others sought to overcome the licensing of the purchase of Native-American lands. Colden was also personally involved. He had various tracts of land, and in 1761 the Board of Trade wrote to the king suggesting that he was granting lands more for his own benefit than for the people in general.

Land dealing in colonial New York was a lucrative business. At a time of elementary surveying techniques and uncertain legal claims the process was full of uncertain boundaries, exaggerated claims, legal wrangling, land fraud against the Native Americans, personal attacks, political lobbying and personal aggrandizement by landholders and public officials.

The military surveys and the mapping of land transfers created a

13 Detail of a cartouche, from Claude Joseph Sauthier's *Map of the Inhabited Part of Canada* (London, 1777).

bank of geographical knowledge that was given cartographic form in the 1779 *Chorographical Map of The Province of New York* by Claude Joseph Sauthier (1736–1802). The author of the map was born in Strasbourg in 1736 and studied architecture and surveying. By 1767, he was employed by Governor Tyron, who had brought him to North Carolina to plan his governor's mansion and gardens. When Tyron was appointed governor of New York, Sauthier accompanied him. In 1773, he was appointed to run the survey line between New York and Quebec. At about this time, he acquired 5,000 acres in present-day Vermont. His first map of the province was completed in 1776 and his *Chorographical Map* was finished three years later; he also produced maps of the whole region. In 1777, he produced a map of Canada and New England that has an interesting cartouche (see illus. 13). Notice how the cartouche clearly reveals the trade relations that undergird the mapping. My comments made in the introduction about how maps are enframed in wider representations is clearly revealed in this case. The geopolitical and geo-economic relations embodied in the cartouche enframe the map in a literal and a metaphoric sense.

Sauthier started work on his chorographical map in 1773, a time of peace, but it was completed when hostilities had broken out between the British Crown and the revolutionary colonists. It was published by William Faden in 1779 and copies can be found in later editions of

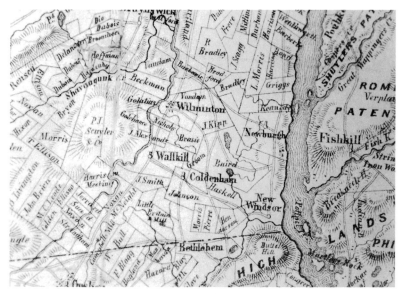

14 Detail of Ulster, Dutchess and Orange counties (the Hudson Valley and edge of the Catskills), from Claude Joseph Sauthier's *Chorographical Map of The Province of New York in North America* (London, 1779).

Jefferys' *American Atlas*.[15] The Sauthier Map is the last major British map drawn of the British province. The map shows a New York province divided into private landholdings (illus. 14). Over the course of 150 years, the land that was shown as tribal land by the Block Map has been mapped and appropriated. Property boundary lines cross the map in a grid of capitalist privatization.

Mapping the Native 'Other'

In all the large-scale maps of North America that we have discussed in this chapter, the Native-American presence was a major focus of attention. The Native Americans were an important source of information, trade goods (especially furs) and vital links in competing chains of alliance with European powers. Native-American villages, names and tribal locations were a significant feature in the maps.

In the New York State area, the Iroquois were a major presence and appear on all the large-scale maps, sometimes given the more formal designation of Nation of Iroquois, Five Nations or Six Nations. The maps of the province by Holland, Montresor, Pfister and Sauthier all show details of the Iroquois presence. In Sauthier's Map, for example, all the land west of Lake Oneida had the designation in block capital letters 'THE SIX NATIONS INDIANS COUNTRY'.

The Iroquois were an important military and economic power whose careful diplomacy and ability to wage war made them a significant enough feature of the geopolitical landscape to merit notation in all of the maps of the time. Their territory lay between the British, formerly the Dutch, and the French. They had resisted defeat from the European powers. Indeed they were a strong and powerful nation that had to be given respect and some deference. The Iroquois both played a delicate game of diplomacy and undertook brutal acts of warfare to maintain their position.

After the Treaty of 1763, the French no longer posed a threat in the New York area. The Iroquois, however, continued to pose issues of political control and political management. These issues were outlined in a 'memorial' (memorandum) written by the Reverend Charles Inglis, who was then the assistant minister of Trinity Church in New York. Inglis's pamphlet, *A Memorial Concerning the Iroquois*, was sent to Secretary of State Lord Hillsborough.[16] The memorial gives a brief history of the Iroquois as a powerful force and friend of the British in the conflict with the French. Inglis draws attention to the fact that the Iroquois have 2,000 fighting men and that 'Such a multitude of people, if reduced to Order and Civil Life and attached to us by ties of religion would evidently be a great acquisition to the Community.' Inglis wanted to Christianize the Iroquois and presented a scheme to the Secretary of State that would bring them under the control, influence and power of the British authorities. 'The conversion of these Indians,' hoped Inglis, 'will entirely secure their friendship.' Inglis proposed that two missionaries, to be approved by the Society for the Propagation of the Gospel in Foreign Parts, be sent to reside at Conajohare (now Canajoharie) and Oneida; that schoolmasters be attached to six villages covering the Mohawk, Onondaga, Cayuga and Seneca tribes; and that a college be established in Oneida for bright young Native Americans to be educated into the ministry.

A map was drawn to accompany the memorial, no doubt to aid in the identification of the places named (illus. 15). The map, like the memorial, is also part of the discourse of control. Two landscapes are shown in the map: a Native-American landscape and an Anglo-European presence. The map shows the territory of the Six Nations spreading across the Finger Lakes region, with tribal names, villages and pathways clearly shown. In the far west, the mapmaker writes that information was drawn from 'my Journals and the Sketches of intelligent Indians and other Persons'. Native-American land titles in the

15 Guy Johnson's *Map of the Country of the VI Nations* (roughly the area between present-day Buffalo and Syracuse), from Rev. Charles Inglis's *A Memorial Concerning the Iroquois* (1771). New York State Library.

Adirondack region are reported in the text. 'This Country belongs to the Oneidas'; 'The Boundary of New York not being Closed this part of the Country still belongs to the Mohocks.' This last phrase and especially the 'still' are indicative of a sense of flux, a feel of transition, of one landscape about to be superimposed on the other. The other landscape depicted is the Anglo-European presence shown up the Hudson River and extending along the Mohawk Valley up to the boundary with the Six Nations. Here are located the forts along the Mohawk Valley: Ontario, Brewerton, Stanwix, Hunter and Johnson, and Fort Edward and Fort George on the upper Hudson. Along these valleys, settlements and churches are highlighted. The map has most detail along the Mohawk; the map is centred there because it is the location of the Johnson lands.

Sir William Johnson (1715–1774) came to America in 1738. He ran an estate for his uncle in the Mohawk Valley but soon began to build up holdings of his own. He bought and sold land, gave leases to Irish, British and German settlers, and traded with settlers and Native Americans. He developed a strong relationship with the Iroquois, especially the Mohawk, who named him Warraghiyagey, 'one who does much business'. The relationship was overlaid with personal connections. He lived with Molly Brant, a Mohawk woman with important tribal connections; they had four children together. Johnson was a land speculator, a trader, a British imperialist and an ally of the Iroquois. It was sometimes a difficult set of mixed roles, but Johnson was successful in extending his personal fortune, defending British interests and trying his best to get a fair deal for the Iroquois. He became an important go-between for the British authorities and the Six Nations. He was made provincial Native-American agent responsible for providing arms and supplies to the Iroquois during the conflicts with France and was successful in persuading the Iroquois to side with the British during the conflict with France. Johnson's importance on the frontier is reflected on the map: Johnson Hall is shown at the same scale as forts and entire settlements.

The map was drawn by his son-in-law Guy Johnson (1740–1788), who, on his father-in-law's death, became the Northern Superintendent of Native-American Affairs. He organized the Iroquois to fight on the British side during the Revolutionary War.

The two landscapes are separated by a line that at the bottom of the map is described thus: *The Boundary Settled with The Indians in 1768.* This boundary was agreed upon on 5 November 1768 at Fort Stanwix, just west of Johnson Hall. Present at the meeting were representatives of the Six Nations, Shawnees and Delawares, as well as governors of New Jersey and New York, and commissioners from Virginia, Pennsylvania and other colonies. Benjamin Franklin was in attendance. In return for $50,000, the Native Americans ceded a vast territory, almost 1 million acres, including land in New York, Kentucky, West Virginia and Pennsylvania. The Native Americans needed the money; a series of crop failures had put them in dire straits. They also knew that they were losing their land in encroachments and shady land deals. By signing the treaty with its fixed boundary line, they hoped to secure their borders. In 1769, Simon Metcalf had the responsibility of surveying the line of division. On the other side, the British secured vast lands. They balked at the price. King George III thought the sum was 'very unreasonable'. Johnson argued that it was a great deal and that he had struggled to get the line drawn so far to the west. In 1769, the treaty was ratified by the British Crown.

If we look again at the map, we can see one landscape pushing up against the boundary line. The forts and settlements are spreading along the Mohawk Valley. The survey line existed on the map. For the Six Nations, the land sale was considered enough to halt further demands, and the line was to hold back the tide of colonists and land dealers. We can see this map as one of the last cartographic witnesses to a deal that was destined not to last. After the Revolution, the line would not be so much breached as completely obliterated. One landscape and one people was going to dominate. It was not the Six Nations.

4 Representing the New State

In 1775, after more than 150 years of colonization, most of the New York countryside remained wilderness. Only a handful of settlers had moved more than a few miles from the seashore or the Hudson–Mohawk Rivers. During the next 50 years the borders of the state were fixed, the land transferred to private hands, and millions of acres brought under cultivation.[1]

The Iroquois landscape and presence that figured so largely in Johnson's 1771 Map was soon to be destroyed. In a little over five years after the map was made, the region and country were engulfed in the Revolutionary War. The Iroquois tried to remain neutral. They had long experience of following a precarious path between competing powers; for the previous 150 years, their expansion and contraction had taken place against the wider background – and sometimes foreground – of French and British competition. This time, however, they could not avoid taking sides. The Confederacy of Six Nations was split. The deaths of some important Onondaga chiefs in 1777 meant that important go-betweens were no longer in place, and the traditional coherence of the confederation fractured along tribal lines. The Cayugas, Senecas, Onondagas and Mohawks sided with their traditional allies – the British Loyalists – while the Oneidas and the Tuscaroras, influenced by the missionary Samuel Kirkland, fought with the Rebels. At the 1777 battle of Oriskany, a small village outside of Oneida, Loyalist and Rebel forces, with their attendant Iroquois allies, fought a bloody battle. For the first time in generations, members of the confederation fought against each other; Senecas and Mohawks against Oneidas. After the battle, the Loyalist Senecas attacked an Oneida village; in retaliation, the Oneidas burned down some Mohawk villages. Iroquois legend has it that the subsequent travails of the people and their land was the direct result of breaking the Great Peace at Oriskany.

Oriskany was a turning point in the northern campaign. It helped to break the British siege of Fort Stanwix and laid the basis for the British surrender at Saratoga, French recognition of the new country and the eventual victory of the United States. The conflict continued after Oriskany. The Iroquois were involved in various skirmishes along the frontier at Wyoming County and Cherry Valley in 1778. At Cherry Valley, 30 people were killed by a joint British–Iroquois force and the town was destroyed.[2]

The Americans sent two military expeditions into the Iroquois heartland. One was led by General Sullivan, the other by General James Clinton. Washington's letter to Sullivan stated that 'the immediate objects are the total destruction and devastation of the settlements'. The two forces met up at Tioga Point in August 1779, and their combined force of 3,200 men set about creating havoc and destruction. The expedition entered the following villages: Kanawaholla, Catharinetown, Kendia, Kanadeseago, Skoiyasew, Shenanwaga, Kanadaigua, Honeoye, Kanaghawas, Gathtsewarohare and Chonobote. Here are extracts from an officer's manuscript journal:

Aug. 30th
. . . large detachments sent off this morning to destroy the corn, beans.

September 2d.
About 3 o'clock came up with the army at the town and encamped.

3d.
Destroyed it, together with the corn, beans, &c., and decamped at 8 o'clock in the morning.

4th.
This day and yesterday passed several corn-fields and scattering houses, which we destroyed as we passed along.

8th.
The army employed this day in destroying the corn, beans &c. at this place [Kanadeseago], of which there was a great quantity.

13th.
Decamped this morning at 5 o'clock; marched to the town, where we were employed in destroying the corn, &c. until noon; from this place Lieutenant Boyd, of the rifle corps, was detached with fifteen or twenty men to reconnoiter the next town, seven miles distant. Killed and scalped two Indians in the town.

21st.
Decamped in the morning, passed Kanaia, and encamped about two miles above. This morning detached Lieut. Col. Dearborn, with two hundred men, to destroy the corn and settlements along the south side of Cayuga Lake.

28th.

Col. Butler with his detachment arrived, having destroyed a vast quantity of corn, beans, apple-trees &c. on the east side of Cayuga Lake, and burnt three towns, among which was the capital of the Cayuga tribe. This day Colonels Cortland and Dayton detached with large detachments to destroy corn; the former taking his route up the Tioga branch, to which place he was detached the day before, and destroyed large fields of corn; and the latter taking his route downwards, and destroyed such as the army left undestroyed in going up.[3]

All the houses were destroyed, all the corn was burned, all the crops and fruit trees were cut down. At Chonobote, 1500 fruit trees were cut down. At Skoiyasew, eighteen houses, corn and apple trees were destroyed. The villages were left in ruins, the foodstocks were destroyed, the land was laid to waste. It was a calculated attempt at extermination. As Sullivan noted:

Corn gathered and ungathered, to the amount of 160,000 bushels shared the same fate, their fruit trees were cut down, and the Indians were hunted like wild beasts, till neither house nor fruit-trees, nor field of corn, nor inhabitant, remained in the whole country . . . there is not a single town left in the country of the five nations.[4]

The destruction of the foodstock meant that hundreds of Iroquois men, women and children were later to die of starvation and scurvy. Two centuries later, a name would be given to this form of activity: ethnic cleansing.

After the war, the lands of the Iroquois fell into the control of the New York State legislature through a series of treaties. At the 1784 Treaty of Fort Stanwix, the Iroquois were forced to relinquish traditional rights to their land; most of the land was transferred to New York State. One of the delegates reminded the Iroquois that 'you are a subdued people'. In 1785, even the tribes friendly to the Revolution, the Oneidas and Tuscaroras, were forced under duress to sign away all the land now composing the three counties of Chenango, Broome and Tioga. In 1788, the Onondagas were forced to cede all their land except a small reserve. Under the 1788 treaty, the Onondagas received 1000 French Crowns for millions of acres. It was probably the best the chiefs could do. The negotiations were conducted by a weakened side against a power that wanted land. Even this small island was overwhelmed; through subsequent treaties of 1793 and 1795, in 1817 the small reserve was turned into a tiny reserve. The result was almost the complete annihilation and destruction of Iroquois culture and presence. In the space of only a few decades, a once-proud people were reduced to being marginalized, aliens in their own land, shunted off to tiny reservations. The quote at the beginning of the chapter, seen against this background, is almost ironic – if it were not so appallingly misinformed. There was no wilderness waiting the progressive force of the United States: it was land owned and cultivated, a land that was central to a whole people's sense of themselves, of who they were; a source of material sustenance, cultural significance and spiritual meaning. The scale of the land loss is staggering. In 1784, the Oneidas 'owned' 6 million acres in central New York; by 1990, they had control of just 32 acres. Their land was first laid to waste and taken from them, then surveyed and mapped before being given away or sold off.

Mapping the New State

Surveying the transformation

The transformation of the 'wilderness' involved a mapping. In 1784, the state of New York appointed a new Surveyor General and allocated funds for the mapping of territory. New York State was one of the few states to employ a surveyor general and underwrite the costs of mapping and surveying. The man appointed to the position was Simeon DeWitt (1756–1834). It was a position he was to hold for the rest of his life. The subsequent mapping of the state is intimately bound up with this man, his projects and his methods.

Simeon was born on Christmas Day in 1756 in Wawarsing, New York. His family was of Dutch stock and he could trace his lineage in the New World to Tjerck De Witt, who appears in the records for the first time when he got married in the Dutch Reformed Church in New Amsterdam on 24 April 1656. Simeon's father was a country physician of modest means who sent his son to college. Simeon attended Queens (now Rutgers) College in New Brunswick, New Jersey, which had been established by the Dutch Reformed Church in 1766 and had become a centre of republican sympathies. DeWitt's studies were interrupted in 1776 when the British landed at Sandy Hook, occupied New Brunswick, burned the college and dispersed the students. DeWitt returned home, where he and his father soon signed the Articles of Association as approved by the New York State Committee. DeWitt joined a local, hastily formed regiment and saw action at the Battle of Saratoga. After the battle, the unit was disbanded and DeWitt returned home again to continue his studies of surveying and mathematics.

To conduct war, it is essential to have accurate maps. Good maps allow commanders to move their forces efficiently, to have some idea of the disposition of enemy forces and to plan marches, sieges and military manoeuvres. The Continental Army had limited maps. Washington wrote to Congress in 1777:

The want of accurate Maps of this Country which has hitherto been the Scene of War, has been a great disadvantage to me. I have in vain endeavoured to procure them, and have been obliged to make shift ... if Gentlemen of known Character and probity, could be employed in making Maps (from actual surveys) of the Roads, Rivers, Bridges and Fords over the Mountains and passes thro' them, it would be of the greatest advantage.[5]

There was a pressing need for solid geographical information. Congress agreed, and later that year it appointed Robert Erskine as Geographer 'to Survey the Roads and take Sketches of the Country where the Army is to Act'. Erskine needed help and, in 1778, he wrote to DeWitt offering him the position of assistant and the pay of 'two dollars a day, a horse and one ration when at camp, and travelling expenses when employed at a distance from it'. DeWitt accepted. Under Erskine's leadership, over 114 numbered maps were drawn, consisting of almost 300 separate sheets. DeWitt was actively involved, and together they prepared accurate road maps.

Erskine died of pneumonia in 1780. Washington wrote to Congress in support of DeWitt for the vacant post, and at the age of 24 he was appointed as Geographer in Chief. He carried on the survey work and mapping begun by Erskine. The Erskine–DeWitt maps provided much-needed information for the Continental Army.[6]

In 1783, DeWitt proposed that the surveys and maps be pulled together into a complete map of the war theatre. He also suggested a nationwide mapping programme, carrying into peace-time the surveys initiated during the war. He even offered to fund the publication of maps already in his possession from his backpay arrears. Washington agreed, but Congress refused to authorize the funding. Disappointed at the lack of support and no doubt angry at the delay in getting his backpay, DeWitt returned to New York where he became Surveyor General of the state in 1784, a post he was to hold until his death.[7] His offices were at the old State Hall in Albany, where he lived first at 149 Court Street and later at 146 State Street.

On his appointment in 1784 as the state's first Surveyor General, DeWitt had two main tasks. The first was to draw the boundary between Pennsylvania and New York because the old boundary was set only in the eastern region. Between 1786 and 1787, survey teams 'ran the line' to ensure accurate measurement. On the New York side of the line, measurements were taken by DeWitt and Generals Schuyler and Clinton; on the Pennsylvania side, were Andrew Ellicott and the astronomer and mathematician, David Rittenhouse. The survey teams marked monument stones every mile along the 42nd parallel. The second task was to survey the former Iroquois land that had come under the control of New York. The land needed to be surveyed for it to be divided up into townships and individual lots; it was to be allocated both on the open market and for military service.

During the Revolutionary War, the state legislature had offered land in return for military service. Under a 1781 act, colonels were to receive 2,000 acres for three years' service; captains and surgeons, 1,500 acres; lieutenants, 1,000 acres; and privates, 500 acres. The state needed men but had little money – land was the accepted currency. In 1782, even more generous allocations were made, and 2 million acres of land were set aside on former Iroquois territory for disbursement to military servicemen. Two military tracts were established in New York State: the old military tract in the north and the new military tract in central New York.[8] The new military tract consisted of 1.5 million acres. DeWitt sent two surveyors in 1789 to survey it; his cousin, Moses DeWitt, and Abraham Hardenberg. They surveyed the land and divided it up into numbered townships. To encourage settlement and civil society, 3,200 acres in each of the 64,000-acre townships were set aside for support of highway building and to endow churches and schools. Few ex-soldiers took advantage of the scheme; most sold their land warrants to speculators.

One of the first major mapping exercises undertaken by DeWitt was the 1792 map of central New York State. This map shows a land that has been measured, named and numbered (illus. 16). A mathematical order has been imposed upon the land. The comparison with the Johnson map (illus. 15) shows how complete the transformation was from Iroquois land to land that had been appropriated, surveyed and parcelled out.

The map is very detailed, a hallmark of DeWitt's careful cartography. Counties and townships are shown and 'Indian' reservations are depicted (illus. 17). The landscape bears the imprint of different landholding systems. The map shows individual landholders, Native-American reservations, purchases and patents. Land disposal in New York at this time was rarely to small farmers; land was generally allocated to large speculators who subdivided their large tracts. Land speculation was a major industry in which fortunes were made and lost. William Cooper created a family fortune from land speculation near Otsego Lake, and DeWitt's map clearly shows Coopers Town at

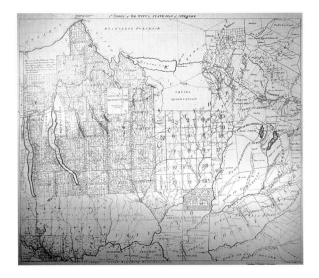

16 Simeon DeWitt's map
of central New York State,
A State Map of New York
(New York, 1792).

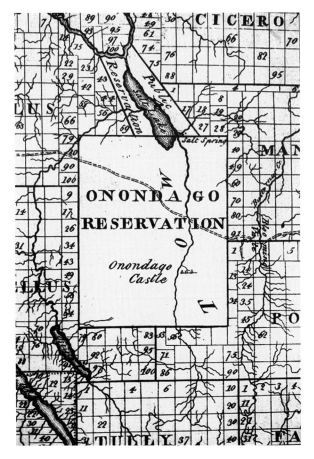

17 Detail showing the
Onondago Reservation (the
area around Syracuse), from
DeWitt's *State Map of New
York* (illus. 16).

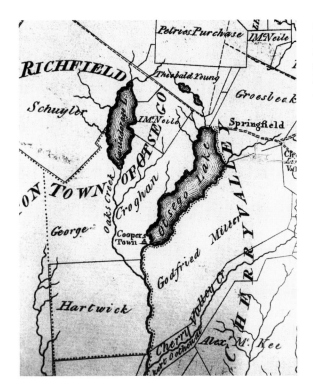

18 Detail showing Otsego Lake and Coopers Town, north of the Catskills, from DeWitt's *State Map of New York* (illus. 16).

the base of the southern tip of the lake (illus. 18). His son, James Fenimore Cooper, would one day write of the coming of white civilization to this part of the world with a nostalgia for the last of the Mohicans.[9] Fortunes were also lost. Alexander Macomb and Robert Morris, who both acquired millions of acres in the state, were bankrupted. Morris's holdings along the southern border with Pennsylvania are indicated on DeWitt's Map. Landholders could lose money if land sales were slow, interest rates rose and income could not generate enough to pay the debt.

The new military tract was an exception. Land was set aside for veterans of the revolution. Notice on the map how the military tract is geometrically subdivided into small units. The military tract was carefully surveyed, numbered and named. The names have a classical influence: Galen, Aurelius, Ulysses, Fabius, Homer. These classical allusions amused city slickers and European visitors. DeWitt was mocked in the press for the classical names: how dare he use such august names for such an uncivilized part of the country. *An Ode to Simeon DeWitt* appeared in the *New York Evening Post* and *National Advertiser* in 1819 that mocked his 'everlasting monument of pedantry and folly':

Surveyor of the western plains
The sapient work is thine –
Full-fledged, it sprung from out the brains;
One added touch, alone, remains
To consumate the grand design.
Select a township and christen it
With thy unrivall'd name, De Witt
Soon shall the glorious bounties bless us
With a fair progeny of Fools,
To fill our colleges and schools
With tutors, regents and professors.

DeWitt did not have sole responsibility for naming the townships. Members of the Land Office at meetings in 1790, 1791 and 1792 designated the names. The classical allusions are interesting. After the bitterness of the Revolutionary War, there was very little public sympathy for English or 'Indian' names. The exceptions were the townships of Locke and Milton, named after Englishmen but of republican sympathies; the founding fathers saw themselves as heirs to Locke's political philosophy. Classical names avoided the English or Indian connections yet laid claim to the great intellectual tradition of the Western world.

DeWitt was also personally involved in the great land grab. He amassed land at the head of Cayuga Lake from 1794 onward and was the absentee landlord of the area that became the town of Ithaca, naming it after the Greek island. He subdivided the land into lots and maintained a controlling interest on the subsequent development of the town. He stipulated leases, employed agents to collects rents and order evictions, gave lots to banks to encourage commerce, and was involved in the promotion and the construction of the Ithaca–Owego Railroad. DeWitt was a classic land developer, buying land cheap then encouraging improvements and urban growth.

The 1792 map was eventually to be just one of six sheet maps of the state completed in 1802. In the latter half of the 1790s, DeWitt was involved in a major survey of the entire state. DeWitt drew upon various sources for this map: sketch maps, boundary surveys and landownership maps. In 1797, he asked township supervisors in the southern part of the state to provide maps of their townships and information on a wide range of things, including landforms and climate as well as farming techniques, inventories of mills, and the number of houses, taverns, doctors and churches. All of this information was summarized in a large map of the state. At one inch to approximately five miles, it was the most detailed and accurate map of the state to date. It was over 12 x 4 feet, a massive artifact that covered the entire state. With a prime meridian set in New York, although longitudes were also noted for Philadelphia, Washington and Greenwich, the map showed rivers, lakes, some mountains and marshes. The physical environment, however, was not the major focus of the map. Landholdings, towns, townships, ironworks, mills and roads were clearly shown. The emphasis of this map was on the progress of civil society. It is a map that celebrates the forward march of progress and identifies the marks of economic growth. The material in the 1802 map also provided the basis for the smaller-scale 1804 map that was published at one inch to fifteen miles. This is a map of civil government; counties and townships are named and numbered (illus. 19). There is no Native-American presence shown on this map. From 1792 to 1804 the indigenous population disappeared from cartographic representation.

19 Detail showing New Paltz, the Hudson Valley and the edge of the Catskills, from Simeon DeWitt's *Map of the State of New York* (New York, 1804).

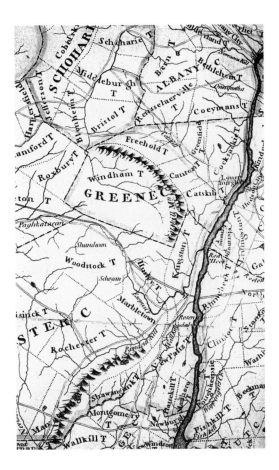

DeWitt's 1802 map was one of the first officially sponsored state maps. In 1803, the New York Senate, no doubt prompted by DeWitt, resolved that a copy of this map should be sent to each and every state governor. DeWitt still had a dream of a national mapping programme and felt that his map was a good model for other states to copy.

Although the 1804 map was DeWitt's last cartographic contribution that he was directly involved in, he continued to supervise and sponsor numerous other mapping projects. Let us consider three of the most important.

Mapping the city

DeWitt was one of the three commissioners involved in the mapping of New York City. The New York Assembly passed an act in 1807 'to lay out streets, roads and public squares of such width and extent as to them should seem most conducive for the public good'. The other two commissioners were John Rutherford and Governeur Morris. The commissioners were allowed four years to undertake surveys and produce maps. The resultant maps and plan, published in 1811, laid a grid system over the island of Manhattan. Many were appalled by the geometric austerity; *Harper's Magazine* noted:

The magnificent opportunity which was given to the Commissioners to create a beautiful city simply was wasted and thrown away. . . they clapped down a ruler and completed their Boeotian programme by creating a city in which all was right angles and straight lines.[10]

This geometric pattern owes a great deal to DeWitt's influence. A mathematician and surveyor, he looked to draw straight lines and impose geometric order. The commissioners' map was less a depiction of what existed; rather like a musical notation, it was the physical form of a future performance. The development of the city followed along the grid pattern laid out in the 1811 map.

Surveying the Canal

One of the biggest public works in the history of New York was the construction of the Erie Canal. It had been first proposed in 1791 by Governor George Clinton. In 1808, DeWitt was told to make a survey of the waterways between the Hudson River and Lake Erie. In 1810, the legislature provided $3,000 for a board of commissioners to survey the canal route. There were six members, two of whom were Simeon DeWitt and his cousin, DeWitt Clinton. The others were Governeur

Morris, Stephen van Rensselaer, William North, Peter Porter and Thomas Eddy. The members were patricians, landholders, politicians, and land speculators. They decided upon a route after intense negotiations and deal making. Opened in 1825, the canal had a dramatic effect; along its route, land values increased and urban growth was stimulated. Freight costs from Buffalo to Albany were cut by almost 90 percent, there was easier access to markets and goods, and emigrants moved along its path. It soon paid off its initial construction costs and laid the basis for the sustained economic growth in central and western New York and led to the primacy of New York City over Philadelphia.

The Burr Atlas

DeWitt also provided official sponsorship of one of the earliest state atlases. The *Atlas of the State of New York* was published in 1830. It was the second state atlas produced in the United States; the very first was the 1825 *Atlas of the State of South Carolina* produced by Robert Mills.

Although DeWitt provided information and sponsorship and put his powerful influence behind the project, the producer of the atlas was David Burr (1803–1875). Born in Bridgeport, Connecticut, Burr was admitted to the New York State bar in 1824, but he never practised law. In 1825, he was appointed to head a survey team in the state. The opening of the Erie Canal promised economic growth for central and western New York. Voters in the southern tier, fearful of being left out, lobbied for a road between the Hudson and Lake Erie. Governor DeWitt Clinton recommended that a survey be undertaken to identify a route. Three parties were sent out into the field. Burr was in charge of one of them.

DeWitt was the moving force behind the scheme to produce a state atlas, using his considerable power and influence to generate official support. In 1827, the legislature passed an act that gave official support and included the defrayment of costs of production and full access to public documents. David Burr drew upon the road surveys, the canal surveys, DeWitt's maps and the other maps held and produced by the state. To ensure accurate information, DeWitt wrote a circular letter to each town supervisor requesting that corrections, revisions and updates be made and submitted to him.

The atlas was published in 1830 although it bears the date 1829. On the title page the subtitle contains the deferential note that it was *Projected and Drawn under the Superintendence and Direction of Simeon DeWitt, Surveyor General*.

The Burr Atlas is a landmark document that constitutes one of the most precise cartographic records of the state. It contains a general map of the state, a large plan of New York City, and maps of each county. There is also a substantial written and statistical text. The long introduction begins with a boosterist flourish:

In presenting to my fellow-citizens an accurate and complete geographical view of a State reputed the richest and best cultivated in the Union, and at the same time rapidly progressing in all those improvements that distinguish civilized man, and presage his advance in national progress, no apology, it is presumed will be required.

The atlas is suffused with this triumphalist belief in progress and the forward march of history. In the introduction, Burr notes that his antecedents were the 1779 map by C. J. Sauthier and the 1802 map by Simeon DeWitt. He suggests that there is a need for more accurate maps because the 'progress of industry and art have produced still greater transformation'.

The atlas has a narrative. After the introduction, there are sections on statistics and government, internal navigation and a topographical sketch. The first map is a large-scale map of New York State with profiles of the Erie, Champlain and Seneca canals in the lower left, followed by a beautiful two-sheet map of New York City. The atlas also contains a statistical table of the whole state that gives for each county the acreage, population, numbers of schools, livestock, mills, domestic manufactured goods, distance from Washington and Albany, and latitude and longitude from Washington. The section on mills is broken down into grist, saw, oil, fulling, carding machines, cotton, factories, woollens and ironworks. It is clear that the rise of industry is a matter of great importance. A detail from the map of Onondaga County (illus. 20) highlights the railroads, roads, canal and saltworks around the city of Syracuse.

There is a map of each county with an accompanying statistical table. The map shows townships, roads and mills, while the table is a reprise of the material in the general state table. The atlas has a uniformity of style and expression. It looks like a modern atlas; it is a modern atlas and the forerunner of the many state atlases to come.

In 1839, the atlas was reprinted by Stone and Clark, who used the same plates and key but added a new introduction and made additions to the plates. Post offices and railroads were now depicted, expanded towns and new settlements were added to the maps, and more detailed topography was included, especially to the counties in the Adirondacks. A comparison of the 1829 and the 1839 versions reveals railway construction, urban expansion and continued population and economic growth.

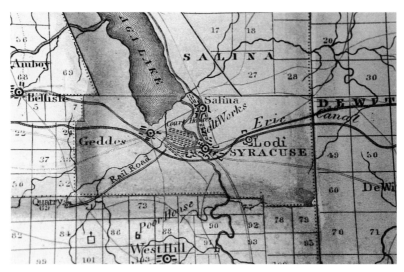

20 Detail showing Oswego Lake and Onondaga County near Syracuse, from David Burr's *Atlas of the State of New York* (New York, 1839).

The Burr Atlas marks a major change. The whole state, the major city, each and every county is depicted in a uniform style and scale, with accompanying standardized statistical information and narrative. The state is given shape and form and substance in the atlas. All the counties are now joined together, a civil union is complete, all the land is subdivided, the marks of progress are recorded and celebrated. The atlas celebrates and documents the hegemony of the state: there is no Native-American 'wilderness', and the march of progress is noted as the location of canals and towns, and signs of economic progress – such as mills – are all marked and recorded. The state has been captured, rendered complete and whole, civil society is cohesive, and the capitalist economy is functioning. The atlas is an embodiment of mathematical representation, statistical understanding and political hegemony.

It is instructive to compare the Block Map and the Burr Atlas (see illus. 1, 3). One is an attempt to understand the territory in order to make a claim. The Native-American presence is richly detailed and recorded. The Burr Atlas now covers the whole state in a grid of latitude and longitude, civil divisions and connections by railroads, roads and canals. Civil divisions blanket the land, the state has been represented, and industry is recorded and celebrated. Native Americans are absent and unrecorded. The land has been fully appropriated, surveyed, mapped, narrated and statistically described. The atlas not so much describes the state as represents it in a triumphalist narrative of control and victory, subject to explanation and understanding.

David Burr went on to make maps of other states, including Delaware and Maryland, Indiana, Wisconsin, Vermont, Ohio, Georgia and Alabama, Florida, Kentucky, New Jersey and Virginia, as well as a map of the United States in 1833. He produced an atlas of the world in 1836, published by Hall in New York. He was appointed Topographer to the US Post Office and in 1838 became Geographer to the House of Representatives of the United States. After a brief spell as surveyor to the state of Florida, he returned to Washington as Geographer to the US Senate. He was named the first Surveyor General of the Utah territory.

Simeon DeWitt died in Ithaca in 1834. At his death he was still the Surveyor General of the State of New York. He died in the town that he had developed, assembling land and encouraging economic and population growth. The town was situated in the land of the Cayugas that had been taken over by the state and then surveyed and mapped under DeWitt's supervision. Appointed at the end of the Revolutionary War, his tenure included: the first surveys of Iroquois land prior to their reallocation; the first detailed maps of the new state; an influential map of New York City; the surveyed routes of the new canals; and the first atlas of the state. DeWitt's tenure marked the territorial hegemony of the new state and its embodiment in maps and atlases. Under DeWitt the state had been given its representation. This was not a neutral representation (it never is) but one marked by a mathematical order, the defeat of the Native Americans and the disbursement of their land, a celebration of economic growth, land development and the forward march of an American history.

PART II

Representing the Republic

5 A New Mode of Thinking

Till the year 1784 ... the geography of this part of the world was unwritten, and indeed very imperfectly known to any one. Previously to this period we seldom pretended to write, and hardly to think for ourselves. We humbly received from Great-Britain our laws, our manners, our books, and our modes of thinking; and our youth were educated as British subjects, not as they have since been, as citizens of a free and independent nation. The Revolution has proved favorable to science in general among us; particularly to that of the Geography of our own country.[1]

The American Revolution constituted a break with the past, a break with Britain, a break with London. The rupture was both political and intellectual. The colonial connection was one of economic ties and of political power but, as the above quotation implies, also one of 'modes of thinking'. Britain had not only economic and political power over its New World colony, it maintained cultural hegemony. Books were imported from Britain, ideas were diffused out from the imperial centre and the manners and mores of élite colonial society had their origin in Britain. While the Revolution created political independence, cultural independence was more difficult to achieve. The North American colonials had forged a distinctive culture from the stream of diverse migrants making their way in the New World. But until the Revolution a distinct culture was the result of pragmatic adjustment, not a conscious endeavour.

The search for national identity in the new republic involved experiments in fine arts, architecture, fiction, science, philosophy and linguistics. Shortly after the Revolution, Noah Webster demanded that 'Every engine should be employed to render the people of the country national, to call their attachment home to their country; and to inspire them with the pride of national character.'[2] In this chapter, I concentrate on the important, though less discussed, 'mode of thinking' of geographical description and cartographic representation. Part of the making of the new republic was in and through its geographical representation. The construction of a national identity involved the creation of a national geography.

When he established the American Philosophical Society in 1743, Benjamin Franklin proposed that there be seven members: a physician, botanist, mathematician, chemist, 'mechanician', natural philosopher, and geographer. Most of the categories would still be appropriate for a similar venture planned today, albeit with engineer for mechanician and physicist for natural philosopher. One category stands out today – that of geographer. It was, however, not surprising at the time. There was an intense interest in geographical issues and concerns. A second look at Franklin's seven categories shows that there was no historian or political scientist, no economist or social scientist. The list was dominated by the natural sciences, with geography as the sole representative of what we now call the social sciences. Geography had a much broader definition then than it has now; it encompassed history, government, economics and public events. To be interested in geography was to be interested in the broad sweep of social affairs. Geography, with its wide definition, was an important part of the discourse of informed public opinion. A geographical discourse was an essential ingredient of literate public opinion and broader general knowledge.

But the geographical concern was not simply a result of the broad sweep of geography. The narrower concerns of cartographic representation, mapmaking and geographic description were also important. Geographic concerns were at the very heart of the public discourse of the educated classes; issues of geographic representation were a vital part of the intellectual life of the territory on either side of the revolutionary divide. Maps, cartography and geography were part of the intellectual fabric of colonial America. On 4 August 1731, James Logan, loyal British subject of Philadelphia, walked into the provisional Council of Pennsylvania carrying a copy of Herman Moll's atlas, *The World Described*, published in London in 1720. To express his fears about the western border with the French, Logan took out the ninth map of the atlas, *A New Map of the Northern Parts of America*, which showed French claims to Carolina and Virginia and their designs on lands bordering Pennsylvania. Logan was worried about French encroachment into 'British' territory and anxious that they would woo the Indians away from allegiance with the British. The fact that he used a map to demonstrate his point assumes a level of graphical literacy in the assembly and an assumption of cartographic comprehension among the political élite.

Benjamin Franklin embodied the intense interest in geographical issues and concerns. As clerk of the Pennsylvania Assembly, he had installed into the assembly halls the 1733 map of North America by Henry Popple. This huge map of eastern America, drawn in 1733, was one of the first maps to represent the interior of the continent (see Chapter 6). The map hung in Independence Hall as late as July 1776 when the Declaration of Independence was signed. Franklin not only collected maps and atlases, he also made maps. In February 1732, he published a map of the new boundary between Maryland and Pennsylvania. He was concerned with travel, discoveries and increasing geographical knowledge. He crossed the Atlantic eight times, lived in Paris and London, travelled in Europe and the United States. He met and communicated with explorers and travellers. He met the English explorer Captain James Cook and wrote a passport that gave Cook safe passage with us seamen during the Revolutionary War.[3]

A reading of the *Pennsylvania Gazette* in the eighteenth century reveals that maps were important. This semi-weekly newspaper was published from 1728 to 1845 and in the colonial period and the early years of the republic was one of the most influential newspapers. Maps were regularly advertised for sale in its pages. On 27 May 1742, a notice appeared that 'Lately imported and to be Sold by Reese Meredith' was a whole list of goods, including narrow shalloons, white flannel, snuff, tobacco boxes and maps. They were regularly mentioned in the list of goods to be sold at auction. A notice of 24 April 1746 recorded that 'Just imported and to be sold by Andrew Oswald at Mr. Joseph Turner's Store in Front St., Philadelphia: Maps of the 4 quarters of the world; maps of the whole globe; maps and prospects of the city of London.' Maps were part of the material culture. A notice of 27 June 1730 proclaimed: 'Books lately brought over and are to be Sold at the printers hereof The Complete Geographer; or the Chorography and Topography of the Known Parts of the Earth. With added maps of every country.' Maps were also part of the educational discourse. Thesophilus Grew took out an advertisement on 26 October 1754 to publicize his teaching abilities and included 'Reading, Writing, Vulgar Arithmetick, Mensuration and Geography' in his subjects to be taught.

Geography books and maps were an important part of the importation of culture but some maps were also produced in the colonies. In October 1748, a note appeared in the *Gazette* concerning the production of a map of Pennsylvania, New York and New Jersey: 'Lewis Evans in now engraving here and in great Forwardness ... gives us every reason to expect the Geography of these parts of America will be rendered sufficiently expert.' This was a quiet come-on and on 21

February 1749, a small notice reminded subscribers that 'the map is formulated'. The notice of 28 February gives a list where subscribers may make payment and that of 4 May asks late subscribers to hurry up and make their payments. A further notice appeared on 12 July and, because he must have been left with unsold maps, a more general sale of the map appears on 3 August.

The Evans Map was the exception rather than the rule. Cartographic production reflects and embodies economic and political power. The British empire not only annexed territory, it also surveyed, measured, mapped, represented and portrayed this territory for a variety of purposes, including military intelligence, social control and cultural appropriation. In the seventeenth century, the continent of North America was mapped by the Dutch, English, French and Spanish. By the eighteenth century, the Dutch had dropped out and by the end of the eighteenth century, the French were no longer a force. On the eve of the American Revolution, the cartographic representation of North America was not a monopoly of the British, but it was dominated by them.

The Reworking of Imported Geography

Books and the ideas in the books were eagerly consumed in colonial society. Much of colonial trade was in books and texts. Even after the Revolution, books written and published in Britain were sold in the major cities of the new Republic. Intellectual independence was difficult to achieve; the intellectual life in the new republic was dependent on the importation of books and ideas from Britain. The reprinting of books first published in Britain was the bread–and–butter trade of the early American printing industry. To create national identity, the imports from Britain had to be transformed.

Guthrie's Geography

One of the most popular geography texts before and even after the Revolution was known simply as *Guthrie's Geography*. William Guthrie (1708–1770) was born in Brechin, Scotland. He was an eager educator who wrote general histories and translated Cicero. His most famous work was his geography text. His first geography book was entitled *General View of geography ... or an attempt to impress on the mind of a school-boy a general idea*. It first came out in 1769 and proved very popular. A second edition entitled *A new geographical, historical, and commercial grammar; and present state of the several kingdoms of the world … Illustrated with large maps* soon followed. The title soon became known as *Guthrie's Geography* and numerous editions appeared: the third in 1771, the 24th in 1827, and even as late as 1842 new and revised editions were sold. *Guthrie's Geography* survived long after William Guthrie died. The name recognition assured publishers of a steady market for updated versions. It grew to a massive text; the 1795 (fifteenth edition) had 956 pages and 25 maps and contained chapters on planets, the earth, empires, climate and the history of nations. The largest section was a description of the different countries of the world. To keep up with the expanding geographical knowledge, subsequent editions led off with the latest discoveries. The 1795 edition, for example, had 164 pages of 'New discoveries'.

In the later editions, there is explicit acknowledgement of an interconnected world and a global economy: 'In considering the present state of nations, few circumstances are more important than their mutual intercourse.' This is chiefly brought about by commerce, 'The prime mover in the economy of modern states'.[4] The global connections are still described from a particular place. The writing is centred in Britain in two ways. First, Britain is roundly praised: 'The people are opulent, have great influence, and claim, of course, a proper share of attention.'[5] The reference to 'proper share of attention' is to head off any ideas that the country is suitable or ripe for revolution; social stability is assured by the phrase. This was an important message at the time of the American and French Revolutions. Second, the world is centred on London by the establishment of the prime meridian there. At the end of almost all of the book's editions there is 'A New Geographical Table', an early gazetteer giving the names of places alongside their province, country, continent, latitude and longitude. London is the first meridian (illus. 21). The world is ordered from a British perspective.

Guthrie's Geography contained a series of maps. The 1788 eleventh edition had 21 maps whereas the 1795 fifteenth edition had 25. There is no map of the United States as such in either volume; it is included in a map of North America. The 1793 edition has a general map of North America that includes present-day Canada, the United States and part of Mexico (illus. 22). Although Canada is noted, there is no naming of the United States. The latter is pushed up against a clearly depicted Canada and a vast wilderness beyond the Mississippi. The individual states have indistinct boundaries with no obvious claims nor connections to the huge western lands that have Spanish or English names. The map depicts the United States as a ragtag group of small

Lincoln,	Lincolnshire,	England,	Europe	55-56N.	03-30W.
Lima,	Peru,	South	America	53-15N.	oo 27W.
Liege,	Bish. of Liege,	Netherlands,	America	12-01 S.	76-44W.
Limoges,	Limoges,	France,	Europe	50-37N.	05-40 E.
Lintz,	Austria,	Germany,	Europe	45-49N.	01-20 E.
Lisle,	Fren. Flanders	Netherlands,	Europe	48-16N.	13-57 E.
Lisbon,	Estremadura,	Portugal,	Europe	50-37N.	03-09 E.
Lizard Point,	Cornwall,	England,	Europe	38-42N.	09-04W.
Louisburg,	C. Breton Isle,	North	America	49-57N.	95-10W.
Limerick,	Limerickshire,	Ireland,	Europe	45-53N.	59-48W.
Litchfield,	Staffordshire,	England,	Europe	52-35N.	08-18W.
Loretto,	Pope's Territ.	Italy,	Europe	52-43N.	01-04W.
Loxpon,	Middlesex,	England,	Europe	43-15N.	14-15 E.
Londonderry,	Londonderry,	Ireland,	Europe	51-31N.	1st Merid.
Louveau,	Siam,	East India,	Asia	50-00N.	07-40W.
Louvain,	Austr. Brabant	Netherlands,	Europe	12-42N.	100-56 E.
Lubec,	Holstein,	Germany,	Europe	50-53N.	04-49 E.
St. Lucia Isle,	WindwardIsles	West Indies,	N. Amer.	54-00N.	11-40 E.
Lunden,	Gothland,	Sweden,	Europe	13-24N.	60-46W.
Luneville,	Lorrain,	France,	Europe	55-41N.	13-26 E.
Luxemburg,	Luxemburg,	Netherlands,	Europe	48-35N.	06-35 E.
Lyons,	Lyons,	France,	Europe	49-37N.	06-16 E.
M Acao,	Canton,	China,	Asia	45-45N.	04-54 E.
				22-12N.	113-51 E.

21 Extract from the gazetteer, or 'New Geographical Table', in *Guthrie's Geography*, fifteenth edn (London, 1795).

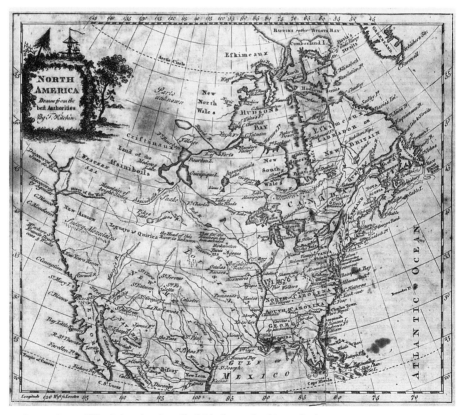

22 A general map of North America, from *Guthrie's Geography*, thirteenth edn (London, 1793). The Library Company of Philadelphia.

states clustering along the eastern seaboard. The map exaggerates the size of Canada and the west and 'shrinks' the new republic to minor prominence. For an empire that has just lost its colonies it is fitting that the upstart new republic is not given pride of place, its own name, or continental significance. The map is full of Native-American names, especially in the west, which is depicted as peopled, full of potential allies and trading partners. It is not an empty wilderness ripe for US expansion but a populated land, a place already inhabited.

Guthrie's Geography, the most important and widely read geography text immediately before and after the Revolution, had an explicit awareness of an interconnected world and a global economy. It was, however, still written from the British perspective. Britain was praised, and the United States was given the cartographic condescension of being included as North America. The geography text of the time did not ignore the United States, but it gave the new nation less than major prominence. The construction of an independent, national geography meant this text had to be given an 'American' perspective.

Mathew Carey

An important figure in the development of an American perspective was Mathew Carey (1760–1839), whose life and work spanned the first flowering of book publishing in the United States. He was born in Dublin on 28 January 1760 to the family of a hard-working baker who ensured a good education for all of his five sons. From an early age, Carey was fascinated by printing and publishing. Against his father's wishes he apprenticed himself to Thomas McDonnel, bookseller and publisher of the *Hibernian Journal*, an anti-English, pro-American publication. Throughout his life Carey expressed the political sentiments espoused in this journal. He was consistently anti-English.

In November 1779, Carey published his first pamphlet; it was on reform of the penal code. He wrote it to help the passage of a bill through the Irish Parliament. To advertise it he printed a handbill *To the Roman Catholics of Ireland*, which was seen by the authorities as seditious and, in the ensuing uproar, the bill was defeated. Now he was distrusted by both sides; the English saw him as a dangerous radical while the Irish Catholics were angry at him for defeating their bill. Carey was spirited away to France by his father. There he met Benjamin Franklin and the Marquis de Lafayette. He returned to Ireland in 1780 but was soon again in trouble. In 1783, he established the *Volunteer's Journal*, an anti-English publication that had the second highest circulation in the country. A year later, an unflattering cartoon of a powerful politician got him in trouble, a libel action was brought against him and an arrest was ordered by the Irish Parliament. On 7 September 1784, with the threat of legal action and imprisonment hanging over his head, he sailed for the United States.[6]

On the first day of November 1784, Carey arrived in Philadelphia – then the largest city in the country and the centre of printing and publication. Philadelphia had one of the most sophisticated and cosmopolitan populations in the country. It was the leading city of scientific and medical knowledge, as well as commerce. There was a relatively large population of readers and potential book buyers. Already in the centre of political debate, it was soon to become the temporary capital of the new republic.

Philadelphia's dominance in book publishing lasted until the middle of the nineteenth century. The city was home to a large number of printer–publishers, the most famous was Benjamin Franklin. Between 1740 and 1776, a total of 42 printers were at work.[7] There was a large market for English books and Scots, like Robert Bell, who came to the city in 1767, sold books by auction. Book publishing was dominated in the eighteenth century by the printing of books first published in England, especially London. The same book printed in Philadelphia sold for half the price of the imported book from London. Piracy was a widely accepted practice in the Philadelphia book trade. Domestic copyright was established only in 1830–31, and the United States dragged its feet over international copyright until 1891.

Carey began his publishing career in the city by publishing a newspaper, the *Pennsylvania Evening Herald*. The first issue came out on 25 January 1785. Carey was the first to publish extensive transcripts of the debates in the General Assembly. Despite its parochial title, the newspaper spoke out against regionalism and sectional factionalism in the country. The editorial line was national unity and the identification of ties that bound the citizens of the new country together, rather than the issues that forced them apart. The newspaper spoke out for national consensus and cohesion. The newspaper was very successful, circulation increased and, in 1786, Carey (along with five other partners) launched the country's first national magazine – the *Columbian Magazine*. This too was a success, but the profits were so small that in January 1778, Carey started a rival journal, *The American Museum*, in which he published American writers and original pieces, poems and essays as well as reprints from other newspapers.

A major problem for any national journal at this time was the difficulty of distribution. Long distances, rudimentary transport linkages, the sparse distribution of outlets and their complete lack in much of the country all made the venture difficult, and costs were barely covered. *The American Museum* was very popular; in fact George Washington wrote a glowing letter to Carey in 1788, which Carey promptly used in advertisements. The magazine promoted American writers, followed a patriotic line and was popular with the Federalists. The magazine made Carey's national reputation and helped lay the backbone of a national distribution system of agents. Carey had produced the most successful national magazine and in the process had helped in the creation of a 'national' audience now used to thinking in 'national' terms. However, the costs were high and the profits very low; despite its high reputation the magazine folded in 1792.

With the demise of the magazine, Carey tried his hand at other ventures in the book trade. He started to import books from Dublin, Edinburgh and London. He also began to publish books. In 1794, Carey published *Guthrie's Geography*. He pirated the work and paid no royalties (at that time there were no copyright laws). He published 2,500 copies of the book, a huge amount at the time and one of the largest undertakings in American publishing. Only Carey could take such a risk because of his reputation and distribution network. He hoped to use his national reputation and the national network of agents he had used in distributing his magazine to sell so many copies. He borrowed heavily to pay for the printing. It was a gamble to publish so many copies of such an expensive book; it sold for $16 – a hefty price tag – on subscription. Among the subscribers were George Washington, Benjamin Rush and David Rittenhouse. It was an important element in the library of the political and intellectual élite of Philadelphia. However, sales were slow and, by 1796, Carey's debts were mounting. Carey then had a stroke of fortune. He made contact with Mason Locke Weems (1759–1825), an Episcopal minister and book salesman who roamed up and down the eastern seaboard and into the backroads of the interior preaching and selling books. Weems had a feel for the market as well as the 'gift of the gab'. He knew what would sell and how to sell it. Carey hired Weems to collect orders for *Guthrie's Geography* and all of Carey's copies were eventually sold. Weems had solved the distribution problem by travelling the country and using his formidable oratory to sell the books.[8] Carey earned $40,000 from the geography text.

Some changes were made between the British version and the American version of *Guthrie's Geography*. The biggest change was the written section on the United States and the maps. Carey got Jedidiah Morse to write a section on the United States. When the

1795 British *Guthrie's* noted, 'No country in Europe equals England in the beauty of its prospects, or the opulence of its inhabitants,' Carey's edition noted that 'England swarms with beggars'. The change in orientation, the writing from a different place, is encapsulated in the change in the gazetteer: now longitude was given from Philadelphia rather than from London (illus. 23). There was no fixed prime meridian at the time, no international agreement; this was to come much later, at the International Meridian Conference of 1884. There is no natural prime meridian of longitude. Unlike the equator, which fixes the latitude with a natural phenomenon, the first line of longitude is entirely a social construct, a construct that reflects nationalism as well as science. By putting Philadelphia as the prime meridian, Carey was making a statement: the new republic was going to have its own measuring of longitude.

Carey's edition of *Guthrie's Geography* also involved changes in cartographic representation. Not only did Carey get new maps drawn, but they formed the basis for some of the first atlases produced in the republic. In the second volume of *Guthrie's*, published by Carey in 1795, there were 47 maps, and these formed the basis for Carey's 1795 *American Atlas* (21 maps) and his 1796 *General Atlas* (47 maps). All the maps are marked *Engraved for Carey's American edition of Guthrie's Geography improved*. Many of the engravings were done by Samuel Lewis, a writing and drawing master of

Pau	Bearn	France	Europe	43-15
St. Paul's Ifle	South	Indian Ocean	Africa	37-51
Pegu	Pegu	East-Indies	Afia	17-00
Peking	Petchi-li	China	Afia	39-54
Pelew	Iflands	Pacific	Ocean	7-00
Pembroke	Pembrokefhire	Wales	Europe	51-45
PENSACOLA	Weft Florida	North	America	30-22
Penzance	Cornwall	England	Europe	50-08
Perigueux	Guienne	France	Europe	45-11
Perinaldi	Genoa	Italy	Europe	43-53
Perth	Perthfhire	Scotland	Europe	56-22
Perth-Amboy	New-Jerfey	North	America	40-30
Perfepolis	Irac Agem	Perfia	Afia	30-30
St. Peters' Fort	Martinico	Weft-Indies	N. America	14-44
St. Peter's Ifle	North	Atlantic Ocean	America	46-46
PETERSBURG	Ingria	Ruffia	Europe	59-56
Petropawlofkoi	Karntfchatka	Ruffia	Afia	53-01
PHILADELPHIA	Pennfylvania	North	America	39-56
St. Philip's Fort	Minorca	Mediterr. Sea	Europe	39-55
Pickerfgill Ifle	South	Atlantic Ocean	America	54-42
Pico	Azores	Atlantic Ocean	Europe	38-28
Pines, Ifle of	N. Caledonia	Pacific Ocean	Afia	22-38
Pifa	Tufcany	Italy	Europe	43-43
Placentia	Newfoundland Ifle	North	America	47-20
Plymouth	Devonfhire	England	Europe	50-21
Plymouth	Maffachufetts	New-England	North America	41-46

23 Extract from the gazetteer, or 'New Geographical Table', in *Guthrie's Geography*, first edn (Philadelphia, 1794).

Philadelphia who exhibited landscapes, still-life and watercolour drawings from 1795 to 1817. While most of the maps of the world and countries outside of the United States remained the same, those produced by Carey for his edition of *Guthrie's* and for his *General Atlas* and *American Atlas* constitute a major change in geographic representation. Philadelphia, like London, was used as the prime meridian of longitude. Many of the maps used a dual system with Philadelphia at the top and London at the bottom. The cultural and scientific dominance of London meant that it was used in a uniquely parallel system that reflected national aspirations and an awareness of the power in international scientific discourse.

Both the *General Atlas* and the *American Atlas* contained only maps; there was no text. They were collections of maps taken from a variety of sources and had little consistency in scale or key. These atlases, however, represent a significant departure from the usual cartographic collection. They contain maps of all of the states as well as of the United States. The state maps differed in style. In the *General Atlas*, for example, the map of Tennessee was taken from a survey by General Smith (illus. 24). The army was concerned with mapping as a form of surveillance of the Native-American population, which comes over clearly in the map; the key features identified in the key are public roads, Native-American boundaries, Native-American towns, and the width of rivers. The map of New York, in contrast, was drawn by Samuel Lewis and includes roads, towns and rivers in a more 'civilian'-style map. The differences reflect different

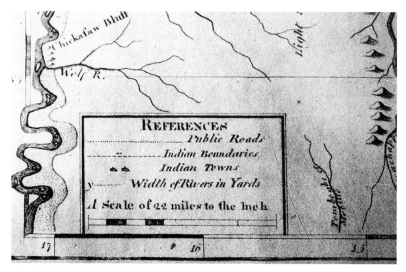

24 Detail from the map of Tennessee in Mathew Carey, *General Atlas* (Philadelphia, 1796).

authors but what is of interest is that they are brought together in the one text. We now take this for granted but, at the time, pulling them together was a political act, both implying and embodying the coherence of the different states. It is not too fanciful to suggest that the atlases helped the states to become united. A text of coherence helped in the creation of a political consciousness that put more emphasis on the 'united' rather than on the 'states'.

Carey also used the maps from the atlases to produce a pocket atlas in 1796, which had maps of the United States and the states. Entitled *Carey's American Pocket Atlas*, it was published by Lang and Ustick in Philadelphia. The text was brief, only a page or two of general geographic description. In this atlas, there was a more consistent style of representation that ran through the state maps, which showed roads, mountains and towns. The text also gave Carey opportunity for nationalist sentiment. On p. 12, he noted:

America endured every cruelty and hardship from her inveterate and powerful enemy ... lost many lives and much treasure, but gloriously delivered herself from a foreign dominion, and obliges her haughty foe to yield her arms, what she would not grant to her petition.

The Revolutionary War was not an historic event dulled by time. It was recent enough to provoke sentiment, intense feelings, and nationalist outbursts.

The cartographic representations in Carey's atlases are important in two respects. First, they give a new depiction of the United States. Compared to the condescension shown in the British edition of *Guthrie's Geography*, the new nation is now given its own prime meridian. Second, the individual states are brought together. We now take the 'united' in the United States of America very much for granted. It was not a foregone conclusion that the states would or could be united. A cartographic representation of them in a single volume, however, embodied the sense of them sharing the same national destiny. National atlases did not cause national unity, but they were an important part in the creation of a national consciousness among the political élite.

Carey was a publisher and a patriot. He went on to publish more books and atlases. A bibliography of his work lists over 1500 separate publications.[9] Between 1792 and 1799, he was one of the most important publishers of his time; at the height of his powers, he employed almost 150 people in Philadelphia. His geography texts were not incidental to his life and work. They were published because there was a market and Carey was indeed a businessman; but he was also a patriot, eager to represent his adopted country in a vigorous and independent manner. He could read a market and know there was a demand for 'American' material. *Guthrie's Geography* and the atlases were not only publishing ventures, they were acts of nationalism. The book and the atlases were widely distributed and became important elements in the libraries of the cultural and political élite in Philadelphia and the wider nation.

Dobson's Encyclopaedia

Not all the reworking of imported intellectual material involved a new geographic representation. We can consider a counter-example. An important category of book that informed educated public knowledge was the encyclopaedia. The signal literary product of the Enlightenment, encyclopaedias gave the literate a classified and ordered view of the world. Twenty-one encyclopaedias were published in the United States before 1831 – nineteen of them were reprints and revisions of British encyclopaedias while two were translations from German.[10] Even the titles could be misleading. For example, the *Encyclopedia Americana*, published 1830–33, was a translation from German. The *Edinburgh Encyclopedia* published in New York in eighteen volumes over the period 1813–31 had the subtitle *And now improved for the greater satisfaction and better information of the people of the United States*. These encyclopaedias were indicative of the reliance on Europe for information and knowledge.

The first encyclopaedia published in the United States was by Thomas Dobson in Philadelphia in 1798.[11] Its eighteen volumes were based on a third edition of the *Encyclopaedia Britannica*, 'considerably revised and expanded with new material'. It was entitled simply *Encyclopedia; or A dictionary of arts, sciences and miscellaneous literature ... The 1st American edition*.

Like many of the printers of the time, Dobson was born outside the United States. He was born in Scotland near Edinburgh in 1751. We have records of him in Philadelphia by December 1784 and, by 1788, he is one of the city's largest booksellers. He retired in 1822 and died the next year at the age of 72. His career in Philadelphia spanned 1785 to 1822 – important years. Dobson was for a time the most prominent printer and publisher in the United States. He straddled the periods of a cottage industry with very small press runs to an industry of mass printing and the rise of professional writing. He saw the establishment of homegrown printing, which took on a national crusade with printers advertising their wares with patriotic appeal to support US manufacturing and to show that scientific advances were occurring faster in the United States. Dobson was part of this nationalist rhetoric. He was a patriotic idealist. Religious works were an important part of his printing output; he stocked the works of liberal Christians and the printed works of the Universalists, but it is for his *Encyclopedia* that he is best remembered. It was published at a time of chronic political and economic instability, annual bouts of yellow fever, poor transport and a sparse supply of readers to pay for books. The *Encyclopedia* was sold through the subscription method, using the network of agents and sellers that had been used before in 1774 to sell accounts of Captain Cook's first voyage. The *Encyclopedia* was a significant achievement in the development of book printing and organized knowledge in the United States. Dobson used and defended the alphabetical arrangement which, in one light, can be seen as a metaphor of order in a period of turmoil.

There were both differences and similarities between the British original and the American edition. While the vast bulk of the text remained the same, there were significant differences. In particular, Dobson hired Jedidiah Morse, and we will discuss him more fully much later, to rewrite the section on America. The additions included a change in the writing of the Revolution. Whereas the British edition saw the war as a result of the secret machinations of French emissaries who stirred up dissatisfaction, Morse explained the clash resulting from Britain's desire for power and Americans 'abhorrence of oppression ... love of liberty ... quick sense of injury' (chap. 1: 576). The American edition in effect was presenting an American perspective, an American interpretation. There were some oddities; for example, the Declaration of Independence was not cited because it was associated with the controversial politics of Thomas Jefferson. It had yet to achieve the status of national icon and was still part of the partisan politics of the day. Whereas the British edition contained many biographical entries, the American edition did not insert the stories of any Americans, reflecting a continuing deference to Britain.

The reworking of the imported work was limited to rewriting their history. The geography remained very much the same – and this is especially true when we look at cartographic representation. Geography had a substantial section in this encyclopaedia (illus. 25). Defined as 'doctrine or knowledge of the earth', geography took up pp. 630–60 of vol. 7, compared with geometry, which constituted pp. 661–86. The geography entry had sections on measuring the earth, the history of the subject, the construction of meridians, latitude and longitude, map projections, and how to use celestial and terrestrial globes. Inserted alongside the geography entry was a double-hemispheric

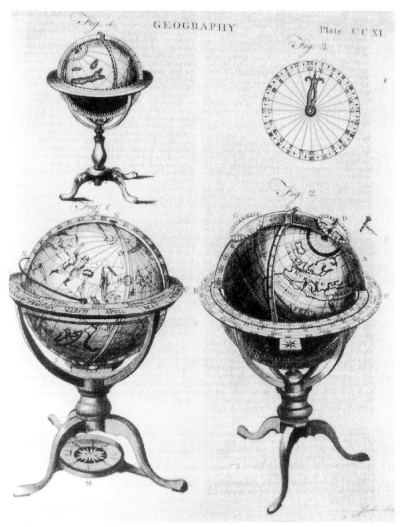

25 Illustration from the 'Geography' entry in Thomas Dobson's first American *Encyclopedia* (Philadelphia, 1798).

map of the world. The latest discoveries refer to the South Pacific islands, which are shown in some detail, and the journeys of Captain Cook and Lord Mulgrave are traced on the map. In the western hemisphere (illus. 26), the area now known as California is still shown as New Albion, a direct naming by the British. This is a British map, centred on London (the prime meridian is written as Meridian of London), showing the journeys of British explorers and British names in the New World. This first American encyclopaedia still bears the imprint of a British cartographic influence.

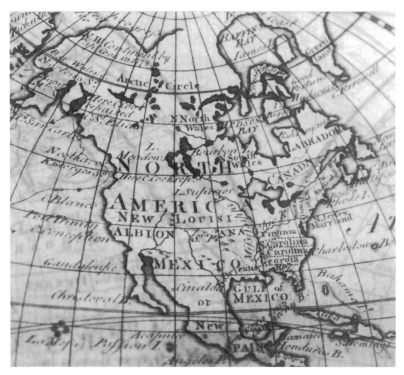

26 Map of North America, from Dobson, *Encyclopedia*.

Despite political independence the new republic still had the difficult task of creating a national identity. An important part of this
endeavour was the construction of a national geography that included
geographic description in a comparative narrative as well as a distinct
cartographic representation. The creation of an 'American' geography and 'American' cartographic representation was an integral part
of the need to create an intellectual independence from Britain and
forge the necessary cohesion over disparate states and regions. The
contrasting examples of *Guthrie's Geography* and Dobson's *Encyclopedia* shows that the construction of national geography was an
important though not hegemonic project. While geographical matters
were also expressed in Britain and throughout Europe they had a
particular resonance in the new republic, where exploration and
national identity, territorial expansion and national legend, geographic
description and national myth went hand in hand.

6 The Father of American Geography

Geography is either universal, as it relates to the earth in general; or particular, as it relates to any single part.[1]

Jedidiah Morse has been described as the Father of American Geography. The title may seem strange because few have heard of his name. He was born in 1761 and died in 1826. He is a distant figure, long dead, and now rarely read or quoted. A portrait of him, by his son, shows a thin-faced man scribbling at his desk (illus. 27). His books lie unread in research libraries; for those who make the effort to search him out, his style can grate. His religious and political beliefs have a harsh, moralizing quality that does not fit in well with current concerns of pluralism and cultural diversity. And yet he has a strange resonance with many modern readers. He wrote in a time when objectivity was not the focus of academic devotion, in a time of religious dispute, when the country was identifying its heart and soul, when conspiracy theories were accepted by many, and when political disputes were mean and fractious. Sound familiar?

And yet a disservice would be done if we were to try to make him too modern and to see his concerns merely as forerunners of our own. He wrote his geography about and from a particular place. He wrote in his own time of current concerns. His is an authentic voice, opinionated and idiosyncratic. And it is his position at the heart of these concerns that makes him so important. His geography texts were some of the most widely read and published books of any kind of their time. He wrote best-selling books and widely read pamphlets; he was a figure of some import at a time when the United States was more states than united and when a distinct intellectual tradition was emerging in the new republic. He was the most important figure in the construction of a 'national' geography at the turning of the eighteenth into the nineteenth century.

Jedidiah Morse was a Congregational clergyman and writer of

27 Samuel Morse, *Jedidiah Morse*, 1810, oil on millboard. Yale University Art Gallery, New Haven, CT.

geography books.[2] He was born in Woodstock, CT on 23 August 1761. After his graduation from Yale College in 1783, he decided to enter the ministry. He remained in New Haven for two more years studying theology and to support himself, he wrote a school textbook on geography: *Geography Made Easy*. First published in 1784, it proved immensely popular. It was aimed at an American audience and was decidedly patriotic in its praise of the United States and persuasive in its argument that a distinctly American geography should be written and read. There were few competitors; it was one of the first national textbooks produced in the new republic written by a native-born who sought to both describe and praise the new country. It was the first geography book written and printed in the United States. The book went through many editions and for the rest of the century was reissued on a regular basis; the second edition came out in 1790, the third in 1791, the fourth in 1794, the fifth in 1790 and the sixth in 1798.[3]

In the preface, Morse notes:

No national government holds out to its subjects so many alluring motives to obtain an accurate knowledge of their own country, and of its various interests as that of the UNITED STATES OF AMERICA ... To discharge the duties of public office with honor and applause, the history, policy, commerce,

108

productions, particular advantages and interests of the several states ought to be thoroughly understood. It is obviously wise and prudent, then, to initiate our youth into the knowledge of these things, and thus to form their minds upon correct principles, and prepare them for future usefulness. There is no science better adapted to the capacities of youth, or more likely to engage their attention than Geography ... This part of education was long neglected in America. Our young men, formerly, were much better acquainted with the Geography of Europe and Asia than with that of their own country ... Till the year 1784, when the first edition of this school Geography was published by the Author ... the geography of this part of the world was unwritten, and indeed very imperfectly known to any one. Previously to this period we seldom pretended to write, and hardly to think for ourselves. We humbly received from Great-Britain our laws, our manners, our books, and our modes of thinking; and our youth were educated as British subjects, not as they have since been, as citizens of a free and independent nation. The revolution has proved favourable to science in general among us; particularly to that of the Geography of our own country.[4]

The book is in two parts. The first, 'Elements of Geography', includes material on general geography: solar system, globes and maps, volcanoes, political divisions of the world. The second part of the book is a regional geography describing the different parts of the world. The emphasis is firmly on North America, which takes up pp. 53–246, while Europe (pp. 247–312), Asia (pp. 315–38) and Africa (pp. 340–58) are given short measure. The historic description of the United States follows the conventional view of a land of darkness awaiting the light of European presence:

When North-America was first visited by Europeans, it might be regarded, except Mexico, as one immense forest, inhabited by wild animals, and by a great number of savage tribes, who subsisted by hunting and fishing.[5]

The largest section, devoted to the United States, is by far the largest entry; it is entitled 'Independent America or, The United States' and is full of nationalist praise for the people, a 'free and vigorous yeomanry' and the political institutions. With reference to the War of Independence:

Thus ended a long and arduous conflict, in which Great Britain expended near a hundred millions of money, with an hundred thousand lives and won nothing. The United States endured great cruelty and distress from their enemies; lost many lives and much treasure; but finally delivered themselves from a foreign domination, and gained a rank among the nations of men.[6]

Each state of the union is given detailed description, including situation and extent, boundaries, population of counties (according to the

1810 census), the face of the country (i.e. physical geography) and a listing of bays, lakes and rivers, soil and productions, minerals and fossils, manufactures and commerce, education, cities and towns. Some mention is also made of Native Americans. For example, in the New York entry he writes of 'the remains of the Six Confederated Nations ... their whole number is supposed to be about 6,000 souls' (out of nearly 1 million). Under Georgia he has a longer description of the Native Americans and notes that the Creek Indians are 'a hardy, sagacious, polite people, extremely jealous of their rights'.[7]

Although it is a geography text, there are few maps. There is only one of the United States and that follows the delineation of Buell. Maps increased the cost of the books, and Morse was in the equivalent of the mass market. Morse's national geography was a word picture more than a cartographic presentation. Subsequent editions of the book, however, contained maps. In the earlier editions, the maps were British maps simply reprinted. The later editions drew upon a more nationalist cartographic representation. Illustration 28 is a map of the United States taken from the 1819 edition. Compare this with illus. 22 and note how the United States is now given a more prominent representation. The individual states are enumerated. There is still a British influence: the longitude is given from Greenwich as well as from Washington, and the New Albion notation in the Far West is a distant echo of British imperial claims.

Morse's text reflects the extent and knowledge of the Republic at

28 Map of the United States, from Jedidiah Morse, *Geography Made Easy* (Utica, NY, 1819).

the time. Only a few pages are given to describing Louisiana, with the terse note that:

The boundaries of Louisiana, as purchased by the United States in 1803 are not settled; its extent of course, cannot be ascertained. It is estimated, however, to contain nearly a million square miles ... The number of inhabitants in this immense country, exclusive of Indians was reckoned in 1800 at about 60,000 of whom about 13,000 were slaves. In 1810 the whole population was 97,401. The number of militia was about ten thousand men.[8]

There was a concern with general education and the scientific principles of a general geography, but the emphasis of the book illustrates Morse's desire to create a national geography – not a body of knowledge that was socially neutral and devoted to abstract principles of reasoning, but rather a body of knowledge that would ensure legitimacy and support for the country, provide an ideological apparatus for civic education and national cohesion, and a text to inculcate moral virtues and values. His geography text was not just an academic book; it was part of a wider, deeper attempt to create a morally correct American citizenry.

His descriptions were not separate from his religious beliefs and moral standards. Under cities and towns he noted, 'New-orleans in the licentiousness of its morals, rivals the corruption of the old world.' Morse saw New England as the source of American democracy and the container of solid, enduring values of Christian worship and hard work. He praised the yeoman farmer of New England and took a more jaundiced view of the slave owners in the South. The South, in the moral geography that underpinned his regional geography, was a place of feckless, indolent people lax in morals and ripe with sin. His moralizing was a constant in his descriptions of Southern regions and cities.

The year after *Geography Made Easy* was published, Morse was licensed to preach. His working life then followed a dual track, sometimes overlapping, sometimes in conflict. He became a Congregational minister. After preaching in Georgia and New York, he accepted a position at Charlestown, MD, a position he held for over 30 years. Morse took an active role in the religious debates of the day. He was a profoundly orthodox Calvinist who organized against the liberal Christians, the Unitarians. He opposed the election of Henry Ware to a professorship at Harvard in 1805, he launched and edited a magazine – the *Panoplist* – which preached the orthodox position, and helped to found the Andover Theological Seminary in 1808. He was unremitting in his attack against what he saw as the inroads of the liberals and was instrumental in forcing out the Unitarian churches from the Congregationalists. He was also involved in evangelical missions. He helped to found the New England Tract Society in 1814 and the American Bible Society in 1816. He was secretary of the Society for Propagating the Gospel among the Indians in North America.

Morse was also a professional geography writer. *Geography Made Easy* was so popular and successful that Morse earned a place as the pre-eminent geographical commentator of the new republic. Travelling south to take up a temporary preaching position, he stopped off in Philadelphia in 1786 and met Benjamin Franklin, to whom he outlined his plan for a comprehensive geography of the new world. Later on the same trip, he dined with George Washington. He remained a lifelong supporter and admirer of Washington. His next book, *American Geography*, was published to coincide with Washington's inauguration.

American Geography was the comprehensive book he had sketched out to both Franklin and Washington. Published in 1789 by Shepard Kollock of Elizabethtown under the title *The American Geography or A View of the Present Situation of the United States of America*, it was dedicated to the governor of the state of New Jersey, William Livingston. In the preface, Morse noted:

Europeans have been the sole writers of American Geography, and have too often suffered fancy to supply the place of fact, and thus have led their readers to errors, while they have professed to aim at removing their ignorance. But since the United States have become an independent nation, and have risen into Empire, it would be reproachful for them to suffer this ignorance to continue; and the rest of the world have a right to expect authentic information. To furnish this has been the design of the author of the following work.[9]

Having distanced himself from the Europeans and asserted the intellectual independence of the United States, Morse goes on to reinforce the civic virtue of the book:

Every citizen of the United States ought to be thoroughly acquainted with the Geography of his own country, and to have some idea, at least, of the other parts of the world ... this book offers them such information as their situation in life may require; and while it is calculated early to impress the minds of American Youth with an idea of the superior importance of their own country, as well as to attach them to its interests, it furnishes a simplified account of other countries, calculated for their juvenile capacities, and to serve as an introduction to their future improvement in Geography.[10]

This book is, as the title suggests, almost entirely about the United States. After a ten-page introduction that deals with astronomy, winds and tides, the book discusses the discovery of America with special emphasis on describing the War of Independence. The section on the United States (pp. 34–136) starts off with boundaries and contents and discusses recent history in imperialist language: 'Americans celebrated the establishment of their Empire.' There are descriptions of Washington in the most glowing of terms. Morse even provides us with a typical day in the life of Washington: 'rose at sunrise, worked on papers before breakfast of at seven hot-cakes and tea, visited farms returned at two to dress for dinner, at three had single dish and between half pint and pint of Madeira wine'.

There are only two maps in the book – one of the Southern states and one of the Northern, a division that reflected political differences as much as cartographic convenience. The vast bulk of the book, pp. 142–473, is a description of the states. Each state is described in standard terms, boundaries, rivers, etc. and then in a range of topics that vary by state. Massachusetts has sections on 'Witchcraft Infatuation' and 'Quaker Persecution' while Connecticut has a section on the war between Mohegans and Narragansetts. A long description of the states may seem commonplace to us now, but remember that Morse was writing when only the first president of the United States had been inaugurated. Federal power was new, untried, and distrusted by many. To write a book with all the states grouped together was to join them together in a narrative of national cohesion; it was a conscious political act.

Morse's book is a marvellous description of the states just after independence. The narrative is varied and covers physical geography as well as economic issues. It is more of a ramble, loosely structured, full of both description and hope. Phrases such as 'the soil is fertile and will support population' become both a description and a prescription in the forward march of progress. It is a delightfully unstandardized, idiosyncratic – and sometimes enlightening – account of the states. Writing of South Carolina, Morse notes: 'The probability of dying is much greater between the 20th of June and the 20th of October, than in the other eight months of the year.' Morse gives two reasons: low marshy country and 'a more operative cause in producing disease is the indolence of the inhabitants'.

A consistent theme in Morse's writings, and particularly evident in his *American Geography*, is his distaste for what he saw as the idleness of the white South. He attacks slavery especially for its corruption of the ethic of hard work among the slaveowners. A dissipate, slaveowning South is continually counterpoised against an idealization of his home state of Connecticut, which has the largest single entry. The state and New England in general, with its family farms and hardworking people, are seen as a perfect model for American democracy.

In contrast, the South is a pit of iniquity where indolence, gambling and drunkenness predominate. Morse did not so much describe America but passed moral judgement on the different regions and peoples of America. The judge viewed the world from a small New England state of orthodox, God-fearing, Congregationalist, hard-working family farmers. Morse wanted to write a national geography, but his writings reinforced the perceived differences between the various parts of the country.

The style is different and sometimes difficult for a reader looking at the material over 200 years later. It is a mélange of flat physical description with personal asides and moral judgements; not the more uniform style we are used to today. Nowadays in travel writing we either have the straight description or the more personal observation. Reading Morse is as if P. J. O'Rourke was also giving us detailed discourses on latitude and longitude figures or as if *Fodor's Guide* suddenly started to write about the indolence and immorality of the men who live in Georgia. In the discourse of early travel writing, population statistics are mixed with hopes for agricultural improvement, and social criticism and recent political history are included with asides on ancient history, all liberally laced with religious remarks and high moralizing. It is a rich mix of observation, description, hopes and fears, history and geography, high moralizing, expressions of moral outrage, economic analysis, ethnography and botany all rolled into one continuous journey. It is the wide-open, singular eye compared to the narrower, standardized visions of later writings; the broad sweep compared to the narrow focus; the large painting where impressionism, cubism and realism are jumbled together, and the abstract and figurative are juxtaposed. It is a highly personal style, with the narrative moving along as it takes us on a tour where our loquacious companion is alternatively scientific, opinionated, moralizing, politicizing, evangelizing, nationalizing. To read these narratives is to be overwhelmed by a sense of authorial presence that can tire and disorientate the modern reader.

The book was enormously popular. It was distributed throughout the country, giving Morse a national and indeed international reputation. The book became the standard geography text at a time when there very few other school textbooks of any kind. Geography texts were the mini-encyclopaedias of their day, covering the range of physical and social sciences, history and government, politics and biology. Morse's text was a vital element in the school socialization of generations of American schoolchildren.

Ralph Earl (1751–1801) was an itinerant artist who travelled through Connecticut and Vermont painting portraits of the the gentry and well to do. One of his paintings, entitled *Mrs Noah Smith and Her Children*, painted in around 1798, depicts a domestic interior (see illus. 29). The family is arranged in a straight line; the eldest boy is shown with a riding crop, a boy is shown with an open book in his hands, another boy with what looks like marbles, a girl holding a posy of flowers and Mrs Smith with baby in her hands. It was a standard design technique of the time, the family shown with representative objects that reflect their gender, age and stage in life cycle. It is a stylish piece, a good example of that flat, non-perspective style that marks it as American folk art. The boy second from the left holds a book which shows a double hemispheric map. Although we cannot be absolutely sure, it is my guess that the book is a copy of a Jedidiah Morse Geography book.

The success of Morse's text assured him a pivotal position in the world of ideas in the fledgling republic. He was hired by Thomas Dobson, on the strength of *American Geography*, to rewrite the entry on America for his new encyclopedia. Morse's article was later sold as a separate volume. Morse rewrote the entry on America, taking a

29 Ralph Earl, *Mrs Noah Smith and Her Children*, *c.* 1798, oil on canvas. Metropolitan Museum of Art, New York (gift of Edgar William and Bernice Chrysler Garbisch).

more anti-British line when it came to recent history and espousing his moralizing on Southern manners and lifestyles.

American Geography went through numerous changes and editions. It was first published in 1789 with 534 pages, and in 1793 the work was enlarged to 1,250 pages and published in two volumes as *The American Universal Geography*. The book expanded to almost 1,500 pages in later editions. A massive book it also became an important part of the emerging publishing industry. And it is at this point and place that Morse crossed paths with Mathew Carey. Just as Carey had invested heavily in publishing *Guthrie's Geography*, a second edition of Morse's *American Universal Geography* was being published by Isaiah Thomas in Boston. At that time, most publishers sold only in their own regions. Morse's book, however, was capable of selling nationally, and Thomas looked around for co-publishers. It was a huge two-volume edition with 28 maps and charts, much bigger than *Guthrie's* but much less expensive; moreover, Morse's book was better suited to an American audience. So despite his interest in *Guthrie's Geography*, Carey took a third of the entire second edition, publishing it in 1795–6, and sold it throughout Pennsylvania and the South, no doubt calling on the help of the indefatigable Mason Locke Weems.

Morse's career as a geography writer blossomed and flourished. The *American Universal Geography* became so popular that it was published by booksellers around the country in a massive national publishing venture that created the distribution network of a national publishing system. Morse's national geography was an important element in creating a national book market. The text also included some major printing innovations that we now take for granted. The book soon got so big that an index system was introduced, one of the first for any book published in the United States. Readers could use the index to look up the name of a place or person and find the appropriate page numbers.

The text went through changes as it went through its various editions. For example, in the seventh edition, published in 1819 by a variety of publishers around the country, Williamsburg was described more flatly as 'situated between two creeks ... The streets cross each other at right angles, and there is a handsome square of about 10 acres in the centre of the town.' A harsh judgement was no longer passed on Southern cities. New Orleans, for example, was described as a place that 'produces sugar, lemons, oranges and figs'. And the men of Bermuda, previously castigated for indolence, are described simply as, 'The inhabitants are generally seafaring men'.

The descriptions have been softened. We lose the P. J. O'Rourke and gain Fodor's.

The *American Universal Geography* was always poorly illustrated with maps. The earliest editions still had *New Albion* indicated across northern California. Morse tended to use standard English maps and although the longitude was changed from London to Philadelphia and later Washington, the whole emphasis of the text was on the words and not the maps. However, the book was so successful that maps could be sold using the name. The 1805 fifth edition was accompanied by a *New and Elegant Atlas Comprising all the New Discoveries to the Present Time Containing Sixty-Three maps. Drawn by Arrowsmith and Lewis*. This atlas was published at the same time in Philadelphia, Baltimore, Washington and Norfolk. It is a beautiful little atlas with a pleasing uniformity. The atlas represents the state of geographical knowledge and US power at the time. The map of the United States is only from the eastern seaboard to just west of the Mississippi; west of the Mississippi is simply blank, and the map does not extend to the Pacific. In the maps of the states that follow the national map, longitude is given both from London and Philadelphia. There is some variation in style for the different states. New York has mountains, towns and counties while some other states have only road maps. The Ohio map, a frontier state at the time with land being appropriated for settlement, has a finely engraved plat system (illus. 30). The map of 'Louisiana' reflects a hazy geographical knowledge of the West and the Rocky Mountains (illus. 31). It was produced before information from the Lewis and Clark expedition restructured US knowledge of that area.

In the later editions of his works, Morse was helped by his family. He had married Elizabeth Ann Breese of Shrewsbury, NJ in 1789. They had eleven children but only three survived infancy: Samuel, Sidney and Richard. The boys helped their father with the later editions of his *American Universal Geography* and with his other writings. The eldest son, Samuel Finley Breese Morse, who worked on successive editions of *The American Universal Geography* and developed innovations in cartographic printing, went on to become an artist and famous inventor; he invented a system of communication in 1832 that still bears his name: the Morse code. Through the work of Samuel we have pictorial records of the family (see illus. 27, 32).

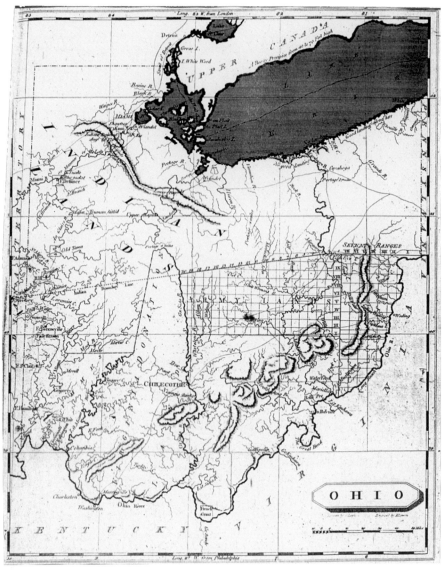

30 Map of Ohio, from Aaron Arrowsmith and Samuel Lewis, *New and Elegant Atlas Comprising all the New Discoveries to the Present Time Containing Sixty-Three maps* (Philadelphia *et al.*, 1805).

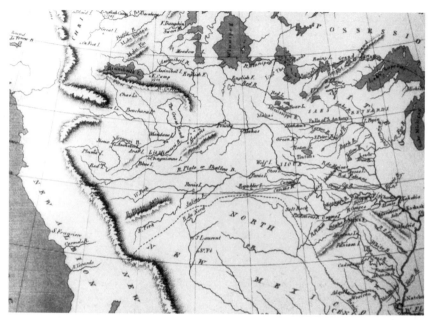

31 Map of 'Louisiana', from Arrowsmith and Lewis, *New and Elegant Atlas...*

32 Samuel Morse, *The Morse Family*, *c.* 1809–10, watercolour, gouache, pen and ink on paper.
National Museum of American History (Smithsonian Institution), Washington, DC.

Criticisms

Morse's work did not go unchallenged. Despite, or perhaps even because of the popularity of his *American Universal Geography*, there were critics. In 1792, James Madison wrote a letter to Morse complaining of the tart description of gentlemen in Virginia, which Madison took as untrue and offensive. The most sustained attack came in a 60-page pamphlet published in 1793. Authored by James Freeman and entitled *Remarks on The American Universal Geography*, the main objections were the lack of uniformity in method and plan, inconsistencies and contradictions, inaccurate maps, poor judgement and obvious prejudices, appearance of haste and carelessness, mistakes and omissions. Freeman criticized Morse's use of Philadelphia as the first meridian.

It is to be regretted that Mr. M. should reject the Royal Observatory at Greenwich, with which most men of science in America are familiar. His intention may be to compliment the capital of the United States, But whilst Philadelphia continues the first city in America for populousness and wealth, it can derive little honour from being the beginning of latitude. A first meridian ought to be a precise point. But Philadelphia is an extensive city; and Mr M. has not informed us, from what part of it he reckons.[11]

Freeman makes an important point. Although placing Philadelphia as the prime meridian may make a nationalist point, it is less than accurate because there no precise point identified. Morse does not say where exactly in Philadelphia the measurement is taken from. Freeman goes on: 'But whether Mr. M's plan be good or not, he frequently deviates from it. For beside Philadelphia, he has three other first meridians; Washington, London and the Observatory at Greenwich.'

The pamphlet is a sustained attack on Morse's accuracy. Freeman criticizes the use of the aggregate figures of average length and breadth for the country as a whole and for each state. The critique is persuasively written and well argued, giving a detailed account with page number of errors and inaccuracies. Freeman takes so much time over correcting the errors because as he writes, Morse's book will 'probably circulate through every part of the United States. It will be read in families, and taught in schools'.

Freeman presents himself as the voice of rational objectivity; he criticizes Morse for his cavalier use of figures, his sloppiness and his moralizing. When Morse described the men of Bermuda thus, 'at home they are indolent', Freeman sees this is as

… dull and illiberal satire. To listen to every exaggerated account of the faults of a town or state, and then to publish it in a system of geography, may demonstrate his hatred of vice, but it affords no proof of his judgment or candour.

This pamphlet takes issue with both the empirical errors and the sanctimonious moralizing and sweeping generalizations used by Morse. At first blush, the debate highlights the distinction between a religious moralizing and the beginnings of an objectivity. Freeman won the argument in the long run: we now hold objectivity above moral fervour, at least in most academic debates. Freeman was not, however, an objective critic. He was the liberal rector of King's Chapel in Boston, and in 1790 he was involved in a controversy with Morse. Freeman had edited a song for children that Morse claimed had wilfully edited out all allusions to Jesus. Morse attacked Freeman in the newspapers. Freeman's pamphlet can be seen as one more retort in his acrimonious exchange with Morse.

Morse's moralizing offended many people, especially those most affected. In *American Universal Geography*, Morse described Williamsburg thus: 'Everything in Williamsburg appears dull, forsaken and melancholy–no trade, no amusements, but the infamous one of gaming, no industry and very little appearance of religion.'[12]

One person was so incensed that he even took the trouble of printing an open letter in a pamphlet entitled *A letter to the Rev. Jedidiah Morse Author of the American Universal Geography*. It was published in 1795 by Thomas Nicholson – 'By a citizen of Williamsburg' – in Richmond. The author begins by questioning the title of Morse's work. 'I had some difficulty in understanding, not being sufficiently versed in Philology to comprehend that *American* Geography could be *universal*, or *Universal* Geography confined to *one* of the four quarters of the globe.' The citizen then attacks Morse 'for wantonly aspersing the moral character of a set of people' and goes on to say that Morse plagiarized Thomas Jefferson's *Notes on Virginia* to describe Virginia in the geography text. Much less disguised as an academic critique than Freeman's pamphlet, it is more a spirited and partisan counterattack. Even after all these years one can still feel the venom and bile generated in a citizen of Williamsburg.

Nationalist Concerns

The nationalist intent of Jedidiah Morse that was so apparent in his geography textbooks was apparent in his other writings as well. I want to consider just two of them that cast extra light on his enduring obsession and allow us to widen our angle on the so-called Father of American Geography.

On 9 February 1795, Samuel Hall of Boston published a 37-page pamphlet of a Morse sermon entitled *The present situation of other nations of the world, contrasted with our own*. This was his most nationalist tract. He begins with a summary view of the present situation of other nations of the world in contrast with our own. A quick survey around the world revealed the depth of the problem:

France: arisen from the darkness of slavery to the light of freedom ... but the existing state of things, in this great Republick is very unpleasant ... their government is unsettled and revolutionary.

Great Britain: the crisis is awful and unprecedented ... the country is involved in a ruinous war.

The Netherlands: the seat of war.

Poland: still deeper distress.

The Germanick Empire: divided against itself and is probably tottering in ruins.

India: many indications of barbarism and wretchedness.

After this survey of a world in chaos and collapse, he paints a rosy picture of the United States, a country blessed with an 'internal tranquility'. This peace is achieved through 'the possession of constitutions of government which unite – and by their union establish liberty with order' and 'wise and salutary laws which flow from and correspond with free government, free election, patronage and encouragement given to publick and school education, religious and civil liberties, prosperity of all classes of citizens'.

The republic is different from the rest of the world. Other countries measure unfavourably against the new republic. The United States offers, 'if not the *only*, probably the *best* asylum for the oppressed and persecuted by civil and ecclesiastical tyranny'. Morse outlines an American exceptionalism: this country is not just another country in the world, but different, better, designated for a special place. America's unique and special position is the blessing of God. The United States was not just another country, but chosen by God for a special mission. Even for modern Americans this belief is part of the taken-for-granted view of the world; when US presidents end their speeches with God Bless America, a statement that no British or French politician could make in all seriousness, they echo beliefs first mapped out by people like Jedidiah Morse.

But there was another side to Morse's nationalism. The identification of the United States as a special place had as a corollary, in his nationalist theology, a place beset by danger, a place under attack from the forces of chaos and disorder. In 1799, he published a 50-page pamphlet entitled *In A Sermon exhibiting the Present Dangers and consequent Duties of the Citizens of the United States*. It is a rambling discourse. In language that is eerily reminiscent of Senator Joseph McCarthy at his xenophobic worst, Morse claimed, 'I have, my brethren, an official, authenticated list of the names, ages, places of nativity, professions etc of the officers and the members of a Society of Illuminati … consisting of one hundred members.'[13]

The Illuminati were the late eighteenth-century equivalent of the elders of Zion, more a product of fear than analysis, a secret group supposedly dedicated to world domination. In the politics of the time they were associated with Freemasons, free thinkers and anticlerics of the French Revolution. Even in its earliest decades then, the new republic had conspiracy theories and a demonology of evil-doers dedicated to creating chaos and confusion in the promised land. Morse continues, again in language that is disturbingly familiar:

we have in truth secret enemies, not a few scattered through our country … enemies whose professed design is to subvert and overturn our holy religion and our free and excellent government. And the pernicious fruits of their insidious and secret efforts [include] the unceasing abuse of our wise and faithful rulers, the virulent opposition to some of the laws of our country … the industrious circulation of baneful and corrupting books and the consequent wonderful spread of infidelity, impiety and immorality.[14]

Morse called for an end to political connections with France and a strict adherence to the Christian religion to bind together all members of US society. Throughout the 1790s he even believed that Jefferson was an agent of France, a dangerous radical detrimental to the health of the new nation. Morse's 'national' geography was part of a broader nationalism – a xenophobic nationalism – that saw the United States as a special place but a place under attack, beset by conspiracies and internal enemies, whose only salvation lay in establishing a national coherence bound by the ties of the Protestant religion. To construct a national geography implied a nation but also an anti-nation. To the nation that was the light of the world was contrasted an anti-nation of internal enemies and foreign evil-doers.

Morse had two distinct careers. He was both a writer of geography texts and a minister actively pursuing his own agenda. However, his congregation at Charlestown complained of his neglect; they felt he was spending too much time writing his geographies. There were acrimonious disputes over salary. Despite his income from his writings, Morse always seemed to be in financial need as speculations, dealings and litigations used up his money. And he had many liberal enemies, especially over the case of Hannah Adams, a professional writer whose income Morse tried to block. He was a complex man. He espoused a Christian morality but ruthlessly followed the pursuit of material gain; he wanted to create a national geography, but his writings often moralized over the differences rather than the similarities. He worked hard and wrote much, but he was bitter to his enemies and carried out an unremitting religious crusade against the liberals in the church. He was a controversial figure who had neglected and annoyed enough of his parishioners that he was asked to leave his parish, and he did so in 1819. He went to New Haven and spent his last years devoted to Native-American affairs.

On 7 February 1820, Morse received a commission from Secretary of War J. C. Calhoun to make a visit of observation and inspection to various Native-American tribes 'to render a more accurate knowledge of their state and how to advance their civilization and happiness'.[15] Morse was given money to undertake the travels, and in May 1820 he set off with his youngest son Richard. They travelled through the (then) northwest of the country as far as Green Bay. In total they travelled over 1500 miles with Morse in poor health. He fell ill a number of times and had to rest at various places along the way. He wrote poignantly at one point, 'I have endured ... so long a tour, in so hot a season, and far away from my family.'[16] On his return, he wrote his last book, based on the report.[17] It is an odd book. It consists of the 90-page report to Calhoun, followed by a long, 200-page appendix that gives reports of speeches and the names, numbers and residence of the major tribes in the United States. Morse had it published at his own expense.

One of the things that Calhoun asked him to look at was trading relations with the Native Americans. Morse proposed supplying Native Americans through private US traders of good character because this would undermine the power of the British in this area and ensure fairness to the Native Americans. In previous writings, Morse had adopted the standard Eurocentric view of Native Americans common and dominant at the time. Only a few years earlier in the 1819 (seventeenth edition) of his *American Universal Geography* he had described the Knisteneaux: 'Their life is an uninterrupted succession of toil and pain ... Incest and bestiality are common among them.' Now, in the twilight of his life, after an arduous trip and in failing health, he seems to have had a major change. In this last book he starkly suggests that the choice for the United States is either to make the Native Americans full citizens or to give them back their territory. The book is a rambling affair. Accounts are mixed in with letters and oral addresses. It is an undigested book, much like some of his earlier work, sprawling and opinionated but marked by a more open perception of Native Americans. No longer simple savages there is a more mature version of their problems and their plight backed by an acceptance of practical remedies. Morse understands that the heart of the matter is land:

The hunting grounds of the Indians on our frontiers are explored in all directions by enterprising white people. Their best lands are selected, settled and at length by treaty purchased. Their game is either wholly destroyed or diminished as not to yield an adequate support. The poor Indians, thus deprived of their accustomed means of subsistence ... are constrained to leave their homes.[18]

In a speech to the chiefs of the Six Nations in Buffalo on 31 May 1820, he put the matter very candidly: 'The white people will push their settlements in every direction, and destroy your game, and take away your land.'[19]

Throughout his writing, Morse showed an ambivalence towards Native Americans. The dominant theme was a position of superiority, a European classical view that saw them as savages, their life brutal and hard, their society rude. It was a standard view of the time. And yet there was another view; an appreciation that there was not a universal Native American, a unitary being who could be dismissed with an easy sweep. His writings also show an awareness of the differences between tribes and an awareness that raised Native Americans above the level of undifferentiated savages. This is not to suggest he was an early proponent of Native-American rights, because much of his writing has that incipient racism that strikes the wrong note to modern readers, but to dismiss him so easily is to ignore the depth of his ambiguity. In his final work, Native Americans are given a more central position and a more careful analysis. He got to the heart of the issue: land. He had no notion of cultural diversity, and many of his plans involved the eradication of Native-American culture in a 'civilizing mission'. His writing on Native Americans followed a trajectory: at first an easy dismissal and then, more latterly, an appreciation for their position, their struggles, and their enduring presence in this country. There was no resolution to the problem. His solutions, while seeing souls to be saved, did not appreciate a culture to be protected.

Jedidiah Morse died on 9 June 1826. He grew up at a time when colonial resistance to British rule increased; he was fifteen when the

Declaration of Independence was signed; he came into maturity as the new country was establishing political forms of government, civil society and an intellectual independence. He was involved in religious controversy and wrote some of the first geography texts in the United States. His writings percolated through the society. He was a paradox: a religious man who followed material gain and speculated with money; a nationalist who was unremitting in his distaste for the morals and manners of much of the country; a man who held the standard racist line on Native Americans throughout his writings and yet in one of his last works took a much more understanding position. His nationalism, which was expressed in his writing of a 'national' geography, was also expressed in a paranoia of fears of conspiracy. He is both very distant and yet very close. His concerns were of his own time, but they echo, sometimes distinctly sometimes more muffled, down through the years. Morse is a distinctively American voice.

7 A Sensible Foreigner

Part of this territory unquestionably belongs to the United States. To present a picture of it was desirable in every point of view. The map so constructed, shows at a glance the whole extent of the United States territory from sea to sea; and in tracing the probable expansion of the human race from east to west, the mind finds an agreeable resting place on its western limits. The view is complete, and leaves nothing to be wished for. It also adds to the beauty and symmetry of the map; which will, it is confidently believed, be found one of the most useful and ornamental works ever executed in this country.[1]

Three figures are central to the creation of a national geography in the United States in the first half century after the Revolutionary War: Mathew Carey, Jedidiah Morse and John Melish. Carey was first and foremost a publisher; Morse was a geography writer but also a Congregational minister deeply involved in the religious debates of the day. John Melish, in contrast, was a full-time geographer, mapmaker and map publisher. Most of the work in his adult life was devoted to what he termed the topographic representation of the new republic. Like the other two, he was a confirmed nationalist but in his case he was particularly concerned with the economic health of the United States and especially keen to increase tariffs to foster local manufactures and committed to the territorial expansion and westward settlement across the continent. He was an important figure who wrote to presidents and received letters back.[2]

Melish was born on 13 June 1771 in Methven, Scotland. He was proud of his Scots heritage and continued to praise the Scots educational system. Like many Scots, before and since, his early anti-English feelings remained, metamorphizing easily into a later pro-US stance. As a young man he was apprenticed to a cotton merchant in Glasgow who traded with the West Indies and the United States.

An able, ambitious man he established his own business dealings and in 1806, he sailed to Savannah, GA to create an import–export business in which raw cotton from the South was exported to Britain and manufactured goods were imported. He travelled through the country taking extensive notes with a mind to writing a book. He visited Georgia, North and South Carolina, New York, Rhode Island, Massachusetts, Delaware, Maryland, Washington, DC and Virginia. In 1807, he returned to Scotland. His business was badly affected by the deterioration in relations between the United States and Britain, especially the trade embargo that began in 1807 and lasted for fourteen months. In 1809, Melish returned to the United States to wind up his existing business interests. He stayed in New York for a while, travelled the interior of the country and in 1811, settled in Philadelphia, where he remained for the rest of his life and was an important figure in the city's vigorous book and map publishing business.

Before coming to the United States, Melish had read some travel books of the new republic but was very disappointed. They were, he thought, neither accurate nor fair. As he travelled through the country he took extensive notes with the idea of writing a book. It was published in 1812 with the accurate, if prosaic, title *Travels in the United States of America in the Years 1806 & 1807, and 1809, 1810 and 1811*. He wrote 'that the work might embody a complete geography of the United States. This is the first attempt that has come under my observation to incorporate a geographical description of a country in a journal of travels.'3 The two-volume work is a fascinating piece of travel writing. Melish had an observant eye and an easy writing style. The narrative takes the form of his journey with telling insights and observations. In the preface he writes that when judiciously compiled, a travel journal should present a 'living picture' and in this he succeeds. The book contains rich descriptions of people, places, topography, society and economy; recurring themes are trade and commerce, geographic description, an assessment of good and bad in the society, and accounts of meetings with important figures, such as Thomas Jefferson and Tom Paine. Melish met Jefferson while he was still president and he remained an important influence in Melish's professional life. They communicated through the years, and Melish continued to send him his maps and books and took Jefferson's *Notes on Virginia* as the model for much of his own geographical writing. He pressed Jefferson to produce an updated edition of this work. Jefferson took care with his replies to Melish, making observations and comments on the material sent to him. Melish shared many ideas with Jefferson, especially his political sympathies, his anti-English posture, his monotheism, his acceptance of slavery and his changing views on trade.

Melish's book begins with a description of Glasgow and then gives advice to those about to undertake a sea voyage: 'endeavour to have your whole business transacted, so as you may have a few days to spend with your friends', 'a small library of books will be found very entertaining.' And for seasickness he recommended, 'A little chicken broth or water gruel should be freely used; and people should go upon deck as soon as possible.'

The book is full of telling incidents. When travelling in Georgia Melish records:

we travelled two miles when my fellow-traveller stopped to point out the spot where two negroes were executed for killing an overseer. The one was hanged and, the other was burnt to death. I was informed that this mode of punishment is sometimes inflicted upon negroes ... to deprive them of mental consolation arising from the hope that they will after death return to their own country ... When I looked at the scorched tree where the man had been tied, and observed the fragments of his bones at the foot of it, I was horror-struck; and I never yet think of the scene without a pang.[4]

Unlike Morse, Melish has a less overtly moralistic style. In describing Charlestown, he simply notes that:

[it] is elegantly situated on a point of land at the confluence of Cooper and Ashley rivers ... The ground on which the city is built is low, but it is open to the sea breese and is, upon the whole, one of the most eligible situations in the low country. The plan of the city is regular, the streets crossing each other at right angles; but many of them are too narrow. The houses are built partly of brick and partly of wood; and many of them are elegant. They are about 24,000 inhabitants, of whom nearly one half are slaves.[5]

There is an immediacy to Melish's writing, as when he describes New York and notes that the sewerage could be smelled two miles away because it ran openly through the street. Melish uses his particular observations to make more general conclusions: cities should be so constructed as to admit a current of free air into every spot; houses should be removed from all stagnant water; and oxygen should be administered to counteract breathing impure air.

Melish writes in a clear, crisp and direct manner. He is much closer to us in style and disposition than Morse. Morse's style is heavy and full of weighty moralizing and baroque style. Reading Morse you are aware that this is someone writing a long time ago; the style and manner are so distant from modern sensibilities. Reading Melish, in contrast, is like reading a journalist of the past 50 decades; it is direct and personal with an attractive authorial presence. Melish seems more contemporary than Morse.

Running through Melish's *Travels* is a supportive attitude to the United States. Unlike many British, and especially English, travel writers of the time, Melish does not use his book as a vehicle to attack the manners, institutions and customs of the United States. Quite the opposite. He is critical of much in the society but celebrates the positive. He does not vent his spleen on the United States; he is very supportive of the American character. Not surprisingly the book was well received in the United States. A reviewer in *Port Folio* in February 1813 commented:

two whole volumes of travels in America; without any material errors; with no palpable falsehoods; no malignant abuse of individuals; no paltry calumnies on the institutions of the US ... A singular example of the good temper, the sound sense, and the candid feelings which a sensible foreigner has brought to the examination of our country.[6]

Melish sent a copy of his book to Thomas Jefferson, whom he had met earlier in his travels. In a letter he wrote in Monticello dated 13 January 1813, the former president thanked him for the book:

The book I have read with extreme satisfaction and information. As to the Eastern States, particularly, it has greatly edified me ... The candor with which you have viewed the manners and condition of our citizens, is so unlike the narrow prejudices of the French and English travellers ... your work will be read extensively here and operate great good ... I consider it as so lively a picture of the real state of the country, that if I can possibly obtain opportunities of conveyance, I propose to send a copy to a friend in France, and another to one in Italy, who, I know, will translate and circulate it as an antidote to the misrepresentation of former travellers.[7]

The success of his *Travels* secured an important place for Melish in the crowded and competitive book trade of the day.

A National Geography

In Volume 2 of his *Travels* in a small footnote he noted:

Indeed it would very easy to procure materials for a *national geography*, which might be published every ten years, under the auspices of the United States. The profits on the sale of such a work would do more than defray the expense of a national geographical establishment.[8]

The note shows Melish's concern with a national geography and although the scheme was never established, Melish undertook in the rest of his writings to create such a national geography. Later he noted that he had been 'systematically engaged in promulgating geographical information, particularly as related to the United States'.[9]

Melish published a number of diverse geographical works. There were small, gazetteer-like works, such as *A Description of The Roads in*

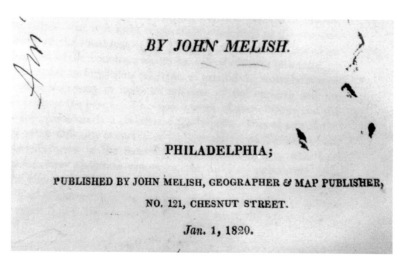

BY JOHN MELISH.

PHILADELPHIA;

PUBLISHED BY JOHN MELISH, GEOGRAPHER & MAP PUBLISHER,

NO. 121, CHESNUT STREET.

Jan. 1, 1820.

33 John Melish's self-description from his pamphlet *Catalogue of Maps and Geographical Works* (Philadelphia, 1822).

The United States, which was published in 1814 with the usual subtitle *Compiled from the most authentic materials.* The title page described the author as 'John Melish, Geographer and Map Publisher, No. 121 Chesnut Street'. He used this description in all his subsequent work, sometimes changing 'publisher' for 'seller' (illus. 33). This was a small pamphlet, no more than 80 pages, which gave distances between the major cities. Ever concerned with accuracy, Melish gave the distance in two columns: one for distance from one town to another and the other for distance from the place of setting out. A pamphlet on road distances may seem nothing out of the ordinary. However, the work involved extensive research and a political agenda. At a time when the road network was rudimentary, the work not only created an important database but gave a sense of national geography: a country linked together by roads was a connected country, a country pulled together by the strands of communication. A good transport network was part of the economic national agenda of the day that would help create an integrated national economy. A small pamphlet on roads was more than just a small pamphlet on roads; it was a statement on national coherence, national economic integration and economic nationalism.

In 1816, Melish published *The Traveller's Directory.* This was a small pocketbook – 8 x 3 inches with 134 pages – and meant for the amusement of the general reader and the enlightenment of the traveller. It contained not only a geographic description but a gazetteer, road map descriptions and a general boosterism of the new territories. The *Directory* gave information on each state, including situation, boundaries, extent, area, face of country (i.e. physical geography), rivers, minerals (described as commodities rather than geological features), soil (with special reference to fertility), produce, climate, and for each county the number of townships and the population of chief towns. The model that Melish was working from was Thomas Jefferson's *Notes on Virginia*. Melish followed a similar classification and order to Jefferson. But whereas Jefferson focused predominantly on his own state, Melish, by bringing all the states together, attempted to show how they were part of a larger national whole. The *Directory* was not simply providing a geographic description; it was suggesting a geopolitical order.

The *Directory* also contained information on the new territories: Indiana, Mississippi, Illinois, Michigan, Northwest and Missouri. Here the tone was less scientific classification and more raw booster-ism. Some examples:

Indiana This interesting country, lately dominated the Indiana territory, may now be considered as a nineteenth state, and such is the fertility of the soil, the salubrity of the climate, and its commanding situation, that it will unquestionably become a very bright star in the galaxy of the republic.

North-West Territory This extensive territory has not yet been organised into a regular government; but it is rising fast into importance. Colonel Hamilton's Rifle regiment stationed at the village of Prairie de Chiens, will check and control the Indians in that quarter.[10]

More than just an academic exercise, the *Directory* gave very practical help to the traveller and settler. Melish included a list of land offices where public lands were sold and a large section on roads, with directions for finding roads and distances in miles from Washington, Philadelphia and other main cities. These data, as noted, were more than information on mileages; they pointed to the connection of the urban system and thus the connection of the country, the cohesion of the national economy and a sense of a national space.

Melish's Maps

Melish also published maps. His 1812 *Travels* contained eight maps, all drawn by Melish in a fine, elegantly understated style. This was the beginning of his career as a mapmaker and map seller. By the end of the decade he had an establishment that employed over 30 people. Melish produced a variety of maps that are marked by an understated elegance and refined style. Making and publishing maps at different scales, Melish built up a catalogue of maps listing over 60 items, including maps of states, cities, the United States and the world. He published his first large-scale map of the United States in 1813 at a scale of 1 inch to 100 miles. It sold for one dollar – and it sold well.

Melish's map accompanied his 1814 pamphlet *Documents relative to the negogiations for peace between the United States and Great Britain*, published in Philadelphia. The negotiations between these two countries took place in Ghent in 1814 to end the war that had started in 1812. The pamphlet consists of documents, especially letters between Secretary of State James Monroe and US representatives (Quincy Adams, Bayard, Clay and Russell). The British wanted a revision of the boundary line between the United States and British colonies and a definite boundary to be settled between the United States and the British Native-American allies. For the British, establishment of the latter was necessary to secure a permanent peace. In their letter of 12 August 1814 to the Secretary of State, the American delegation resisted the British claim for a Native-American boundary: 'The proposed stipulation of an Indian boundary was without example in the practice of European nations ... no nation observed a policy more liberal and humane towards the Indians than that pursued by the United States.'

The Native-American boundary was a major sticking point and the British suspended the meetings. In the protocol of 8 August 1814, it was established that 'the peace be extended to the Indian allies of Great Britain, and that the boundary of their territory be definitively marked out, as a permanent barrier between the dominions of Great Britain and the United States'. Melish's map contains the division of the continent into land of the republic and Native-American land. Illustration 34, for example, depicts the area around Fort Adams; the land of the United States is the shaded area on the right of the map. Melish sent a copy of the map to Jefferson, who wrote back:

It was an excellent idea; and if, with the documents distributed by Congress, copies of these had been sent to be posted in every street, on every town-house and court-house, it would have painted to the eyes of those who cannot read that reconquest is the ultimate aim of Britain.[11]

In 1816, Melish produced another large-scale map of the United States. At 1 inch to 50 miles this map covered 89 x 144 cm.[12] It was a massive map and was meant for public display. The new republic had found its epic representation. Its position in an imperial struggle is hinted at in the title of the map: *Map of the United States with the contiguous British and Spanish Possessions*. The title had the usual claim *Compiled from the latest and best authorities By John Melish*. The map

34 Detail of
Louisiana (the
surroundings of
the border post of
Fort Adams,
Natchez and the
future site of
Vicksburg), from
John Melish's
1813 map of the
US.

gave longitude from Washington and London and included Lewis
and Clark's wintering places among the Mandans. In a letter from
Monticello, dated 31 December 1816, Thomas Jefferson thanked
Melish for the map: 'it is handsomely executed, and on a well-chosen
scale; giving a luminous view of the comparative possessions of
different powers in our America.'[13]

In the course of his geographical studies, Melish was frequently
led to regret that there was no map in existence presenting an entire
view of the US territory, and he formed the opinion that a map of the
United States in connection with the British and Spanish possessions,
constructed with special reference to the events of the war, would be
a 'special desideratum in geographical science'. When he planned the
map, Melish intended to draw it no further west than the Rockies. But
when he drew the map, he added two western sheets to take the map
to the Pacific Ocean (illus. 35). In a flourish that predates (yet echoes)
the doctrine of Manifest Destiny Melish notes:

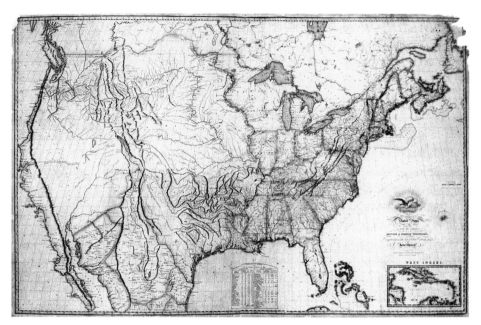

35 John Melish's *Map of the United States with the contiguous British and Spanish Possessions* (Philadelphia, 1816).

Part of this territory unquestionably belongs to the United States. To present a picture of it was desirable in every point of view. The map so constructed, shows at a glance the whole extent of the United States territory from sea to sea; and in tracing the probable expansion of the human race from east to west, the mind finds an agreeable resting place on its western limits. The view is complete, and leaves nothing to be wished for. It also adds to the beauty and symmetry of the map; which will, it is confidently believed, be found one of the most useful and ornamental works ever executed in this country.[14]

From 'sea to sea' was a confident act of cartographic appropriation. Comparison between the 1813 map and the 1816 map shows the scale of the appropriation. Melish saw the 1816 map as 'a convincing proof of the rapid progress of geographical science, and of the fine arts in the United States', but it was also an act of geopolitical dominance.

The map was also used to accompany a small pamphlet written and published by Melish in 1816, *Geographical description of the United States with the contiguous British and Spanish Possessions, Intended as an accompaniment to Melish's Map of These countries*. The pamphlet is a geographical description of each state, including latitude and longitude, boundaries, area, counties, number of townships, population and a list of post offices with miles from Washington. The latter inclusion is not accidental; again it is a symbol and measure of national cohesion and federal authority.

What was the significance of post offices and why do they appear on so many maps and gazetteers of the time? During the early days of the republic the postal system was the only form of long distance communication. No other institution had the capacity to transmit such a large volume of information on such a regular basis over such an enormous geographical expanse.[15] It was the information super-highway of its day. It was also an instrument of the federal govern-ment. In 1816, almost 70 per cent of all 4827 federal employees were employed by the post office. This percentage remained even as the absolute figures increased through to mid-century. The postal system, for all intents and purposes, was the federal government. The central authority was weak in most regards, but the postal system reached far into the hinterland and postmasters were one of the few federal appointments. In 1828, the United States had 74 offices for 100,000 inhabitants; the United Kingdom had seventeen, and France had four. The post office became the central administrative apparatus of the central government. Congress used post offices to transmit newspapers, letters, pamphlets and government documents to keep constituents informed. For Washington, this ensured the allegiance of the population. For James Madison, it provided the citizenry with a means to monitor the abuse of power. The postal system also gave merchants the only reliable means of transmitting information, bills of exchange and money throughout the country. This system was the internet, the information superhighway and the national banking system of the entire country. It linked business, connected consti-tuents with politicians and provided the threads that bound together a fragile alliance. When Melish showed post offices, he was represent-ing an important federal institution that shaped the boundaries and contours of American public life and civic society. *Geographical Description* is the country measured, identified, surveyed.

In 1820, Melish produced his largest map of the United States: a large-scale map, 1 inch to 50 miles. It was beautifully and finely engraved by John Vallance and H. S. Tanner. The map was meant to be hung; it was a public display representing the country. It contains a picture of the American eagle and the national motto, *e pluribus unum*. However, longitude is still given from London on the bottom of the map and from Washington on the top.

Information on the Far West is fragmentary and drawn primarily from the findings of the Lewis and Clark expedition. To the east of the Mississippi, towns, roadways and canals are depicted; to the west of the Mississippi, only rivers and crudely drawn mountains are shown.

The 1820 map is a continental map full of the promise of the new west: vacant, inviting, capable of taking more population. The general statistical table, located in the bottom left of the map, gives area and population and inhabitants per square mile. The current population of the territory is given as 18,629,903, yet Melish asserts that it is capable of supporting 500 million people. This map is not only a geographical description; it is a national celebration, a map reflective of continental exploration and indicative of continental expansion.

America in the World

With his large map of the world that was first published in 1817 and revised in 1818, Melish put the United States in a broader context. This world map is large (91 cm x 123 cm), elegant and austere with a delicate typography.

The map expresses a wonderfully balanced piece of cartography, subtle colours, elegant typescript, charming and well-drawn cartouche; it strives to achieve a sense of restrained good taste as well as scientific truth. The map has a nautical bias: there is a compass rose with names given to 32 compass directions; islands are well represented; the coastlines are very detailed; and it contains the traces of voyages of explorers, including Captains Cook, Vancouver, Clerke and Governor. It is a self-conscious scientific document, yet the cartouche has nymphs who have dividers and are studying a globe (illus. 36). This is a late baroque touch but with a scientific purport: the world as object of study. The cartouche is an echo of baroque sensibilities that foregrounds the world of science. On the lower left there is an explanation of how to find the distance from one place to another with compasses. The map also contains statistical tables; the world is given numerical order, divided into continents, subdivided into countries, with data on area, population, length and breadth in English miles. Longitude is given from Washington, yet the map as a whole is centred on London; the United Kingdom is at the centre and the United States is on the left periphery.

With the publication in 1818 of *A Geographical description of The world Intended as an accompaniment to The Map of The World on Mercator's projection*, published by John Melish and Samuel Harrison, this map was given a written accompaniment. The book discusses the map, including the problem of map projection, before going on to deft descriptions of different parts of the world:

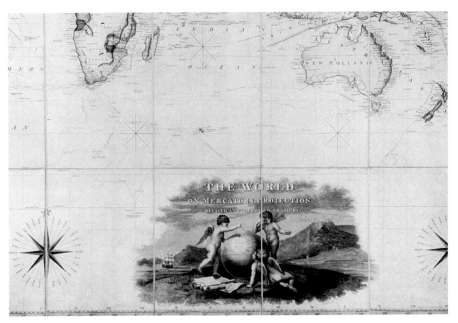

36 A cartouche, from John Melish's *The World on Mercator's projection...* (Philadelphia, 1817; rev. edn 1818).

Tripoli
Very little known: a great part of the country appears to be desert. There are no rivers of note ...
Agriculture is in a poor state, and famines are frequent.
Government Despotic.
Education. In a wretched state.

Nubia
Inhabited by a deceitful and ferocious people.

China
The population of China seems to be entirely primitive.

Japan
Laws are very superior and justice speedily executed. There are few crimes committed and few punishments inflicted.
Education abounds with schools for the education of youth who are taught without chastisement and stimulated by bright examples.

Hindostan
Religion is an artful system made up by cunning priests to gull the multitude.

Mexico
Education Indifferent.

Poland
The government is despotic; the laws arbitrary; and public education can be little valued where the people are slaves.

Ireland
Government Assimilated to that of England, but administered more under the system of spies and informers.
Laws Principally made and administered to favour the rich. The poor are in a wretched state.

Scotland
Education Under excellent regulation, by means of the parish schools, which were established before the union with England.

All these descriptions are marvellously pithy and opinionated. This is not a value-free description; it is judgemental and makes for entertaining reading.

An American Nationalist

Throughout all his works from 1812 until his death, Melish was very much an American nationalist. He not only described the United States but celebrated it, praised it, compared it favourably with every country in the world. He did not, however, renounce the land of his birth – Scotland. He praised it in his geographical writings and was connected to other expatriates. Many of the engravers and printers who worked with him were from Scotland, and he also had a more formal connection. Melish was a member of the Scots Thistle Club. Founded in 1796, it was a benevolent society open to natives of Scotland, their sons and sons of members. It was a mutual aid society 'sensibly convinced in relieving each other when in distress'. Members had to be over sixteen and under 45, in good moral character, with a healthy constitution, free from bodily infirmity, of a settled nature and able to earn a subsistence. Throughout the nineteenth century it had a membership of around 350. Many were denied membership. Those allowed in had to pay an entry fee; in the 1820s it was $2. The money was used to help widows of members, to pay for medical assistance, to provide relief for Scottish immigrants and to pay for funerals; the Society had Lots 21 South 1 and 2 East; and 22 South 1 and 2 East in the Philadelphia Cemetery. The Thistle Club was one of the many mutual benevolent societies in which people banded together to provide mutual relief. Melish became a member in 1813 soon after his arrival in the city. He was recom-

mended by James and Andrew McAlpin and retained this membership until his death.[16]

Melish would be described today as a Scots American. The Scots
part gave him a set of connections, a platform of ethnic solidarity and a
network of help and support in the new city. It connected him with the
past to survive and prosper in the present. But the second part of the
double identity guided his work. From his first writing to his last he
praised and promoted the United States. His nationalism took a number
of forms, including economic promotion and economic protection.

Economic promotion

Melish promoted the growth of the United States through a constant
boosterist rhetoric. In his earlier *Travels in the United States of America*, he described the country as 'an immense territory, a great part of
it is still unoccupied, or very thinly inhabited, so that there is room for
the industry of thousands of generations yet unborn'. This notion of
almost limitless expansion was a constant theme in all Melish's writings. He was keen to see the growth and enlargement of the republic.
He was not a narrow nationalist like Morse; Melish wanted to encourage immigration and westward expansion. In 1819, he wrote and
published *Information and Advice to Emigrants to the United States:
And from The Eastern to The Western States Illustrated by A Map of The
United States*. The map that accompanied the book is his usual small-
scale map, which interestingly stops at the 97th parallel with no definite boundary in the north. Longitude is from Washington on the
bottom and from London on the top. The map also has a chart of the
Atlantic tracing the five voyages he made.

It is a small, pocket-sized book, only 144 pages, with a catalogue at
the end listing the other books and maps published by Melish. It is an
enlightening and interesting book:

I have long considered it a matter of importance to prepare a work expressly
for the benefit of emigrants to the United States, and from the Atlantic to the
Western states ... this work is prepared under a conviction that emigration
must go on, and greatly increase. (pp. iii–iv)

The book promotes the United States as 'an independent nation of
great political importance, possessing the best system of government in
the world, and holding out advantages to mankind of very great importance'. In the book, Melish identifies those groups most likely to succeed
in the United States: industrious farmers, mechanics (tradesmen such
as masons and shoemakers), manufacturers (spinners, weavers, hatters,

etc.), labourers of every description, and 'gentlemen of republican principles and manners'. Those who will have more trouble include
merchants, learned professions (lawyers and doctors), noblemen, and
gentlemen of high birth and aristocratic principles (pp. 9–10).

In the remainder of the book, Melish gives directions to those who
wish to emigrate. He tells them to buy his maps and also his *Geographical description of the United States* and his *Traveller's Directory*. Melish
was keen to encourage the settlement of public lands. He identified the
principal land offices. Land sales would give a powerful source of
revenue to a frugal government and farmers would pay no poor rates
or tithes. The mechanics, he suggested, would find the best opportunities in Pittsburgh, Cincinnati, Lexington and St Louis, whereas
labourers would find a great deal of work in the cities. The appendix
includes the US Constitution, with amendments, and instructions on
becoming a citizen. As with all his other work, the writing is clear and
direct and the maps and typeface are elegant and simple.

Economic protection

Melish's nationalism was most vividly expressed in his constant call
for economic protection of domestic industry and manufacturing. It
was a theme that, similar to his mentor Jefferson, shifted over the
years. In his 1812 *Travels*, he included in the appendix of Volume 1 an
essay on the trade between Britain and America that takes a more
free-trade perspective to encourage foreign import of manufactured
goods:

It is in the interest of the people of the United States to receive them [Manu-
factures] so long as they can apply their industry to better advantage in clear-
ing and cultivating their lands, and in applying to other branches of internal
policy. (p. 442)

But in his 1819 *Guide to Emigrants*, he argues that economic growth
will come from protecting national manufactures, especially cotton
and woollen goods. Melish was keen for Congress to enact legislation
that would protect local manufactures. To this end, on 1 January
1820, he printed an open letter to President James Monroe. It was in
the form of a 32-page pamphlet entitled *On the state of the country
with a plan for improving the condition of society*. In this pamphlet, he
refers to the depressed state of agriculture, the near annihilation of
commerce, the unfavourable balance of payments amounting to $120
million, and the fiscal deficiency of $5 million. The reason for all this

economic distress, claims Melish, is neglect in protecting the manu-facturing industry. He argues that there was a pressing need to raise tariffs. Doubling tariffs for most items, such as wine, spirits, molasses, tea, coffee, sugar, salt, hemp, beer, soap, cheese, iron and steel, and shoes, and prohibiting the import entirely of tobacco and cotton goods would solve the fiscal crisis and give net revenue (after collec-tion expenses) of $24 million. These measures would make room for domestic articles, give farmers a market, increase employment and increase government revenue without increasing taxes. He ends the pamphlet with the detailed case of the cotton trade – something in which he had personal experience. He argued that if the United States manufactured, rather than exported cotton, there would be a national gain of $100 million and extra employment for 94,000 men and 94,000 women and children. Efficient protection would ensure economic independence.

Melish returned to this theme in 27-page pamphlet, published on 4 July 1822. It was addressed, like an open letter, to 'Fellow Citizens, the People of the United States' and was entitled *Views On Political Economy*. It was one of the last things he wrote or published. As usual, he begins by promoting his previous publications and then calls atten-tion to his *Map of the United States of America* and *A Description of the USA*, 'believing that you will find it useful and instructive'.

Although small, the pamphlet is packed with information; it gives detailed tables of each state, with data drawn from the 1820 census, giving population and numbers in agriculture, manufacturing and commerce. Melish argued that too few of the citizens of the United States were employed in active industry. The only answer lay in increasing manufacturing industry:

It would be judicious policy, and correct national justice, to exclude the manufactures of all nations who will not indiscriminately receive the produce of our soil and as the manufactures of the country would thereby be materially promoted, a tax could be raised from them to support the revenue; but perhaps the most simple process, for the present, would be to augment the present rate of duties.[17]

Melish quotes Jefferson's comments, with customary approval, that 'manufactures are now as necessary to our independence as to our comfort'.

John Melish died in 1822. He had established a national reputation as one of the foremost American geographers and mapmakers of his day. He provided descriptions and maps of the United States and the world. He wrote in a style that was clear and crisp, and his maps were marked by a simplicity and elegance. With his use of statistics he also prefigured the more empirical turn in both geographical analysis and policy analysis. Melish was a geographer, a mapmaker and a nationalist. All these elements were part of his work. He described the territory of the United States, but this description was also used to boost emigration and national economic self-sufficiency. Through his maps and writings, Melish both described and promoted the economic development, population growth and territorial expansion of his adopted country.

8 Mapmaking in Philadelphia

To trace the features, develop the resources and record the improvements of any portion of the earth, has always been regarded by those desirous of possessing general information, as a topic worthy of peculiar attention; and to no portion of mankind do those subjects present more interesting views, than to the citizens of the United States. Occupying a vast region, yet partially explored, and operating on a system of internal improvements on a grander scale than any other people, they are marching forward to national greatness, with a rapidity unexampled in the annals of the world. These circumstances have caused works which illustrate the geography, topography and statistics of the Union, to be regarded with general attention; and not infrequently, to be liberally patronised.[1]

From the end of the eighteenth century through much of the nineteenth century, Philadelphia was the most important centre for cartographic information and map production in the republic. In these years, Philadelphia was the largest city in the Union, with a concentration of cultivated readers. Artists, lawyers, doctors and academics provided a sophisticated and cosmopolitan audience. The city was the leading centre in the production of scientific and medical knowledge. The cradle of enlightened rationalism in the United States had mapmaking as one of its signal achievements. Foreign-born and American travellers, scientists, publishers and geographers created a forum for geographic knowledge and representation at a time when increased knowledge of the world and the United States was being codified into maps and atlases. A variety of printed maps were produced, printed and distributed in Philadelphia, including atlases, world maps, US maps, and maps of particular cities. There was a community of printers, cartographers and engravers that gave a visual representation of the world for public consumption. Men such as Scots geographer, cartographer and publisher John Melish (1771–1822), engraver and publisher Henry Schenck Tanner (1786–1858) and geographer and publisher Samuel Augustus Mitchell (1792–1868) turned geographical knowledge and folklore into visual images. Quite literally, this community represented the nation and the world to literate society.

For almost a hundred years Philadelphia was the cartographic capital of the United States. Many maps were made, published and printed. After a slow start, the industry grew in the late eighteenth and early nineteenth centuries, reaching a peak in the 1860s and 1870s. By 1876, the industry (including colouring, mounting, surveying, engraving, lithography, printing and publishing) was clustered in the congested city centre around the present site of the Independence National Historic Park. The mapmakers were small establishments, family businesses, independently operated and it was very common for several shops to share the same building. A detailed survey of Philadelphia in 1860–90 identified over 400 firms.[2]

A wide variety of maps was produced, including landownership maps, county and city atlases, fire insurance maps and even reprints of old maps – especially useful in lawsuits regarding property disputes; every important map of the city and surrounding areas between 1683 and 1796 was republished between 1846 and 1895.

The single most important type of map was the landownership map, sometimes termed the cadastral map. These were first produced in the eighteenth century but the dominant form, the county cadastral map, first appears in the first decade of the nineteenth century. State legislatures would often support efforts to map the entire state. Large-scale maps were produced; it was not uncommon to have a map with a surface area of six square feet. The majority of cadastral maps were published in the period from 1840 to 1860. One important cadastral publisher was Robert Pearsall Smith, who published over 100 maps between 1846 and 1865.

The cadastral maps were often produced as wall maps because they were so large; for example, the map of Philadelphia surveyed by D. J. Lake and S. N. Beers and published in 1860–61 was six feet square. The cadastral maps got so large that some printers divided their sheets. In 1861, Henry F. Bridgens divided his map of Berkshire County into different sheets for the various townships. He added an index and bound the sheets together: the landownership atlas was born. By the end of the decade it had replaced the cadastral map. After the Civil War, most of the county cadastral surveys were published in an atlas format (see Chapter 12). Atlases were produced for both counties and cities and, between 1870 and 1877, many communities hired surveyors to map their county for centennial celebrations. By the end of the 1870s, atlases were available for many cities. Griffith Morgan Hopkins published his *Atlas of West Philadel-*

phia in 1872. Hopkins did a lot of work in Philadelphia and in 1875 and 1876, his six volumes of Philadelphia surveys, entitled *City Atlas of Philadelphia*, were published. This atlas gave a detailed ward-by-ward cartographic description of the city. George Washington Bromley worked for Hopkins between 1873 and 1875, and with his brother, Walter Scott Bromley, established a firm in 1885 that produced many maps of the city. From 1885–94 they published an *Atlas of the City of Philadelphia*.

An important source of urban mapping in Philadelphia, as in other large cities, was the need for fire insurance maps. Insurance companies hired surveyors to survey property prior to creation or renewal of insurance policies. In 1852, the first US fire insurance survey was published in New York. In 1857, Joseph Dietrich, Ernest Hexamer and William Locher published two volumes of *Maps of the City of Philadelphia*. To keep up with changes, they provided a correction service; from 1862 to 1873, volumes were corrected each year. This was discontinued in 1873 with the introduction of revised editions. In 1873, Hexamer started publication of a new series 50 feet to 1 inch and by 1912, 38 volumes had been produced.

In the previous chapter, we looked at the work of John Melish. In this chapter, we consider some of the work of Tanner and Mitchell, both important figures in the mapmaking business at the high point of geographic representation in Philadelphia.

Henry Schenck Tanner

While Mathew Carey was born in Ireland and John Melish was born in Scotland, Tanner represents the development of an American-born group of artisans. He was born in New York City but moved to Philadelphia. His brother was a partner in the firm of Tanner, Vallance, and Kearney, which published books, pamphlets and printed maps. Tanner trained as an engraver and worked on the maps that accompanied Melish's *Travels* (1812) and *Map of The United States* (1816). Tanner soon extended his work to publishing and writing. The death of Melish provided an opportunity for a 'geographer and map publisher'; by the 1820s, he had adopted those names. Tanner, like Melish, not only printed and published maps and books but also wrote much of the text (the demarcation between printers, publishers and writers was less rigorous than it is now).

Tanner's first major publishing project of his own was his *American Atlas*, first started in 1819 and published in 1823 as *A New American*

Atlas Containing Maps of the Several States of The North American Union. Most of the writing, drawing and engraving was done by Joseph Perkins (1788–1842), a former banknote and letter engraver, who was born in New Hampshire and worked in the Philadelphia publishing world from 1814 to 1826. The *New American Atlas* has 22 plates. The very elaborate title page shows the first landing of Columbus in the New World from Herrara's *Life of Columbus*. The first map is one of the world drawn on Mercator's projection centred on Greenwich. Despite its title, the atlas follows a typical British pattern of maps of Europe, Asia, Africa and America. However, half of the atlas depicts the states of the Union. There are eleven maps of states and pairs of states drawn on a uniform scale of 17.3 miles to 1 inch. It is a large book (17 inches x 23 inches), not easily transportable. All the maps have lines of latitude and longitude drawn through them. This is a world measured, cribbed and confined, bounded and triangulated, a world under the control and power of numbers. The first written section, entitled 'Geographical Memoir', outlines the labour involved, 'ten years of unremitted application' and Tanner's goal to 'exhibit to the citizens of the United States a complete geographical description of their own country'. The memoir discusses each map and describes the source; the map of New York State, for example, draws upon Simeon DeWitt's 1804 map. The map of each state depicts post offices, distances of state capitals from Washington and distances of county town from state capitol. It is a map of civil society. The atlas concentrates on the connections between states. The principal focus is national cohesion; its main object is the union as a national community. The atlas was popular – despite its relatively high price of $30 – and was continually published in subsequent editions until 1839. It was copied almost in its entirety by other publishers, including S. A. Mitchell.

Tanner published a number of atlases, including *An Atlas of Ancient Geography*. This was a small book, with only sixteen maps, used to 'elucidate the writings of ancient authors, both sacred and profane'. The maps depict the Holy Land, ancient Greece and Rome, and the ecclesiastical divisions of early Europe. It is in modern atlas style with common design elements. All the longitudes are taken from the Fortunate Islands (Canary Islands) and a variety of scales are depicted, including Roman miles, Greek stadium, Egyptian schenes and Persian parasangs. There is no text.

In 1833, Tanner not only published but wrote most of the text of another atlas, entitled *Tanner's Universal Atlas*, which has maps of the individual states. The map of Ohio depicted in illustration 37 shows

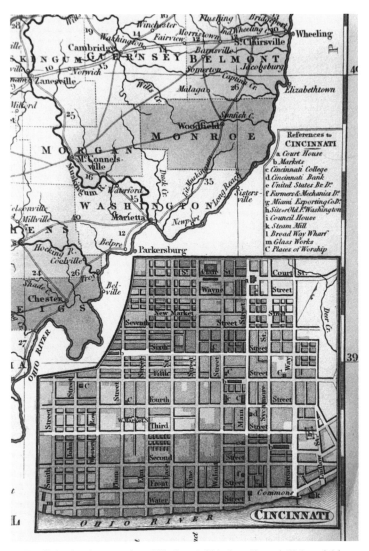

37 Detail showing the street plan of Cincinnati, Ohio, from *Tanner's Universal Atlas* (Philadelphia, 1833).

counties, roads (proposed and existing), towns and canals (proposed and existing). The inserts include a map of Cincinnati with court-house, banks and commercial buildings; steamboat routes with times; and a profile of the Ohio canal. Like many of Tanner's domestic maps, there is an emphasis on transportation, including roads, canals and steamboat connections. In the more detailed picture given in illustration 38 the distances between places are marked along routes.

Previously atlases were collections of maps drawn by different

148

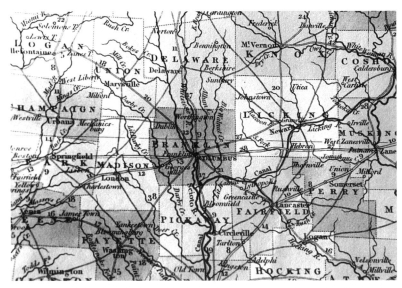

38 Detail of the surrounds of Columbus, from the map of Ohio in *Tanner's Universal Atlas.*

people, at different scales and often pulled together in loose-leaf collections. In Tanner's work we can see the development of the more formal atlas in the US. Tanner was a major figure in the history of US mapmaking.

A more coherent, more formal atlas is his *New Universal Atlas*, published in 1836. There are 117 maps, all with a standard design. There are world maps, maps of the United States and other regions of the world, and then maps of individual states of the Union showing counties and towns. Longitude is given from Washington, although the maps of other parts of the world are given from London. This is a modern-looking atlas: common design, standardized look, with the now-familiar patterns of world maps, maps of the United States and individual states. There is no text.

Tanner published a number of atlases, including *A New American Atlas, Atlas of the United States, A New General Atlas* and *A New College Atlas*. The same maps were used in the different publications. With Tanner we are moving into the era of mass publishing.

Maps of the Republic

Tanner not only published – but was also involved in – the production of maps. His map titles included *Map of The World, A New Map of North America, Map of Europe, Map of Asia* and *Map of Africa*. His market was in the business and educational communities, as noted in

39 The north-west, from Henry Schenk Tanner's *Map of North America Exhibiting the Boundaries Arranged agreeably to the Late British and Spanish Treaties* (Philadelphia, 1819).

his prospectus: 'These Maps will be found highly useful in mercantile establishments, as they present a complete view of the whole world with the most important commercial places, distinctly marked.'[3]

Tanner's US maps reveal much about the changing nature of the nation's territorial expansion. In 1819, he made a map of North America (published by Tanner, Vallance, and Kearney of 10 Library Street), that showed the United States in relation to the territories of Britain and Spain, with longitude from Greenwich on the bottom and from Washington on the top. This is a map concerned with geopolitics. The full title is *Map of North America Exhibiting the Boundaries Arranged agreeably to the Late British and Spanish Treaties*. The map is coloured with territorial markings: British in red, Spanish in yellow and US in green. The Pacific Northwest is left unmarked, ambiguous, still up for grabs. The Missouri Territory extends to the Pacific and the northwest boundary is undefined (illus. 39). The boundary between Canada and the United States was not finally agreed upon until 1846. It was thus left to US cartographers to show the area either as a shadowy, unclaimed area – as Tanner did in his 1819 map – or as an area of the United States, as the fashion became dominant. In his world map of 1831, Tanner clearly shows the United States extending to the 54th parallel.

Tanner also produced large maps of the country for public display. One of the largest was his 1829 *United States of America,* which measured an impressive 117.7 cm x 151.3 cm drawn to a scale of 25 miles to 1 inch. It was engraved by James W. Steele (1799–1879), a native and lifelong resident of Philadelphia who worked for Tanner, Vallance, and Kearney. He also did portrait, landscape and historical engravings but later became a banknote engraver.

After the simplicity of Melish's maps, this Tanner map is more baroque looking, with elaborate cartouches, inserts and statistical tables along each border. It is a very busy map and one gets exhausted looking at it. It has detailed town maps of Washington, Baltimore, Philadelphia, New York, Boston, Pittsburgh, Charlotte, New Orleans and Savannah; inserts of southern Florida and Northwest Territory; and profiles of canals, including Erie, Ohio, Pennsylvania and Chesapeake. The statistical tables presented in the margins include population (divided into whites, free people of colour, slaves) and the numbers engaged in agriculture, commerce and manufacturing; and for each state: area, capital city, major cities, population, latitude and longitude. This is a map and a statistical compendium of progress in the United States. It is a map of progress of civil society, but a society deeply divided into racial categories. The map and accompanying table also represent the geographical representation of difference.[4]

The nation is divided into east and west in terms of representation. The eastern area has county names and boundaries, cities and roads marked off and a dense population. Western lands are shown as vacant. Illustrations 40 and 41 highlight the differences. In looking at the map, there is strong sense of teeming population, progress and civilization in the east, while the west lies open, full of vacant spaces and undefined boundaries. Tanner has yet to represent continental appropriation.

Hung up on a wall, this map would have represented the mark of progress in the east, the increasing density and differentiation of the country, the creeping urbanization and especially the development of canals that marked human control over nature. This was the forward march of history; an elaborate display of city growth, increasing population, density, economic connectivity and specialization, the structure of civil society (county seats and boundaries), and social differentiation. The statistical tables show a nation growing, expanding, urbanizing and differentiating. To read the tables in this wall map is to see difference between north and south, urban and rural, slave and non-slave states, east and west.

The map was accompanied by a memoir, published the same year as *Memoir of The Recent Surveys, Observations and Internal Improvements in The United States*. This memoir carries on the triumphalist tone of the forward march of progress. It describes the making of the map and then devotes most attention to a description of each state, listing the new counties and towns and, what Tanner terms, 'internal

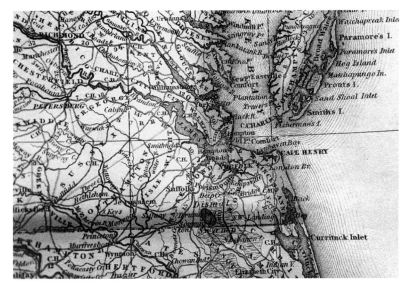

40 Detail showing Richmond, VA, and the mouth of Chesapeake Bay, from Henry Schenck Tanner's map *United States of America* (Philadelphia, 1829).

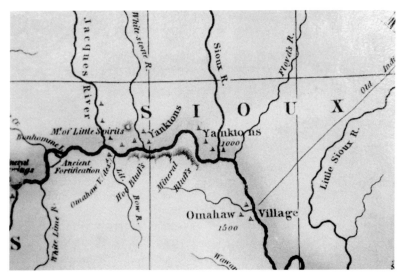

41 Detail showing Omaha (formerly in Indian Territory, now in Nebraska), from Henry Schenck Tanner's map *United States of America* (1829).

improvements'; these are the existing and proposed canals and roads. The map and memoir are concerned with showing the development of civil society, the deepening and strengthening of economic connectivity and the forward march of the nation.

In this memoir, Tanner takes up the issue of longitude, which in his maps had the prime meridian at Washington:

I feel it is incumbent on me to contribute my humble aid towards the introduction into use of the proposed meridian, and therefore selected it as the one best suited to an American, intended for the use of Americans. Boston, New York, Philadelphia and Washington, have each had their advocates in the persons of their resident geographer, who appear to have selected a first meridian for their maps, according as their convenience or fancy dictated. This practice, it is hoped, will be entirely abandoned, since the position of our capital has been determined with sufficient exactness for all geographical purposes ... the City of Washington, as the only legitimate point for our national first meridian ... being nearly in the centre of population ... being also the seat of the general government.[5]

Geographical writings

Tanner also wrote more analytical pieces. My favourite – and one that has been largely ignored – is his *A Geographical and Statistical Account of the Epidemic Cholera from its Commencement in India to its Entrance Into the United States* (1832). Throughout the early years of the republic, and beyond, epidemics were frequent occurrences, often wreaking havoc. Yellow fever and cholera exacted an enormous toll. Tanner's goal was simple:

Among the infinite variety of publications on the Epidemic Cholera, there is none, I believe, which gives any satisfactory account of the geographical progress, and statistical details of the subject ... the gradual extension of the pestilence; its localities; the period of its commencement and termination; the number of human beings which have been subjected to its attacks, and those who become its victims, and other statistical facts were either wholly disregarded ... or given in such a loose and unconnected manner as to render a reference to them at once irksome and unprofitable.[6]

Tanner was writing at a time when statistical techniques were not well developed. Maps and mapping were an important way of identifying causal connections from correlating data. Tanner's book consists of a series of tables listing the number of cases reported, duration in days of the 'pestilence' and the number of deaths in different localities by country. A world map then shows the diffusion of the epidemic from India in 1817. By this method the 'disease may, by reference to the map, be traced with facility, in its westward march, and at the time of its invasion of each country readily distinguished.' He also produced a more detailed map of the United States and New York that shows with small red dots the sites where cholera had broken out. The map provided a detailed chart of the diffusion of the illness that showed how the disease spread along the riverways – up the Hudson and along the Champlain and Erie canals. His map is a detailed example of the diffusion of a contagious disease and his little book on cholera is a fine example of statistical mapping. His work predates the more famous Snow map of London, which was published in 1855, by more than 20 years.

As improvements in transport were making travel easier there arose an important and growing market for guidebooks. In 1834, Tanner published *The American Traveller or Guide Through The United States*. This was a small, pocket-sized volume, ideal for the traveller, giving a brief and concise list of facts. The area, population (including number of slaves), government, legislature, judiciary, physical structure, rivers, productions, internal improvements (railways, canals, etc.) and principal towns are recorded for each of the states. For each large town there is a listing of latitude and longitude, population, public buildings, city government and the most extensive information on travel routes by steamboat, stage and canal boats with distances from place to place. *The American Traveller* is a useful compendium of knowledge. Just one example of many published at the time, the book gave the necessary information for the increasing number of travellers. But it was more than a traveller's handbook – it had a broader purpose: the attention to improvements and civic culture (there is a lot of detailed information on number of elected representatives, who elects judges, the salary of officials, etc.) indicates a concern to highlight a connected country, a governed society and to give a solid introduction to civic culture.

Tanner writes poorly. Unlike the crisper, clearer Melish, Tanner has a stilted style and is more comfortable with statistics and maps than words. The maps in his travel book are excellent as they provide detailed street maps of major cities with a list of public buildings, colleges, coffee shops, churches, banks, theatres and museums.

In his atlases, books and maps, Tanner gave a more visual representation to the expanding country. He highlighted the spatial connections, the growth of civic society and the increasing connectivity and strength of the national economy.

Samuel Augustus Mitchell

Mitchell was born in Bristol, CT in 1792. His father had come to the United States from Scotland as a young boy. Mitchell began his working life as a teacher but soon moved into the writing and publishing of geography texts, maps and atlases. He worked in Philadelphia and was a major figure in the book trade. Mitchell wrote and published atlases, guidebooks and a range of geography school texts. The production of geography texts and maps was an important part of the Philadelphia printing and publishing industry. At the height of the city's commercial success, over 40,000 copies of geography texts were produced annually and the book and map sector employed almost 250 people. There was a growing demand for books, atlases and maps, especially from the expanding school population. Mitchell published for a general public and for the school market. He published geographical readers, geography question books and outline maps. Most of his texts and atlases were reprinted throughout much of the nineteenth century.

Mitchell represents the zenith of geography publishing in Philadelphia. Before him, firms tended to be smaller with low print runs. After him, the publishing industry moved its centre of gravity more decisively to New York while private map publishing became dominated by the Rand McNally company in Chicago. Mitchell represents an important turning point between the early Philadelphia-dominated trade and the rise of the giant firms located outside Philadelphia.

Guides

One of Mitchell's most successful books was his *Travellers Guide Through The United States*. First published in 1832, it appeared in successive annual editions for almost 20 years, achieving such a status that the later editions were entitled simply *Mitchell's New Travellers Guide Through The United States*. The book became a standard reference work; its wealth of information was in an entirely tabular form. The tables were constructed using a very ingenious system which allowed people to travel and take side roads. As befits the new age, the *Guide* is full of adverts from railway companies and contains a sophisticated table of railway systems, mileages and connections that enable travellers to go throughout the country. The country is now a more connected system, not so much described as tabulated.

Mitchell was fascinated by transport improvements. In 1835, he wrote and published *Mitchell's Compendium of Internal Improvements of the US*. It is a small, pocket-sized book that lists for each state the location, length and cost of canals, existing railroads and those under construction. An accompanying map shows states, capitals, towns and particularly roads, railroads and canals – all with distances attached. It is another map of a connected country.

The *Guide* and the *Compendium* are not the opinionated writing of Morse, nor the cool elegance of Melish, nor even the heavy prose of Tanner. The books and guide record the transport improvements and tabulate the distances between places in the country. The earlier guides of Melish and Morse, with their value judgements, are being transformed into the more objective, less personal, more formally empirical accounts that enable travellers to make their own journeys and construct their own narratives.

Maps and atlases

Mitchell also produced maps of the United States. One of his largest was a 1835 map entitled *Mitchell's Reference and Distance Map of the United States*. A large map (326 mm x 1,707 mm), at 25 miles to 1 inch on Flamstead's improved projection, it was designed for hanging. It was a reprint of a previous map, *Map of The United States*, published in 1832 and revised and renamed in a variety of forms. Four engravers worked on this map: Mitchell's usual engraver, James Hamilton Young; J. Dankworth; Edward Yeager, a portrait, historical and map engraver on copper, steel and wood, who was active in Philadelphia during the 1840s and 1850s; and E. Woodward, an engraver of maps and historical vignettes. The map has the characteristic flowery border which appears in many of Mitchell's maps and it is one of the first large US maps to have letters along the margin to help identify a place on the map. The map goes up only to the border of Missouri territory. The inserts include maps of Boston, New York, Philadelphia, Albany, Washington, Cincinnati, Charlestown, New Orleans, Niagara, Rochester, Florida and northern Maine. This is an American map: there is a large cartouche of an American eagle (see illus. 42) and the longitude is given from Washington. The key lists capitals of states, towns, forts, Native-American villages, stage roads, roads and canals. The distances in miles are shown along routes. The map highlights the differences between east and west: east of the Missouri line, towns and counties are depicted whereas in the west, Native-American names and villages are shown.

This was one of the first large-scale maps to be engraved on steel. Previously, engravings were done on the softer copper but there was a limit to the number of copies that could be taken from a copper

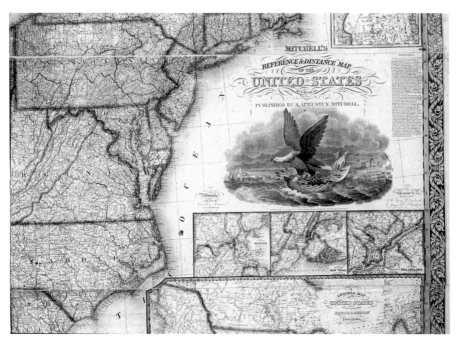

42 Detail from Samuel Augustus Mitchell's *Mitchell's Reference & Distance Map of the United States* (Philadelphia, 1835).

engraving. Steel engraving allowed more copies to be made and meant that the price could be reduced.

Mitchell also wrote a book to accompany this map – *An Accompaniment to Mitchell's Reference and Distance Map of The United States* – which was published by Mitchell and Hinman in 1835. In the preface he notes:

To trace the features, develop the resources and record the improvements of any portion of the earth, has always been regarded by those desirous of possessing general information, as a topic worthy of peculiar attention; and to no portion of mankind do those subjects present more interesting views, than to the citizens of the United States. Occupying a vast region, yet partially explored, and operating on a system of internal improvements on a grander scale than any other people, they are marching forward to national greatness, with a rapidity unexampled in the annals of the world. These circumstances have caused works which illustrate the geography, topography and statistics of the Union, to be regarded with general attention; and not infrequently, to be liberally patronised.[7]

This quotation reveals the triumphalist note behind much of the geographical representation of the time. More particularly, it is indicative of Mitchell's cumbersome, heavy style that sounds like

Latin translated into English, badly. No wonder Mitchell preferred maps and tables to words and sentences.

The *Accompaniment* is particularly concerned with the names of the local and civil divisions of the state. There had been a proliferation of names: by 1830, there were 100 counties and towns bearing the name Washington; 79 Jackson; 73 Franklin; 66 Jefferson. Of the 324 pages, 177 are a consulting index (much like contemporary gazetteers) with name of place, class (town, township, county, district, capital), county, state, reference by letters (so that it can be identified on the map), population, distance from Washington and distance from state capital. There is also a table showing distances between Washington and capital or largest towns in each state. The general statistical picture emphasizes political units, transport connections and distances, and the centrality of Washington. The book is more concerned with statistics than written reports. While there is a similar concern, shared by Melish and Morse, with progress, civil society and the coherence of the Union, the style is different. As with his *Traveller's* Guide, this book was also moving away from the verbal description toward the style and tone of the contemporary gazetteer. The idiosyncrasies of Morse and Melish were being replaced by the blander depictions of Tanner and Mitchell. In both the travel guides and geography texts of the time, there seems to be a move away from the opinionated writing toward the blander, more neutral representations. Mitchell published many atlases for schools and the general public. He often simply copied other atlases. His 1831 *New American Atlas* was a reprint of Anthony Finley's 1826 atlas. In 1845, he obtained the copyright for Tanner's *New Universal Atlas*, which he published as the *Universal Atlas* in 1847. It went through many editions. In 1860, Mitchell's *New General Atlas* was published to replace the *Universal Atlas*. Again, the publication was successful and went through many editions.

The *New General Atlas* is more like a contemporary atlas, with 100 maps and tables with a similar scale (though not exactly – Texas is at 70 miles to 1 inch, Georgia and Alabama are at 40) and a similar look represented by the flower border that surrounds each map.

It is an atlas with an American bias. All maps have Greenwich and Washington as prime meridian. The world map shown on pp. 2–3 is entitled *Map of the world on the Mercator projection Exhibiting the American Continent At its centre*, although 0° longitude is given from Greenwich. Of the 100 maps in the atlas, 68 represent the American continent and 48 of them refer to the United States with a selection of state and city maps. There are detailed street maps of thirteen US

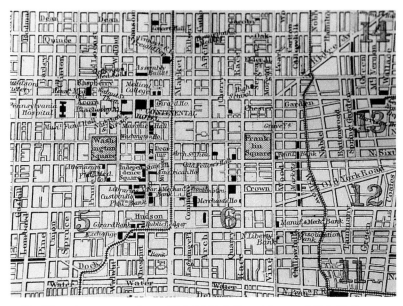

43 Detail from the street map of central Philadelphia in Samuel Augustus Mitchell's *New General Atlas* (Philadelphia, 1860).

cities (illus. 43). The state maps show counties, roads and towns. At the back of the book there are a number of tables, including US post offices, population by state, land routes within the United States and population of cities and countries around the world.

Philadelphia retained its dominant position as the centre of book publishing and map production well into the nineteenth century. In looking at the work of such people as Melish, Tanner and Mitchell, we can see the emergence and evolution of the production of national geography. Melish was publisher, writer and mapmaker. By the time of Mitchell, the division between the different roles is sharper and Mitchell represented an increasingly connected expanding country. He was more of a publisher than a writer, geographer or mapmaker. He bought the plates of others and marketed them for a mass market. His guidebooks are losing the individuality of the earlier books and his atlases look more like modern atlases. With Mitchell we are in the process of moving toward contemporary guidebooks and modern atlases. We also see the emergence of new techniques, such as steel engraving replacing copper engraving. A mass market had been created, print runs are longer, prices are falling. From Melish to Mitchell, we can see the change from a craft industry – in which people performed a variety of jobs and idiosyncratic voices still had a place – to a larger industry where the intellectual craftspeople were replaced by a corporate division of labour. These trends were to continue. By the end of the nineteenth century, the small firms were driven out of existence by the emergence and dominance of the large firms: the Sanborn Map Company of New York City produced fire insurance maps of all US cities; Rand McNally in Chicago produced a variety of atlases and maps; and the US government provided detailed topographic surveys. By the end of the twentieth century, only a few mapmakers survived in the city.

I was working at the American Philosophical Library in 1996 in Philadelphia. I was given a gift from a long-time resident of the city: the 'best map for a visitor of the city'. It was published by Streetwise Maps of Amgansett, NY. Over the course of a century in the shift from local to national map production, Philadelphia had lost its dominance.

PART III

Representing the Nation

9 Inscribing the National Landscape

Among the most important surveying duties is the marking in the field of the lines and corners of the surveys in a distinct and durable manner. These marks, when identified as the originals, placed there by the sworn deputy surveyor of the United States, constitute in fact the survey, taking precedence over field-notes, official plats, or any like evidence, controlling all future proceedings in resurvey, and respected accordingly in proceedings affecting title before the courts of the country.[1]

Before the Constitution of the nation came the mapping of the land. In May 1785, two years before the Constitution was discussed and signed, the Continental Congress passed the Land Ordinance. Its full title was 'Ordinance for ascertaining the mode of disposing lands in the western territory'. Thomas Jefferson had chaired the committee charged with preparing a plan for that western territory. The basic question was what to do with the windfall gain of huge lands. For a hard-pressed republic the answer was clear: sell it off. But to sell it the land had to be surveyed. Always the mathematical rationalist, Jefferson proposed dividing the land into geographical square miles oriented north–south and east–west. Other members agreed with the need for straight-line divisions, although the township unit was reduced from 100 to 36 square miles. A square division was simple, easily undertaken and cheap to survey.

Under the Land Ordinance and successive pieces of legislation, the land was surveyed into a rectangular grid that ran on a north–south (township) and east–west (range) system. A principal baseline and meridian running at right angles to each other were established, carefully measured and used as the starting point for reading off the six-mile square divisions called 'congressional townships'. Each of these townships was divided into 36 squares called sections, approximately one mile square, containing 640 acres. The numbering system is shown in illustration 44. The survey also gave a convenient naming system. Sections could be identified by their township and range numbers; thus section T7N, R2W was easily identifiable: it was seven townships north and two ranges west of the principal meridians.

The sheer size of the country meant that new meridians and principal baselines had to be established. Measurements taken from one baseline needed adjustment because the curvature of the earth meant that the more northerly townships would have been smaller. The survey system counteracted the sphericity of the earth by using new baselines every six to ten townships in lower latitudes and every four to five townships in higher latitudes.

The establishment of meridians and baselines reflected and embodied the growth of settlement. The gold rush in California brought a meridian in 1851. Mormon settlement was aided by and encouraged the establishment of a meridian in 1855 in Salt Lake City. The last one in the coterminous states was surveyed in Oklahoma in 1881.

The mapping also involved a recoding of the territory. Each township survey involved the compilation of filed notes and the production of three manuscript maps of each township. One copy was retained by the Surveyor General, eventually becoming the property of the state, a second copy was deposited in Washington, and a third was used in the local land office.

Not all the land was sold off. Under the 1785 legislation, sections 8, 11, 26 and 29 were reserved for the federal government (the hope was that after settlement and development they could be sold at a higher price) and section 16 was reserved for school buildings. The school section persisted throughout the nineteenth century. Other large chunks of land were allocated to public works; these federal land grants provided the basis for many large schemes, such as the Illinois and Michigan Canal. The government gave 131 million acres of public land to railroads.

The very first surveys were not encouraging. Survey costs were high and receipts were disappointingly low. Better terms could be had from the private land companies. The need for revenue, however, forced the government back into the land-selling business in 1796. Over the years, the minimum size of a purchasable lot was reduced. In 1800, it was reduced from one section to a half-section. Four years later, it was reduced again to a quarter-section and to a half-quarter-section in 1820. This steady reduction in size and liberal purchasing arrangements democratized, in principle if not always in practice, land sales. The appropriation of the vast new lands of the republic was not restricted to the rich and the few. Land was opened up to the modest and the many.

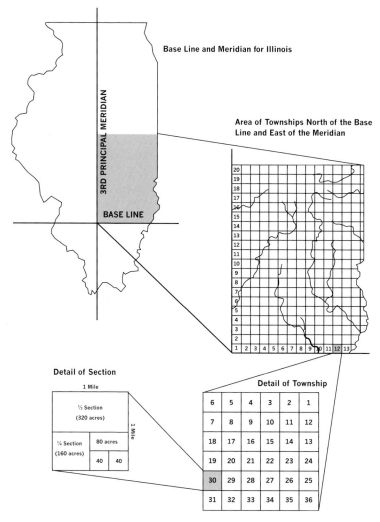

Base Line and Meridian for Illinois

Area of Townships North of the Base
Line and East of the Meridian

3RD PRINCIPAL MERIDIAN

BASE LINE

Detail of Section

Detail of Township

1 Mile

½ Section (320 acres)			1 Mile
¼ Section (160 acres)	80 acres		
	40	40	

6	5	4	3	2	1
7	8	9	10	11	12
18	17	16	15	14	13
19	20	21	22	23	24
30	29	28	27	26	25
31	32	33	34	35	36

44 Illinois taken as an example of the 1785 Government Land Survey. Source: Grim, 1990.

In the wake of the Land Ordinance and subsequent land legislation came the greatest transfer of land in the history of the world. Almost 23 million acres were transferred from the public domain into private ownership. This massive land survey and transfer was overseen by agents of the federal government. In 1812, the General Land Office (GLO) was established to oversee land transactions; in 1836, the Surveyor General was also included in the GLO. The GLO lasted until 1946 before becoming part of the Bureau of Land Management.

The GLO was always sending out circulars with updates on legislation and copies of forms. The GLO sent out a circular to Registers and Receivers of the US Land Offices on 3 June 1838 that drew attention to the 1838 act of Congress granting pre-emption rights to settlers on public lands. Simple forms were used that reflected the grid system of the township and range notation:

I _____ of _____ county _____ do hereby apply to purchase the _____ section _____ in township _____ of range _____… containing …_____ acres according to the Surveyor General, for which I have agreed with the Register to give at the rate of one dollar and twenty five cents per acre, with the understanding that in any case any right of pre-emption shall be suspended thereto, or to any part thereof, under the act of twenty-second of June, eighteen hundred and thirty-eight, the purchase money of the tract of land herein applied for, either wholly or proportionately, as the case may be is to be refunded without interest.

I _____ register of the Land office at _____ do hereby certify, that the lot above described contains _____ acres, as mentioned above, and that the price agreed upon is one dollar and twenty five cents per acre.

Register

The standardized simplicity of the forms and the locational identifiers of the township and range system meant that the land was easily and quickly disposed of.

One of the greatest single pieces of legislation was the Homestead Act of 20 May 1862. Any adult who filed papers for a $10 fee could claim 160 acres; on occupancy of the land for five years they received the land for free. This act applied only to surveyed lands. There were laws that allowed settlement on unsurveyed land, but claims had to file notice of settlement at the District Land Office. These forms were also simple:

I _____ of _____ do hereby apply to enter, under the provision of the act of Congress approved May 20, 1862, entitled ' An act to secure Homesteads to actual settlers on the public domain,' the _____ of Section _____ in Township _____ of Range, containing _____ acres.

Over 10 million acres were allocated under this act by the end of the century. The map shown in the 1866 annual report of the GLO showed a landscape in the making. Large areas of the Midwest and Far West had been subdivided. The map recorded the work done to date and implied the work yet to be done.

The post-Civil War annual reports of the GLO published in Washington provide a good record of the mapping of the national territory in the last third of the nineteenth century. They consist of a report by the commissioner of the progress to date and reports from the Surveyor Generals in each of the states. A brief perusal through these reports provide a fascinating account of the work of the GLO and of the surveying of a national territory of 1,500 million acres.

In the annual report of 1866, published in 1867, Commissioner Josiah Wilson reports on his ten surveying departments and 61 land offices. By 30 June 1865, 474,160,551 acres had been surveyed, and 991,308,249 of public land was still unsurveyed. Wilson records the lack of progress in New Mexico, assigning the cause: ' No field operations have been prosecuted in that Territory during the last fiscal year, on account of the hostility of the Indians.[2] The report even discusses the problem of combining French measurements in Louisiana with the standard US measurements because there were still land divisions in that state that used the old French system. The commissioner reported that the appropriate translation was 72 French feet equalled 77 US feet.

The annual reports also contain the reports of the Surveyor General for each state. Some of them go into great detail. For example, the Surveyor General of Colorado and Utah, one John Pierce, gave a detailed written survey of his area:

the grasshoppers, which destroyed the crops of the last two years, have left the northern portion of the Territory and gone southward, and are committing some depredations in the southern portions of the San Luis Park, but the main body of the flock has passed beyond the limits of Colorado.[3]

The Surveyor Generals of the individual states were responsible for drawing up contracts with local surveyors. Thus E. Richardson had a contract with the Surveyor General of Washington Territory, dated 1 June 1866, to survey subdivision of townships 8 and 9 range 30 east plus others, combining a total of 540 miles at $10 a mile.

The General Land Office Map

The 1867 report, published in 1868, also included a large map of the United States showing Surveyor Generals' offices, army camps, land offices, railroads, mineral deposits and a detailed diagrammatic representation of the township and range system. Illustration 45 is part of this larger map that was reproduced in the 1867 annual report of the General Land Office (GLO) but was also printed separately as a fold-out map and as a map on rollers. This 1867 General Land Office Map was produced under the direction of J. Wilson, Commissioner of the GLO;

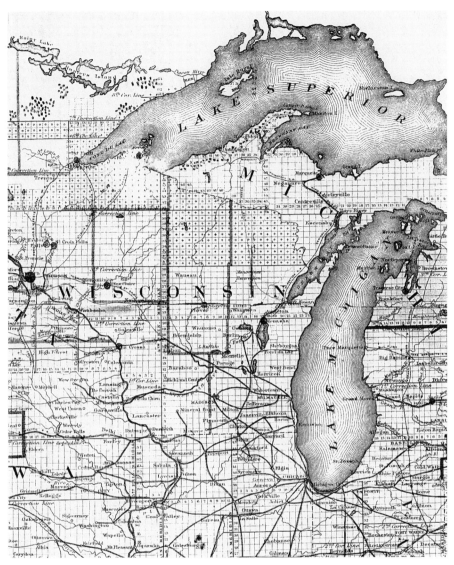

45 Detail of Wisconsin and Illinois, from General Land Office Map entitled *Map of USA and Territories showing the extent of public survey and other details* (New York and Philadelphia, 1867).

the draughtsman was Joseph Gorlinski. Most likely it was based on one drawn for the GLO in 1866 by Theodore Franks. This 1867 'official' map was also published by the private sector, by Bien in New York and Bowen in Philadelphia. The map thus appeared in official publications and was also privately sold as a fold-out map and displayed on rollers. Approximately 500 copies were sold. Its title is *Map of USA and Territories showing the extent of public survey and other details*, and it is drawn at

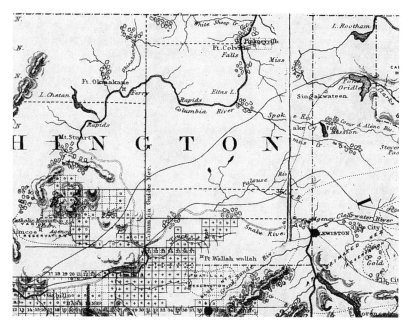

46 Detail of Washington State, from General Land Office Map (1867).

the detailed scale of 60 miles to one inch. The map, meant to be displayed, depicted the creation of the national landscape. It was a large wall map of the continental United States, meant to be hung in offices, that shows the township and range system of land division across the country at mid-century. A map of things done, a map of things still to do. The map is a musical score of the national landscape.

The order of the key is revealing; first comes the Surveyor General's office in Washington, then land office, land grant, and proposed railways, other railroads, a list of minerals deposits including gold, silver, copper, quicksilver, iron, tin, asphaltum, coal and oil. In the western part of the country, US flags are used to represent army forts. The land in the midwest is covered by the grid but how it had yet to be imposed west of Kansas and east of California. The wave of migration has yet to sweep over the western plains.

This GLO map is the aggregate sum of many maps of surveys and land transfers. The importance of maps cannot be overstated in the huge land transfer that occurred in the United States. A map was needed to claim title.

Within one month after filing the map or plat with the recorder of the county, a verified copy of said map and statement is to be sent to the GLO, accompanied by the testimony of two witnesses that such city or town has been established in good faith.[4]

The General Land Office Reports

The subsequent annual GLO Reports are revealing since they indicate the progress of the land survey and land transfer. The report for 1867 noted that since 20 May 1785, 20 principal bases and 23 meridians had been established and in a triumphalist tone, reinforcing the notion of inscribing the national landscape, recorded: 'The framework of the surveying system thus described as meridians and intersecting bases constitutes a scientific structure which has been established over the greater portion of the continent.'[5]

In 1890, commenting after another spike in land transfers, the report noted that in the year ending 30 June, 19 million acres had been disposed of to settlers, to coal and mineral lands, as well as to lands patented to states for educational and internal improvements. Cash receipts were $6,486,210 from sales and $155,132 from fees. The scale of surveying was enormous. Up to 30 June 1890, a total of 986,084,675 acres of public land were surveyed out of 1,815,504,147 (2,836,725 square miles).

In the annual report of 1890, the commissioner noted that the GLO needed more office space and personnel and money. He had a point. Surveying was not cheap: it involved exhaustive, time-consuming survey work. For example, in Montana on 7 December 1889, Rodney W. Page and Newton Orr were paid $10,000 for surveying the principal meridian of Montana and other measures, including the Fort Browning guide meridian. By 1890, the GLO had made 14,000 maps of the United States, 673 maps of states, 482 railroad maps, 482 general maps, 7,800 photo lithograph copies of plats, 197 volumes of field notes prepared for binding and 79 volumes of plats of surveys.

A major silence in the annual reports is the abuse of the system. For discussion of that issue we have to look elsewhere. In his 1879 *Report on the Lands of the Arid Regions*, John Wesley Powell attacked the land surveys for using the contract system. It led, he argued, to shoddy work because surveyors raced to complete their contract. He pointed to the corrupt practice in which surveyors altered claims to appease the highest bidder. Land rings were formed between landowners and surveyors that allowed better access to water and richer soils and to better holdings for those willing to pay off the surveyors. The surveying of the land gave ample opportunity for personal enrichment. The state of Montana had fourteen surveyors from 1867 to 1925, half of whom were either removed from office or forced to resign.

Despite all the problems, the scams and land rings, the surveying and allocation of public lands was an incredible achievement and, like all human achievements, it contained the base as well as the noble. Its participants were knaves and heroes with many in between. The process ' opened' up the land to millions of settlers and laid the basis for the creation of a national landscape. In the 1866 annual report of the GLO this evocative and slightly overblown quote still manages to capture the essence and enduring legacy of the project:

our liberal system of land legislation has extended, and still continues to afford, facilities for opening new farms, founding new cities, holding our incentives for immigration from the crowded capitals of the elder States and from abroad by stipulations for the acquisition of real estate, either agricultural or city property, on terms so easy as to enable the industrious to secure homesteads almost at nominal rates. That system founded by the illustrious statesmen of the revolution . . . has not restricted its benefits to merely the opening rich and boundless fields to individual settlement; in vesting title in local communities for school purposes in every township of six miles; in giving means for the endowment of seminaries of learning and universities; but it has made concessions on a stupendous scale for internal improvements, for opening ordinary roads, for spanning the North American continent with railways, and still further, in meeting the wants of diversified localities by liberal provisions for works of this class to connect centres of trade, and afford rapid means of intercommunication.

The landed estate of the Union is the great inheritance of the American people.[6]

The land survey also entered national consciousness through its usage in atlases and schools. In the last third of the nineteenth century, county, state and national atlases invariably introduced readers to what they termed the Government Land Survey. Diagrams were presented which showed the principal meridians and base lines, methods of subdividing a section and plats of congressional township.

Illustration 47 is a diagram that was used in schools in Iowa at the turn of the century. The figure shows a township with correctional errors and generalized geographic features. The diagram was used to teach basic mathematics, geography and civics.

The township and range system of the land survey was also the basic co-ordinate system of the county plat books that were sold and distributed throughout the country.

Through these different channels the government land survey became a part of a broader national debate and identity.

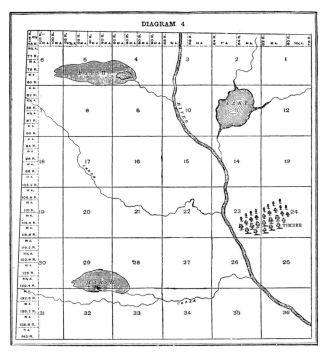

DIAGRAM 4

47 Teaching Map of the Town and Range System.

Inscribing the National Landscape

The surveying of the land also involved a marking of the territory.
The lines were measured with a chain and marked on the land. An act
of 1796 stipulated that 'all lines shall be plainly marked upon trees,
and measured with chains':

Among the most important surveying duties is the marking in the field of the
lines and corner of the surveys in a distinct and durable manner. These
marks, when identified as the originals, placed there by the sworn deputy
surveyor of the United States, constitute in fact the survey, taking precedence over field-notes, official plats, or any like evidence, controlling all
future proceedings in resurvey, and respected accordingly in proceedings
affecting title before the courts of the country.[7]

The land was scratched with the marks of the surveyors. Distance
was measured off in chains 66 feet long. At every 40 chains a 30-inch
wooden post was set in an 18-inch hole to mark the quarter-section.
On one side of the post was marked the township location, on the
other, the range location.

Across hills and river plains, mountains and vast prairies, tiny posts recorded the property divisions. They were difficult to find and for the uninitiated difficult to understand. Locators, often former members of the survey team, would often wait at railway stations to be hired by many emigrants to find their property.[8]

The land was not only surveyed it was marked. The grid was inscripted into the landscape through tiny marks and through patterns of land usage that were moulded by the rectangular survey lines. The lines on the map became the lines on the landscape as roads, boundaries, farms and towns developed and emerged, turning the invisible survey lines into landscape patterns.

Maps are not just reflections. They are not like a mirror whose only function is to show us the 'real' of an external reality. The grids on the map became the grids on the ground; a mathematical modelling of the world rendered real by tiny little posts and palpable by generations of settlers. Maps can also be imagined as musical notations that promote a performance. The maps of the government land survey were the notes that provided the symphony of the national landscape.

Under the Land Ordinance of 1785 and successive pieces of legislation, the great land bounty of the republic was surveyed into a rectangular grid that ran on a north–south (township) and east–west (range) basis. It was one of the largest single acts of territorial mapping – unique in its size, scope and rectangular system – that followed a rigid north–south, east–west orientation across a continent of varying landforms. The surveying of the land created a national landscape; a landscape that embodied the enlightenment legacy in the United States and the enduring power of rational empiricism across the vast lands of the West; a landscape that was easily recognized, easily understood and, in its continental unfolding across the heartland, gave a cohesion to an enormous territory. A vast grid was placed across the land that imposed mathematical order across chaotic geography and created a national identity on a newly appropriated land. It was the triumph of geometry over geography.

10 Mapping the National Territory

> The main object of this exploration will be to obtain correct topographical knowledge of the country traversed by your parties, and to prepare accurate maps of that section. In making this the main object, it is at the same time intended that you ascertain, as far as practicable, everything relating to the physical features of the country, the numbers, habits and disposition of the Indians who may live in this section, the selection of such sites as may be of use for future military operations or occupation, and the facilities offered for making rail or common roads, to meet the wants of those who at some future period may occupy or traverse this portion of our territory.[1]

On the map of the country produced by the GLO in 1867 there is an area in the west that has printed on its surface the phrase *unexplored territory*. By naming an area within the national boundaries yet beyond the boundaries of understanding, surveillance and national power, the map indicated the work still to be done in mapping and describing the national territory.

After the Civil War, the attention of the republic turned west. After the North–South obsession, the East–West axis offered hope, expansion, a new national identity, the basis for a national ideology that transcended the bitterness of the immediate past. But to move into the West you needed to know where you were going and you needed to have monopoly control of the area. For both ventures, precise mapping was a necessity.

To map and describe the West was to bring it under national understanding. Mapping extended surveillance and control. But the mapping was also part of a broader attempt to explain and understand the West. Surveys not only mapped; they collected, analyzed, classified, drew, photographed and painted. The West was re-presented to the military, the scientific community, the politicians and the wider public. The surveys brought the West back to the East, made it part of the national discourses of military, scientific, political and popular understanding. To map the West was to wrestle it from the vague status of unexplored territory and place it in the solid category of national territory.

Early Military Surveys

From 1800 to 1838, much of the mapping of the national territory was undertaken by the military on an informal *ad hoc* basis. This military mapping of the national territory was concerned with basic discovery and national land claims; exploration and mapping enterprises were tied to imperial rivalries and were an integral part in the claiming of sovereignty and the creation of US hegemony over much of the West. The maps produced were claims to territory, paper trails in a quest for imperial expansion. Federal mapping of the territory was a spasmodic affair. Survey teams were sent out on an irregular basis with differing aims, methods and agendas. The most famous is the Lewis and Clark expedition, sent out by Jefferson to find a trade route to the Pacific. There were others. Jefferson also sent out William Dunbar to Louisiana in 1804 and in 1809, Lieutenant Stephen Long explored the region between the Rocky Mountains and the Mississippi in an eighteen-month expedition. His later expedition in 1823 travelled to the St Peter's River. In 1832, Schoolcraft and Allen went to search for the source of the Mississippi River.

In 1838, the Army Corps of Topographical Engineers was established by Congress and charged with the exploration and development of the continent with particular attention to the problems of transportation and the construction of a scientific inventory. From then on through much of the nineteenth century, the mapping of the West was intimately connected to military control, investment opportunities and transport improvements. Early examples include the Fremont expeditions. A second lieutenant in the Corps, John Charles Fremont (1842–8), led three major surveys in 1842, 1843 and 1845 to the Rocky Mountains, Oregon, California and Upper California, respectively. Another Corps mapping exercise was The United States and Mexico Boundary Survey, 1848–53. This survey resulted from the Treaty of Guadalupe Hidalgo, which stipulated such a survey. The survey team included geologists, plant collectors, surveyors and naturalists. Military mapping was becoming more associated with the creation of a scientific inventory as well as political control and military intelligence.

In March 1853, Congress authorized a government survey of all principal rail routes. The Corps was charged to find the most feasible railway route from the Mississippi to the Pacific. The survey came under the control of Secretary of War Jefferson Davis, who sent out four main parties and represented the different sectional interests – a northern survey concentrating on the 47th and 49th parallels led by Isaac Stevens; a survey of the 38th parallel led by Captain John Williams Gunnison; and two surveys along the 35th parallel, one from the west led by Lieutenant John Parke and one from the east led by Captain John Pope. The reports of these great railroad surveys extended knowledge of the botany, zoology, geology and detailed topography of the West.

In their surveys of the Mexican boundary and the Pacific Railroad Surveys, the Corps made major inventories of the West and mapped much of the territory. Two important large-scale maps were produced from these surveys. Major William Emory (1811–1887) compiled his map for the Office of the Mexican Boundary Survey. Entitled *Map of the United States and their Territories Between the Mississippi and the Pacific Ocean and Part of Mexico*, it was made in 1858 at a scale of 1:6,000,000. Lieutenant Gouverneur Warren (1830–1882) published his map, *Map of the Territory of the United States from the Mississippi to the Pacific Ocean*, for the Office of Pacific Railroad Surveys in 1857; the map accompanied Jefferson Davis's final report (illus. 48). These maps, both drawn at the same scale, represent a culminating achievement in the mapping of the West. They represent the most accurate cartographic representation of relief and drainage then available. The large-scale maps show relief, rivers, some routes and occasional Native-American names. The overwhelming impression is of a land measured – and hence brought under both scientific understanding and political control – and now available for development. Warren's map, for example, was the basis for a large-scale commercial map, *The United States West of the Mississippi*, published in St Louis in 1859 by McGowan and Hildt, which highlighted routes to the newly discovered goldfields in Colorado.

Early Geological Surveys

Most historians of the West have focused on the Army Corps of Topographical Engineers and the role of the military in mapping the national territory. There were also, however, more purely scientific expeditions, especially in the geological surveys of the states. While a

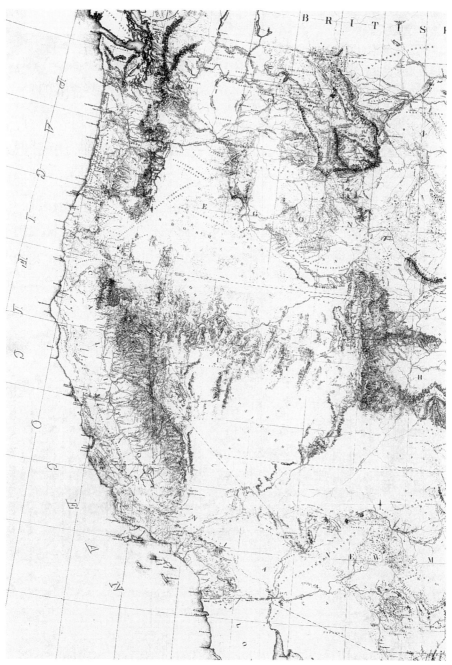

48 Detail of the western seaboard from Gouverneur Warren's *Map of the Territory of the United States from the Mississippi to the Pacific Ocean* produced for the office of Pacific Railroad Surveys (Washington, DC, 1857).

great deal of attention has been paid to the military expeditions, rather less attention has been lavished on the geological surveys. And yet, fully three-quarters of the over 80 scientific expeditions funded by the US government between 1800 and 1861 were geological surveys. Of the remainder, almost all had geologists on the survey teams. In the first half of the nineteenth century, geology had a much broader definition than now; it was the science of the earth before an era of scientific specialization.

At noon on 26 January 1837, Michigan achieved statehood. Two hours later, the new legislature approved a bill to undertake a geological survey. This was the first department of the state created by statute and $3,000 was appropriated for the work. Dr Douglas Houghton was appointed the first State Geologist – a post he held from 1837 to 1845. To cut costs, Houghton signed an agreement with the commissioner of the GLO to conduct a joint linear and geological survey. This was the first instance of cooperation between federal and state surveys. Michigan was not alone in quickly establishing a geological survey. In 1838, Kentucky appointed W. W. Mather as the first State Geologist.

These surveys were seen as an important economic inventory of a state's resources. Agricultural and mining interests could see the advantages in such surveys. Variations in soil quality and the presence of minerals were vitally important pieces of commercial information. The interests of farmers, mining concerns and land speculators coincided with state and federal government interests and the emerging scientific community in a unique combination of scientific curiosity, public policy and material interests to create the first surveys. The story of the geological surveys in this early period is full of interesting, quixotic characters, such as Houghton, who died at age 36 when his boat capsized in a gale on Lake Superior. He was Mayor of Detroit and Professor of Geology at the University of Michigan, and just before his death he was nominated for Governor of Michigan.

Geology was, like geography, a larger subject than it is now. Geological surveys were not restricted to surface geology but included botany, soil science, archaeology and anthropology. A geological survey was a much larger enterprise and a more wide-ranging study than is meant in modern usage. The wider concerns of these early geologists have a legacy. Staff geologists working on the geological survey of New York formed an organization to communicate with geologists working in other states. This led in 1840 to the founding of the Association of American Geologists, which later became the American Association for the Advancement of Science. This remains one of the largest scientific organizations with a wide remit to communicate the works of scientists to a more general audience.

These geological surveys were undertaken at a time when the federal government had a much more restricted role.[2] Before the Civil War, the federal government was small, relatively weak and viewed with great suspicion by many states, especially in the South, where political clout in Congress was used to halt the enlargement of federal government. Not all state legislatures, however, were convinced that the benefits of surveys would outweigh the costs. In New Hampshire, the position of State Geologist was half-time, a state of affairs that lasted until 1987. The survey of that small state was undertaken by professors and students during their summer field trips. In other states, surveys were established and then ran out of funds. The second geological survey of Michigan was established in 1859 but suspended in 1863 due to lack of funds. A third survey was only started again in 1900. In 1860, the California legislature appropriated $20,000 for a state geological survey to provide information on where gold could be found. Josiah Whitney, the appointed State Geologist, hired a number of people, including Clarence King, who subsequently led one of the largest federal post–Civil War surveys. The survey was abolished in 1874 again by the state legislature. Some states have maintained a persistent, if fluctuating, presence. Arkansas commissioned a series of geological surveys in the last quarter of the nineteenth century and throughout the twentieth; the eleventh survey was started in 1978.

The field was dominated in the early years by a small number of people. People such as Douglas Houghton, David Dale Owen, and Charles Jackson were the forerunners to John Wesley Powell, Clarence King, George Wheeler and Ferdinand Hayden (see later sections of this chapter for a discussion of these four). They filled a variety of positions and left a legacy of students. One of Houghton's students was James Hall, the Director of the Geological Survey of New York from 1837 to 1898, who exerted an enormous influence on the development of geology in the United States. Let us consider briefly the life and some of the work of Owen and Jackson.

David Dale Owen

David Dale Owen (1807–1860) was born in Scotland, the third son of the famous social reformer – Robert Owen – who had built a mill town on the banks of the Clyde. The town of New Lanark was an early factory community where the mill owner was as concerned with the education of the workers as with making a profit. The town was considered a model community and people came from all over Europe to see one of the most important and earliest social experiments in urban planning and capitalist-philanthropic social welfare of the industrial age. David was educated in Scotland and went to the United States when his father moved to New Harmony, IN to found a utopian community. David returned to London for most of his further education. He worked as a volunteer on a geological survey of Tennessee and in 1837 was offered the position of State Geologist of Indiana. Two years later, he was in charge of the federal surveys of Wisconsin and Iowa. In 1854, he was appointed State Geologist of Kentucky and undertook fieldwork from 1854 to 1857, publishing the results in a four-volume survey that included beautiful pen-and-ink drawings in his own hand. By 1857, he was also the State Geologist of Arkansas.

In 1852, Owen published a report of a geological survey of three states: Wisconsin, Iowa and Minnesota.[3] This report, made under instructions from the US Treasury, is well worth reading. It is a large text, 638 pages, beautifully reproduced with many illustrations, including woodcuts and engravings on copper, steel and stone. Many of these were done by Owen. Geological reports of that time were not scientific reports as we understand them now. The narrow discourse of dry rational analysis had yet to reach the hegemonic position it has assumed today. Scientists of the day had the luxury of comprehending a number of fields in the arts as well as the sciences. Reports were part science, part poetic description, part travel writing and part reflection on the course of the survey. The modern equivalent is less a scientific paper and more a special television feature on an expedition showing us the origin of the enterprise, the struggle for funding and the emerging personality battles. The early reports are like contemporary National Geographic television programmes rather than modern government reports.

The survey was wide-ranging, including geological surveys, temperature records and estimations of the soil fertility; it was a resource inventory that paid particular attention to the soil, the possibility of agriculture and analysis of the mineral base. But it also comprised many other things, including descriptions of botanic specimens and bird species found in the field and lists of Native-American names. It was not dull scientific reportage. In describing Cold Water Lake in northern Minnesota, for example, Owen notes:

The waters of the lake are remarkably cold – below 40 of Fahrenheit's thermometer. Its chilling effects on the superincumbent atmosphere, condenses its moisture into fine spray, which, floating in the rays of a setting sun, as we viewed it in the evening, presented the most brilliant rainbows . . . During the night of the 4 August, when we encamped on the spot from which the drawing was taken, water was frozen in a tin cup, and the ground was covered with frost in the morning.[4]

The report contains a mixture of discourses: science, aesthetics, poetry and travel writing. It also gives some indication of the difficulties of mapping in the field:

Among the pineries of Northern Wisconsin, and more or less throughout the whole of the designated region, the buffalo gnat, the *brulot* and the sand fly to say nothing of myriads of gigantic musquitoes [sic], carry on incessant war against the equanimity of the unfortunate traveller. I and other members of the corps, when provided with the necessary defence, have had our ears swelled to two or three times their natural size, and the line of our hats marked, all around, by the trickling of blood.[5]

Owen's report is a marvellous example of these early scientific writings; full of observation and commentary, poetry and science, description and intimations. They still make great reading.

Fieldwork in the early surveys was especially arduous. Cholera was a constant danger and supply lines were rudimentary. Owen reports on a survey conducted in 1849: 'We have frequently, notwithstanding the utmost prudence exhausted the last pound of eatables and travelled a day or more without breaking our fasts.'[6] In another instance, while Owen was ascending the Upper Des Moines in 1849, the canoe jerked, a rifle was discharged, the ball smashed into another rifle and three fragments lacerated the deltoid muscle of his left arm. His coat was perforated by a dozen holes. Owen was disabled for weeks, though as he noted, it could easily have been worse and 'this report, in all probability, would have been completed by some one else than its present author.'[7]

Owen's health was badly affected by the years of fieldwork. He suffered from malaria and died early, aged only 53. Like many of the other mapping pioneers, he was a man of many talents: writer, illustrator, explorer and scientist when being a scientist meant interest and skills in a rich variety of subjects.

Charles Thomas Jackson

Charles Thomas Jackson (1805–1888) was born in Plymouth, MA. He graduated from Harvard Medical School in 1829 and had a lifelong connection with medicine; he also developed an interest in mineralogy. He studied both areas at the Sorbonne. On the boat journey home in 1834, he met Samuel Morse, the son of Jedidiah Morse. They talked of their shared interest in electricity; later Jackson claimed that Morse had stolen the idea of the electric telegraph from him. This was a recurring theme in Jackson's life. He was a man of some genius; he was experimenting with a prototype of the telegraph when he met Morse; but so was Morse. Later he was involved in similar controversies with guncotton and surgical anaesthesia. He was a quixotic figure and long involved in personal wrangles. In the midst of all this, he was also involved in geological surveys. In 1837, he participated in surveying the public lands of Maine and Massachusetts under a joint state-federal agreement. He was the first State Geologist of New Hampshire, appointed in 1839, and between 1840 and 1844 undertook surveys of Rhode Island and New Hampshire.

In the 1840s, there was a lot of speculation in mining stock. Northern Michigan was seen as a rich area for making money from mining. Congress wanted to sell off public lands. Jackson had already made geological surveys of parts of this area and was appointed to lead a federally funded survey to report on the mineral lands of northern Michigan. Under an act approved in March 1847, Congress appropriated funds that enabled Jackson to mount an expedition. On 19 June, he received a letter from the Commissioner of the General Land Office authorizing him to draw $2,500 from the US Treasury. His party consisted of two subagents (William Channing and Joseph Peabody), a surveyor (J. Mullet), five men to carry the instruments and two geologists (Professor John Locke and Josiah. D. Whitney). The final report was published as *An Account of a Geological and Mineralogical Survey of the State of Michigan* by Charles T. Jackson in the 1849 annual report of the GLO. It makes fascinating reading. There is a long introduction, part geological and part human history, and then detailed mineralogical and geological data plotted against a township and range map (illus. 49). Descriptions were given according to this system; for example, the area of Township 54 north, Range 36 west was described as having a base of red sandrock.

The report also details Jackson's diary of the survey. Following are entries from 1847:

June 24 Left the Sault Ste Marie for Copper Harbor ... took barometric and magnetic variation readings.

July 2 This day went to Copper Falls mine, on township 58, range 31, section 11 to make an examination of their works, and to explain the mine to my party. On going from Sand Bay, I took a barometric observation on the shore of the lake.

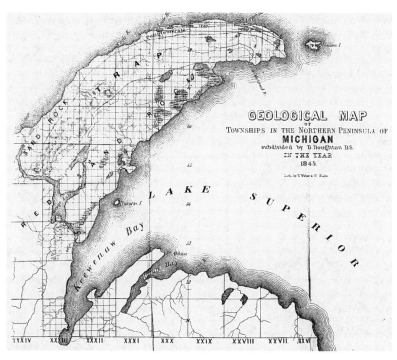

49 *Geological Map of Townships in the Northern Peninsula of Michigan* (1845), from Charles Thomas Jackson's *Account of a Geological and Mineralogical Survey of the State of Michigan* (Washington, DC, 1849).

July 10 Saturday evening, finished my surveys of Lac la belle and Bohemian Company's mines, and was about leaving, when to our surprise Dr. Locke and his sub-agents arrived . . . and informed me that their boatmen had all deserted them, and had set out on foot to return to Copper Harbor. I learned that the mutiny was got up by the boatmen, because Dr Locke would not allow them to make as free use of his sugar as they wished . . . While Dr. Locke remained with me he measured the height of Bohemian Mountain and obtained results within a few inches of those already obtained by me.

Even these brief excerpts give us a feel for the difficulties involved and also for the commitment of the scientists. Even though they had just been stranded, Dr Locke still took measurements of the height of Bohemian Mountain.

Congress had approved money, but getting it was another matter. Jackson wrote to the US Treasury for money but having got nowhere went to Washington on 2 June 1848. Appropriations were held up, he believed, because of the machinations of his enemies. He finally got the money that enabled him to pay his men, purchase equipment to obtain more precise longitude measurement and finance the next year's expedition. Jackson's report tells a tale of mapping in difficult conditions, with recalcitrant workers, a tight-fisted Congress and recurring difficulties that included weather, illness and mutiny. The problems were endemic to the earlier surveys but were no doubt exacerbated by Jackson's temperament, which obviously had traces of acute paranoia. His later years were spent in constant controversy over inventions and patents. In 1873, he went mad or, as the *Dictionary of Biography* has it, 'his mind gave way.' But perhaps you had to be half-mad to attempt such dangerous undertakings. Mapping the national territory was not for the faint-hearted or the timid.

Mapping the West

After the Civil War, attention turned westward. As the 1867 GLO map had it, parts of the West were still unexplored; they were beyond national control and national understanding. The federal government undertook a number of surveys of the West that were to set standards of mapping and that laid the basis for the federal mapping programme and the United States Geological Survey, the organization still responsible for mapping the national territory. Four large surveys, funded by Congress and commonly named after their principal leaders (Hayden, King, Powell and Wheeler) were sent out West. The journalistic reporting and artistic representations of these surveys were reproduced in the expanding magazine and book trade of the time and greatly influenced the Eastern perception of the West. Popular accounts of the surveys were some of the biggest best-sellers of the age. I give a brief introduction to each before elaborating further.

Clarence King led a survey along the 40th parallel. The King Survey (1863–73) covered a large area with most interest focused on geological structure.

The Wheeler Survey was led by Lieutenant George Wheeler. The survey's full title was *United States Geographical Surveys West of the 100th Meridian*. Its terms of reference are noted in the quote at the beginning of this chapter. The survey covered a huge area over the period 1863–73, including California, Colorado, Montana, Idaho, Nebraska, Nevada, New Mexico, Utah and Wyoming. Wheeler produced the first contour maps of the region and developed the quadrant system that the Geological Survey uses to this day. He also produced 27 land classification maps. Wheeler wanted to produce a uniform map of the Western region. In his survey work he established careful measures of longitude and altitude.

Ferdinand Hayden led an expedition into Colorado. The Hayden Survey (1873–6) was concerned with assessing the resource base and land classification. Hayden saw his primary responsibility as publicizing and promoting the West. His reports and maps helped to bring the grandeur of the Rocky Mountains and Yellowstone to wider public attention. The designation of Yellowstone as the nation's first national park owes a great deal to Hayden's tireless promotion.

John Wesley Powell is a legendary figure, whose trip down the Colorado River is the stuff of legend. He undertook two trips. In 1869, he set out down the Colorado with nine men in four small boats. The adventure captured the public imagination and in 1871, he set out again – with federal backing – north of the canyon. In 1878, he published his report on *The Arid Regions of The United States,* which called for the establishment of irrigation cooperatives and the regulation of grazing and farming.

Surveillance: Mapping as control

After the Civil War, the greatest military problem facing the United States was control of the West. Settlers were moving in, and the vast spaces were filled with the competing needs of Native-American tribes and land-hungry settlers. The mapping of the West was not just a matter for scientific curiosity but a question of social control, military dominance and territorial hegemony. Despite all the survey work done before the Civil War, there was still a great need for accurate information. The US Army tried to solve the problem in three ways. First, an exploration officer was assigned to every military department in the West as a sort of intelligence officer gathering spatial information and generating maps. Second, Clarence King, formerly of the California survey, was employed to conduct a survey of the 40th parallel from the California border to the Great Plains in a 100-mile-wide path following the proposed line of a transcontinental railroad. Third, an army officer, Captain Wheeler, was entrusted with a geographical survey west of the 100th meridian.

THE KING SURVEY The King Survey, officially entitled the *Geological Exploration of the 40th Parallel,* was authorized by an act of Congress on 2 March 2 1867. King was to survey territory between the Rocky Mountains and Sierra Nevada, including an alternate route for the proposed Pacific Railroad. King's survey was an army undertaking: the commission was issued by the Secretary of State for War, orders were taken from General Humphreys, the Chief of Army

Engineers, and the work of the survey was dependent on military supplies and military escorts. The survey was led, however, by a civilian and staffed with civilian scientists. The survey, although under nominal army control, conducted itself with greater reference to the emerging discourse of organized science than to the needs of the military.

Clarence King had received this important position at the incredibly young age of 25. He was born on 6 January 1842 in Newport, RI. Graduating from Yale in 1862, he undertook a horseback trip the next year across the continent. On the way he worked in a mine in Nevada, crossed the Sierra on foot and went down the Sacramento by boat to San Francisco. Between 1865 and 1866, he was a member of General McDowell's expedition to desert areas in southern California. He returned East and convinced Congress to fund mapping of the Sierra region from Colorado to California.[8]

King chose men from the world of science as his assistants: James Gardner was chief topographer; the Hague brothers, James and Arnold, were the geologists; William Whitman Bailey was the botanist; and teenager, Robert Ridgeway, was the ornithologist. They were all young men at the expanding edge of scientific research in their fields.

The group sailed from New York on 1 May 1867, crossed the Isthmus of Panama and sailed to San Francisco. In July, they started west into the Sierras in the first season of their survey work. In all, the King team surveyed some 15,000 square miles using the triangulation method. The survey team perfected the use of the new, lighter theodolite. Over the next years, the group mapped the land and collected thousands of geological, botanic and biotic specimens. The work was popularized in King's *Mountaineering in the Sierra*. This book, first published in 1872, captured the majesty of the high mountains and the excitement of the frontier.

The expedition also produced a seven-volume *Report of The Geological Exploration of the Fortieth Parallel;* the first volume was published in 1870, and the final one appeared in 1880. The volumes were both resource inventories, such as *Mining Industry* (1870) and scientific reports, such as *Botany* (1871). In 1878, an atlas was produced by Gardner that included a large-scale map of the Cordilleras of the western United States and ten smaller maps drawn at a scale of two miles to one inch. Relief was shown by hachures, which – while aesthetically pleasing – lacked precision. The major work of the survey report was the volume written by King, *Systematic Geology* (1878), which gave a detailed account of the geological evolution of the region.

The King Survey, while nominally under the control of the military, produced information and data more suitable for science than for military intelligence. The atlas provided a detailed knowledge of the topography of the region, but the work was contextualized with regard to geological science not to military needs.

King was made the first head of the United States Geological Survey (USGS) in 1878. He helped it to become established and appointed its early staff members. King resigned in 1880 to pursue his business interests, but his final years were not so illustrious as his earlier years. He lost money in the 1893 depression, had a nervous breakdown and died in Arizona in 1901.

THE WHEELER SURVEY George Montague Wheeler was born on 9 October 1842 in Hokinton, MA. He graduated from West Point in 1866 and was appointed second lieutenant in the Corps of Engineers and employed in surveying duty in California. He was promoted to first lieutenant in 1867. Four years later, he was given charge of the military survey of territory west of the 100th meridian. The survey, the result of an act of Congress on 10 June 1872, was to be the great work of his life, absorbing all his energies. The survey was designed and planned as a military operation. Its aim was explicitly one of military intelligence. Wheeler was to produce a

mathematically based topographic survey, intended as a connected first survey of a comparatively wild and uninhabited region, more particularly for immediate military purposes. . . . Its origin was the outgrowth of a permanent and legitimate want of the War Department for current topographic information of the vast area west of the Mississippi, within which constant military movements were and are required.[9]

Fieldwork took place from 1871 to 1879 and involved fourteen trips, each ranging from three to nine months. The field trips were often attended by the greatest hardship, deprivation, exposure and fatigue. A vast area was mapped, surveyed, drawn and photographed to make a detailed topographical map of an area of 359,065 square miles. Annual reports of the survey were published from 1873 to 1880, all with maps. Under instructions from the Chief of Engineers, the aim was to obtain correct topographical knowledge; to prepare accurate maps; to gather as much information on physical features of the country, the number, habits and disposition of the Native Americans, possible sites for military operations, facilities for making road and rail, mineral deposits, land potential and measures of latitude and longitude.

The Wheeler survey, like the other surveys, drew extensively on Native-American guides. The notion of intrepid white explorers making their way through the wilderness on their own needs to be replaced by the more accurate picture of them using local people and local knowledge. In his Report, Wheeler notes:

From among the Utes and Pah-Utes found north and west of the Colorado River, it was possible to obtain friendly guides, many of whom proved most invaluable in pointing out the little hidden springs and streams, especially in the Death Valley country, Southwestern Nevada, and Eastern California sections.[10]

The use of such guides did not preclude Wheeler from a distrust of the Native Americans. On the next page of his Report, he noted that 'The fate of the Indians sealed, the interval during which their extermination as a race is to be consummated will doubtless be marked in addition to Indian outbreaks, with still many more murderous ambuscades and massacres.'

The survey cost $691,444.45, produced 41 printed reports, 164 maps and a final report of the expedition that was published in 1889, the capstone of a massive eight-volume report actually finished in 1879 but, due to Wheeler's illness, not completed until 1887. The eight volumes were *Topographical Atlas* (1874), *Geology* (1875), *Zoology* (1875), *Paleontology* (1877), *Botany* (1878), *Archaeology* (1879), *Astronomy and Barometric Pressure* (1887) and the *Geographical Report* (1889). Let us consider briefly the *Geographical Report* and *Topographical Atlas*.

Volume 1, *Geographical Report*, had sections on population, industries, commerce and water. The water deficit in the region was a consistent theme: 'the most superficial estimate shows a tremendous deficit in water, as compared with the amount actually required.'[11] Wheeler wrote of the need for artesian wells and canals. He also used a land classification system that divided land into arable, grazing, timber, arid or barren, and chaparral. He was aware of the various purposes for which this information could be used:

the first use of such results was with the troops in their movements without forage supplies and the next with the General Land Office in conducting their subdivision surveys, while the use has been general for those seeking homes in these regions, and for the capitalist and investor with present or prospective interests therein.[12]

There was also a report of the human geography of the region, including a call for the extirpation of polygamy among the Mormons and a large chapter on Native Americans in which Wheeler saw the inevitability of white settlement on Native-American lands.

The *Topographical Atlas* was part of an ambitious mapping programme. Wheeler's goal was to produce a detailed topographic map of the territory west of the 100th meridian. He surveyed fully one-third of the area and produced 71 topographic maps and seven land-use maps. He succeeded in mapping one quarter of the area west of the 100th meridian. The maps were published individually from 1876 to 1883 as well as in an atlas form. The first atlas, produced in 1874, uses a simple key.[13] The order is revealing; the first symbol is for fort or camp represented by a US flag, and it comes before symbols for settlements, villages and towns.

There are seven categories of topography: craters, buttes, peaks, mesa bluffs, canyons, plateaux, and ranges of mountains. The atlas contains maps at a range of scales, including one inch to eight miles with relief shown in hachures; one inch to four miles also with hachures; one inch to two miles showing relief by contours of different colours. The maps have a dual longitude system from both Washington and Greenwich. The most striking feature of the maps is the beautiful rendition of relief. The hachure system employed is wonderfully evocative of relief with a real artistry in depiction. The Wheeler Survey was more concerned with topographical mapping than any of the other surveys were. Relief was shown by spot measures of altitude and hachures (lines indicating slope and height). This method gives a very strong sense of relief, intuitively much better than contours. There is a grace and elegance to Wheeler's depiction of relief that gives an aesthetic dimension to a mapping exercise. The map also highlights routes through the terrain. As an army officer, Wheeler was concerned with showing the routeways through the country and their ease of travel. The map contains vital military intelligence. The ease of travel (vital military information) is depicted by the routeway key: a line with a stippled line is a wagon road quickly traversed, a straight line is a trail over steep relief and thus impractical for wagon use, and a dotted line is a trail of low relief.

The eight-volume report was Wheeler's life work. He worked on it from 1875 to 1889 and was actively involved in the production of the written volumes and especially of the *Topographical Atlas*. However, in the struggle for dominance in the emerging world of organized and government-funded science, Wheeler lost out. There was duplication in the survey of the West. In 1873, for example, there were two government survey teams mapping the same peaks: Wheeler's and the other from the Hayden Survey. In 1874, the House of Representatives' Townsend Committee on Public Lands looked at the duplication. The methods of the Wheeler Survey were attacked by Hayden and Powell.

In the struggle for power, the civilian scientists eventually won the day. There was also a struggle between the Army and the Department of Interior. A report of the National Academy of Science in 1878 condemned the Wheeler Survey and called for civilian control of mapping and survey work in the West. Wheeler's survey was merged with the Geological Survey but he did not become director. Defeated in the world of scientific politics, the effects of the explorations caught up with him. At his own request, a retiring board found him permanently incapacitated for active service but allowed him to work at his own discretion until 1888. He communicated with national topographic surveys around the world. In 1881, he was the US commissioner at the International Geographical Union Congress in Venice and spent some time studying surveys in Europe. In 1890, Congress approved his rank and pay of major. He died in New York City on 3 May 1905.

THE HAYDEN SURVEY Ferdinand Vandiver Hayden (1829-1887) was born in Westfield, MA. After his father's death, when Hayden was only ten, he went to live with an uncle on a small farm near Rochester, NY. While later studying medicine in Albany, NY, he met James Hall, who encouraged him to go on a fossil-collecting trip to the Badlands. His interest in geology had been sparked into life. He served as geologist in various expeditions and explorations. After the Civil War, he served as a surgeon, renewed his interest in geology and was appointed Professor of Geology at the University of Pennsylvania in 1866. Formal academic life, however, was too restraining for him. He was happiest in the field. In 1866, he was part of an expedition to the Badlands under the auspices of the Academy of Natural Sciences of Philosophy. In 1867, he did a survey of Nebraska for the GLO. The report of the survey was well received and enabled him to obtain more money for further exploration in the Rocky Mountain region.

In 1869, he was appointed to the Geologic and Geographical Survey of The Territories. This survey was part of the Interior Department and marks a shift away from formal military control of mapping and survey work in the West. Hayden had considerable expedition and field work experience when he was appointed but, just as important, he was also well connected with the most important topographers and geologists of the day. In addition, he had the political 'savvy' to get his appropriations increased from $5,000 in 1868, to $10,000 in 1869, and to $25,000 in 1870. He knew how to play the Washington game of building an empire. The expedition that he led in 1870 included 20 men, numerous assistants and the photographer, William Henry Jackson. Jackson accompanied him on subsequent surveys. Illustration 50 is a photograph taken by William Henry Jackson of two members of the Hayden survey, W.H. Holmes and G. B. Chittenden, surveying in 1874.

In 1871, Hayden managed to obtain $40, 000 in federal appropriations to finance an official exploration of Yellowstone. The party

50 William Henry Jackson's 1874 photograph of members of Ferdinand Hayden's geological and geographical survey of Colorado (1873–6). National Archives, Washington, DC.

consisted of scientists, photographers and the great painter, Thomas Moran, who was to fix the images of the scenic grandeur in drawings and majestic paintings. This was not just a scientific expedition but an act of image making, a re-presenting of the West for an Eastern élite audience. Moran created huge canvasses and Hayden wrote extensively. In 1872, he wrote an article for *Scribner's*.[14] These images and words, as well as Hayden's lobbying of friends and acquaintances in Washington, led to Yellowstone being created the world's first national park in 1872. Soon after, a book appeared, perhaps the first coffee-table book on a national park but definitely not the last. The 1876 *Yellowstone National Park*, whose authorship was 'described by Prof. F. Hayden (geologist-in charge of US Government exploring expeditions and illustrated by Thomas Moran [artist to the expedition of 1871])', is a huge book; not so much a coffee-table book, more like a substitute coffee table.[15] In the introduction, Hayden describes a 'world of grandeur and beauty unsurpassed, even by the world-renowned scenery of the Alpine districts of Europe'. There is a nationalistic pride to the description. It is also a promotional text; Hayden describes the best routes for tourists to travel and see for themselves 'some of the most remarkable and instructive features in North America'. Yellowstone Lake is described in glowing terms that combine scientific interest and aesthetic sensibility: 'From whatever point the lake is viewed, a scene of beauty will repay the observer. The student of science, the lover of nature, and the artist can find something of interest on its shores.'[16] The book is illustrated with fifteen large plates, chromolithographic reproductions of water-colour sketches by Thomas Moran, all wide-angle views that give a monumental perspective and heighten the dramatic representation of the landscape. In less than five years, the Yellowstone became less an unexplored territory and more a place photographed, painted, written about, and read about.

Hayden also produced more obviously scientific work. One of his major works was the *Atlas of Colorado*, published in 1877 and based on the results of the fieldwork from 1873 to 1876.[17] The atlas has two series of maps: four sheets at a scale of twelve miles to one inch covering the whole state; and twelve sheets (six topographical, six geological) at four miles to one inch with contours at 200-foot intervals. The atlas is sensitive to wider issues of settlement and development. An economic map identifies agricultural land, pasture land, forest, land above the timber line, and the location of coal, gold and silver. The atlas is wonderfully illustrated with detailed geological sections and six wonderful panoramic views by W. Holmes that each stretch across two large pages. This atlas was an expensive production with wonderful drawings, great maps and good colour. On the title page after Hayden's name comes his title: US Geologist In Charge.

By 1878, Hayden's star had begun to wane in Washington. Secretary of State Carl Schurz, with prompting from Powell, had directed him to make a choice between geology and ethnology. Hayden chose geology, yet it was King who was made the director of the USGS. Hayden became an employee, with less autonomy and less ability to organize his own expeditions. However, as the great publicist of the West and its attractions, his name still carried weight with the wider public. He was marketed as an expert and authority in various publications. In *The Great West*, published in 1880, Hayden's name is used to sell a popular account.[18] The preface praises him with the title 'Professor' and notes that his 'great work of scientific exploration has earned the admiration and praise of the scientific world in general and many eminent men in particular'. This book is a collection of essays drawn from the *New York Independent* and *Tribune* as well as government reports, including Surveyor General reports with the comforting remark that 'The removal of the Sioux from Northern Wyoming have given fresh impulse to settlement in that fertile region.'[19]

This book was published soon after the surveys were sent out. The West had moved quickly from unexplored territory to site of scientific exploration through a boosterist presentation to become an investment opportunity and a destination of tourist travel. This book is part of the selling of the West; the recurring theme is 'to come and see it'. There are still some scientific articles and the overall effect of reading the book is like viewing a place with a wide-angle lens; there is a great mixture of scientific reporting, boosterism, reportage and hints to travellers. Hayden's name gives scientific authority to the project as well as a recognizable name to a reading public. Three years after this book was published, Hayden retired because of ill health. He died in Philadelphia in 1886.

THE POWELL SURVEY The second, purely civilian, survey of the West was led by John Wesley Powell. He was born in 1834 to a devoutly Methodist couple in western New York who named him after the great evangelical preacher and founder of Methodism. In the Civil War, he served as a captain of artillery. At the Battle of Shiloh, he lost his right arm at the elbow. His later adventures are all the more impressive when we consider this disability. In 1865, he was a professor at Illinois Wesleyan College. Like other great surveyors, he was a man of the outdoors and regularly took field trips. He persuaded his university and the Natural History Society of Illinois to fund a museum in Bloomington and managed to secure $500 for a trip to the Rockies to collect samples. He obtained further support from railroad companies, the US Army and the Smithsonian. In 1867, he led an expedition into the Rockies reaching Pike's Peak on 27 July. On his return, he secured funds for another expedition that set out in 1868. Each time, Powell was extending knowledge of the Colorado River as well as making important connections with the business community, members of the scientific establishment and government officials. The second expedition was even visited by a party of tourists, including the Speaker of the House and the newspaperman, Samuel Bowles. Even on his expeditions, Powell was making connections with politicians and newspapermen.

In 1869, Powell obtained financial support for a 1,500-mile trip down the Colorado River. Powell had four special craft built of oak and pine that varied in length from sixteen to twenty feet. Men from his previous trips were signed up and a total of eleven men began their journey on 24 May 1869 from Green River City. Powell later wrote: 'The good people of Green River City turn out to see us start. We raise our little flag, push the boats from the shore, and the swift current carries us down.'[20]

Three months and over a 1,000 miles later, after numerous adventures, including the death of three members by Native Americans, they reached Callville, where they were met by a Mormon family. Powell's trip became the stuff of legend and was carried by all the newspapers and popular journals. He gave invited lectures throughout the country, becoming an orator of force and power. When he went to Washington, he was national hero. In 1869, Congress appropriated $10,000 for the Geographical and Topographical Survey of the Colorado River of the West.

The second survey, with an emphasis on topography and the inclusion of a photographer (E. Beaman) and an artist (Frederick Dellenbaugh) set off, again from Green River City, on 22 May 1871. By 1872, a preliminary map of the Grand Canyon region had been made. Surveys continued until 1879 with emphases on mapmaking, ethnology and land-use patterns. Powell also developed an interest in the farming techniques of the indigenous peoples and the Mormons. He learned from them the practice of an agriculture appropriate to the dry conditions. He also developed a lifelong interest in the languages and belief systems of the indigenous people. Powell's second expedition mapped the human resources as well as the natural landscape.

A number of publications emerged from the survey work. Powell produced two major works of geology, *Exploration of the Colorado of the West* (1875) and *Report on the Geology of the Eastern Portion of the Uinta Mountains* (1876), as well as *Introduction to the Study of Indian Languages* (1877). Other members also published; Grove Karl Gilbert, lured from the Wheeler Survey, produced *The Geology of the Henry Mountains* (1877) and Captain Clarence Dutton wrote *The High Plateaus of Utah* (1880).

Powell also published more general works that sought to influence public policy. In 1873, he was appointed special commissioner to investigate the condition of the plateau Indians. The report, published in 1874 with fellow commissioner G. Ingalls, advocated moving Native Americans to reservations where they could learn techniques and skills. The Native Americans were to receive education, health care and property. Powell wanted them weaned away from their nomadic lifestyle and acculturated into what he deemed a higher form of development. In 1879, he also published *Report on the Lands of the Arid Regions of the United States*, in which he argued that techniques of farming developed in the humid West were not appropriate for the arid West. A scientific approach was needed, he maintained, that included a careful mapping and classification of the land. The standard 160-acre holding that was the basis for settlement in the rest of the country should be abandoned in favour of smaller, 80-acre holdings organized into irrigation districts with farmers encouraged to form cooperatives. Powell drew heavily upon his experience with Mormon settlement patterns and farming techniques, which had devolved more communal forms of water management. A fundamental element of Powell's report was that water rights should not be easily privatized, traded, bought or sold. Powell was mapping out not just a new land but a new society; an ecologically conscious and communally organized society that drew its inspiration from the Mormon experience and the tenets of Methodism all combined in Powell's own hard-won vision. Powell went to the West as an explorer but returned as a prophet.

Representing the West

In a comparatively short period, from 1867 to 1880, the notation of 'unexplored' that appeared on the GLO's 1867 map was rendered obsolete. By the end of the 1870s, the territory had been not only explored but mapped, described and classified. The territory was represented in hachures, contour lines, geologic sequences and biotic taxonomies, photographs, paintings, illustrations, articles scientific and general, and books both technical and popular. The mapping of the territory was part embodiment and part metaphor of the incorporation of the West into national discourses of science, politics and national identity. The great surveys represented the West to a broader public. King, Hayden and Powell, in particular, realized they were in a competitive position, jostling for funding, power and a dominant position in the emerging scientific establishment. The illustrators, painters and popular writers were not just doing a public service; they were part of a struggle for dominance.

These surveys were also great publicity campaigns. On the production side were the purveyors of Western imagery eager to get their message across in word and picture. On the consumption side was an expanding reading public for whom the reports from the Western surveys combined the adventures of science and exploration with swelling national pride about the wonders of the American landscape. And in between was the burgeoning magazine sector. Popular illustrated magazines such as *Harper's, Aldine* and *Scribner's* carried stories of the surveys with engravings and photographs from the expeditions.[21] From the viewpoint of surveys in the West through the magazine distribution network to the readers in their homes, a national landscape was represented and celebrated. In newspaper reports, magazine articles, photo albums, books and commentaries and exhibitions (the 1876 centennial exhibition in Philadelphia had a large area devoted to topographic representation of the mountain West), the Western landscape was represented, packaged, commodified and consumed.

The West was 'captured' in maps, paintings, photographs and books, and brought back East. The great landscape painter, Thomas Moran, for example, accompanied Hayden into the Yellowstone and painted huge canvasses of scenic wonder. The artist William H. Holmes accompanied both the Hayden and Powell surveys, and his topographic drawings are statements in both scientific and aesthetic representation.

Photographs were an important medium for transmitting images of the West to an Eastern audience. Timothy O'Sullivan, a professional photographer whose images of Gettysburg fixed many people's images of the Civil War, was one of the first photographers to represent systematically the West. O'Sullivan went with the King expedition and later with Wheeler. A field photographer became an essential position in the great surveys. Hayden employed William Henry Jackson while

Powell used first E. O. Beaman and then Jack Hillers. The work of these photographers concentrated on the West of scenic grandeur and grand geologic architecture. They were forerunners of Ansel Adams.[22]

The West was also represented in books designed for a popular audience. One of John Wesley Powell's last books was *Canyons of the Colorado River*, first published in 1895. In the preface, Powell explains that his first exploration down the Colorado had been the theme of much newspaper writing. He wanted to set the record straight. The book was based on previous work; the four articles he had written for *Scribner's* in 1874 and various reports published by the federal government and the Smithsonian, especially the 1875 *Exploration of the Colorado River of the West and Its Tributaries*.[23] There was still a popular demand. 'I have received many letters urging me that a popular account of the exploration and a description of that wonderful land should be published by me.' Powell's book is a delightful read. Clearly written and wonderfully illustrated the book, written well after the surveys had been completed, provides a fitting full stop. The excitement of exploration, the scientific understanding, the broad gaze that incorporated geology, topography, botany, and ethnology, the visual representations of people and places are all captured in Powell's book (illus. 51). Science, exploration, representation. The West has been described, explained, mapped, represented. The West as a place of grandeur, a natural monumentalisms quickly disseminated around the country and percolated through the community. The West was not only mapped, it was given a place in the national imagination.

Centre of Representation

The federal mapping of the West had wider consequences. A national centre of representation was established and at its heart was the federal government centred in Washington. William Goetzmann has calculated that between 1840 and 1880 the federal government was spending between one-quarter and one-third of its budget on the funding of scientific enterprises and their publications. The vast majority was being sent out West on exploration/mapping exercises. This level of support reflected an incredible federal subsidy to organized science, the arts and the printing and publishing industry that dwarfs anything to come, including the New Deal. Ron Tyler has estimated that in this period the government issued 25 million images of the American West, including illustrations and maps.[24] Government grants enabled scientists to pursue and develop a scientific discourse

51 Illustration of the Colorado River, from John Wesley Powell's *Canyons of the Colorado River* (Meadsville, PA, 1895).

and paid for the work of painters and engravers. Government contracts also stimulated the development of the mapmaking, printing and engraving industries.

Much has been written about the four post–Civil War surveys. A map of their travels shows meandering and interlocking paths across the Western states (illus. 52). From Oregon to New Mexico and from Montana to Arizona, the surveys wend their way through the territory; mapping and measuring, recording and classifying, painting, sketching and photographing. Just as important would be a map that shows where this information was sent to. Popular accounts were published in newspapers and journals in New York, Philadelphia and Boston. The scientific reports were read in the universities and

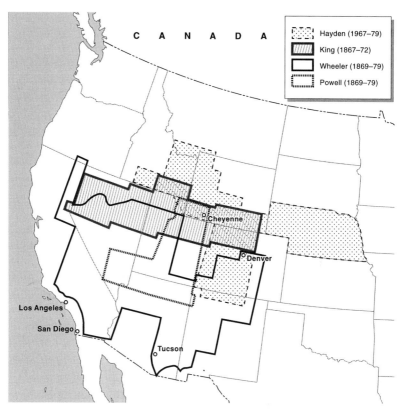

52 The Great Surveys — Hayden, King, Powell and Wheeler.

meeting places of an organizing and organized science. The reports were sent back, published and discussed in Washington. A map of the surveys would be incomplete without a map of Washington at its pivotal centre; the source of funding, legitimacy, dissemination and discussion. The mapping of the West involved the representation of the West as well as the creation of Washington as a centre. Bruno Latour has written about centres of calculation in the history of science.[25] In the last third of the nineteenth century, Washington emerged as a centre of representation.

The centralizing tendency was not smooth. Rivalry between the surveys came to a head in 1874 in a House Committee on Public Lands. The congressional hearing of 1874 brought to light the conflict between the Army and the Interior Department and the personal jealousies of the leaders of the surveys. A five-year debate ensued in which alliances were made, enmities solidified and scientists fought for recognition, funding and power. It marks the beginning of the era of Big Science. Scientific pursuits moved from personal obsessions to publicly funded endeavours tied to notions of national interest. In 1878, Powell, Hayden and Wheeler had to submit reports to the House Appropriations Committee, which in turn asked the National Academy of Science to appoint a special committee to review the reports. The special committee, packed with friends of King and Powell, reviewed the reports and effectively decided (surprise, surprise) to discontinue funding of the Wheeler and Hayden surveys. Powell now had greater power and he suggested a plan to rationalize the mapping programme: a Coast and Interior Survey for geodetic work and a United States Geological Survey (USGS).[26] In 1879, Congress authorized the establishment of the USGS. Congressman Hewitt of New York, one of the principal authors of the legislation, said in 1879, 'What is there in this richly endowed land of ours which may be dug, or gathered, or harvested, and made part of the wealth of America and of the world, and how and where does it lie?' In 1879, President Hayes signed the bill that gave birth to the USGS. King and Hayden jostled for position, but King was better connected than Hayden. King was a partner with Congressman Hewitt in three ranching enterprises, and his friends and Hayden's enemies had direct access to President Hayes.

Clarence King was appointed the first director of the USGS in 1879. He lasted only a year before resigning to devote attention to his mining and ranching interests. Powell took over in 1881, expanding the staff and seeking to establish a topographic map of the West. He introduced the *USGS Bulletin*, still published today, and folio atlases starting in 1874 at four miles to one inch. In 1882, Powell received authority to survey the whole country.

The ambitious mapping programme outlined by Powell was not only a goal but a vital inventory for the land classification and reform outlined in his 1878 report. However, resistance against his preservation and irrigation plans came from powerful Western land interests. Heavy cuts in his budget led to his resignation in 1894, although he continued as head of the Bureau of Ethnology until he died in 1902. The USGS National Center in Reston, VA is the John Wesley Powell Federal Building.

The mapping of the West and especially the four great surveys laid the basis for the government mapping of the entire territory. From the four surveys emerged the beginnings of Big Science and, in particular, the United States Geological Survey – the main government organization still responsible for mapping and cartographically representing the national territory. From these nineteenth-century endeavours emerged a scientific community closely tied to government and federal policy.

11 Constructing the National Community

Only the more thoughtful, however, fully recognize how closely and extensively the prosperity of a country depends upon the existence of accurate maps of its domain with general facility of access to them.[1]

Nations have been described as imagined communities. They are imagined in maps. National communities are pictured in maps. The varied communities that make up a nation are cartographically represented, sometimes misrepresented and often unrepresented.

Throughout the nineteenth century, but particularly in the last third, a series of county, state and national atlases were produced in the United States. Technological improvements in printing created cost reductions that made the distribution and purchase of atlases available to a wider public. It is legitimate to speak of a cartographic explosion brought about by more available cartographic images and their wider and deeper consumption. The maps represented communities and in turn, communities were shaped and formed by the consumption of these maps. The maps represented and embodied imagined, real and observed communities.

The County Map

A basic unit of local government in the United States is the county. It has constituted the cellular structure of political society for over 200 years. Most of the nation is now covered by approximately 3,000 counties. Rural counties provide the basic services of the provision of law and order, road maintenance and public health; semi-rural counties also include library provision. Urban counties provide a range of services, including street lighting, sewage disposal and garbage disposal. County electorates vote in a range of officers: coroner, county attorney, county treasurer, sheriff and the board of education. The county is a unit of government that is more direct, more personal and more tied to the Jeffersonian notion of participatory democracy than the much larger and more distant state and federal units of government.

Before improvements in transport and communications, counties were a very important level of political organization. They were the smallest geopolitical unit and more accessible to citizens when transport and communication were more difficult and expensive. The county unit was a fundamental organization and demarcation of political-social space that helped to create local communities by giving a civic focus to matters of shared interest and public concern. These political units became social units as people had to come together to organize their public lives and deal with matters such as the maintenance of law and order, education and health. Counties became communities. This transformation, however, was always an unequal and an uneven affair. The rich and powerful, as in all things, tended to have a disproportionate share of local power. Not all the people in the county were directly involved in public life and political affairs. Local business interests dominated both the economic and political scene. Yet, there was a rhetoric of community and the explicit creation of community consciousness through the interweaving of civil society and political organization at the county level. One important element of this connection was the production and consumption of county maps.

The evolution of county mapping is depicted by Michael Conzen as a five-stage process (Table 1). Prior to 1847, county maps were experiments in mapping and graphic design. Lithographed wall maps of counties appear in the 1840s and mark what Conzen refers to as the proto-professional period. The county maps that appear in the middle of the nineteenth century were produced on subscription and sold for about $5. The standard scale was one inch to one mile. They were large, meant for display on a wall. They often showed landownership patterns as well as the names and locations of residents and prominent physical features, roads and streams. Around the borders, the names and pictures of prominent business people and their businesses were often displayed. People would pay up to $30 for this privilege and advertising opportunity. In effect, these county maps provided a cartographic record of the county and its inhabitants. The geopolitical unit with members of its civil society, business and farming communities were graphically displayed. People were put in their place, literally and metaphorically. The county map was a graphic communication which linked the members of propertied civil society through shared spatial depiction.

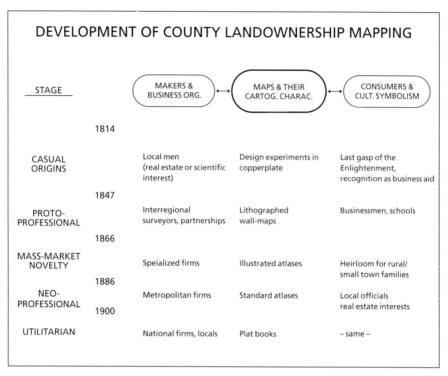

DEVELOPMENT OF COUNTY LANDOWNERSHIP MAPPING

STAGE		MAKERS & BUSINESS ORG.	MAPS & THEIR CARTOG. CHARAC.	CONSUMERS & CULT. SYMBOLISM
	1814			
CASUAL ORIGINS		Local men (real estate or scientific interest)	Design experiments in copperplate	Last gasp of the Enlightenment, recognition as business aid
	1847			
PROTO-PROFESSIONAL		Interregional surveyors, partnerships	Lithographed wall-maps	Businessmen, schools
	1866			
MASS-MARKET NOVELTY		Speialized firms	Illustrated atlases	Heirloom for rural/ small town families
	1886			
NEO-PROFESSIONAL		Metropolitan firms	Standard atlases	Local officials real estate interests
	1900			
UTILITARIAN		National firms, locals	Plat books	– same –

Table 1 Source: Conzen, 1984.

An important figure in county wall maps was Robert Pearsall Smith.[2] Smith was an entrepreneur who attracted investment and organized the process of county map production. He was interested in both lithography and mapmaking. Over the period 1846–64 he sponsored over 150 maps through the Northeast. Smith started the tradition of including all inhabitants on county maps, not just the major landowners and prepaid subscribers. Smith had a notion of cartographic democracy. His ultimate goal was to produce county maps as a basis for state maps which in turn would be a basis for a map of the entire nation in which all inhabitants would be mapped in a cartographic endeavour that showed everyone in their place and a place for everyone. All citizens would be located on a map, a spatial depiction of a democracy.

The County Atlas

The large-scale county map had its drawbacks; it was large, bulky and difficult to transport and store. It was only one surface and thus advertising revenue was limited. These problems were overcome with the development of the county atlas.

County atlases were produced in the United States as early as 1814 but the so-called golden age occurred between 1850 and 1880 when they reached their peak of detail and design exuberance. Over 5,000 county atlases were produced and their coverage was particularly strong in the Northeast and Midwest. The atlases, by showing all landowners, bind people together in the same text. This gives a sense of community but also identifies inequalities in wealth, status and landholdings. The county atlases, in particular, are a rich source of information since they identify individual landholdings. In effect, they provide a map of local communities.

County atlases were often sold on a subscription basis. An agent of the company producing the atlas would drum up support among the local élite. Sometimes they would be successful in getting the official endorsement and help of the county boards. Canvassers would then be dispatched throughout the county to sign up subscribers. A typical subscription would cost about $10 and subscribers would be listed in the final atlas. Larger subscriptions were required for a portrait of a person and a depiction of their property, farm or business. Sometimes $160 could be charged for a large spread. The atlas also contained a list of patrons and their residence and business. In *An Historical Atlas of Lee County Iowa*, for example, the list also includes their country of birth and sometimes the date when they came to the county. Thus J. W. Johnstone of Keokuk was an undertaker who came from Pennsylvania in 1840; Van Grieken was a photographer who came from Holland in 1854; and the longest county resident was the sheriff of Keokuk, an R. P. Creel who came from Kentucky in 1836.[3] The county atlases are a treasure trove of information.

The average cost of producing an atlas was between $10,000 and $15, 000 – the actual mapping and surveying costs were only about 15 per cent of total costs. Most of the information was copied from official maps and tax lists and fieldwork rarely took more than a few days. The printing and selling of the atlas constituted the bulk of the costs but it was a lucrative business as, on average, 1000 copies would be sold. Companies concentrated their efforts on counties with a minimum population of 20,000. The average receipts for each edition were $25,000 made up of basic subscriptions and the added charge for more prominent displays. While not all landowners bought a copy, some – especially those with full-page spreads – bought many copies to distribute to friends and clients. A clear profit of at least $10,000 was not unusual. When companies were surveying and drumming for business in adjacent counties as they swept through entire states, the average costs were reduced while receipts were kept high. The well-organized firms could map up to a dozen counties in a single season; profits of almost $16,000 per edition, for efficient operations, were easily attainable. One publisher, Alfred Andreas, made a profit of $17,000 on his *Atlas of Peoria County* published in 1878. Publishers, especially in the lucrative Midwest market, were taking in total receipts of over a $1 million in the 1870s.

The production of county wall maps was centred in Philadelphia; however, county atlases for New England and Middle Atlantic states were produced in Philadelphia and New York City. In the last third of the nineteenth century, the atlases of Midwest counties were produced not only in Philadelphia and New York but also in the Midwest. Alfred Andreas established his own company in 1869–70 after many years as a successful salesman in Davenport, IA. In 1873, the company moved to Chicago.

Firms would specialize in the county atlas market and there was often a specialization in regional markets. The Edward brothers, for example, did county atlases of Missouri and Kansas. Family firms and partnerships dominated. The Beers (Silas, Daniel, Frederick and James) were involved in a variety of enterprises from 1864 to the beginning of the twentieth century. Frederick W. Beers produced over 80 atlases from 1866 to 1886 and covered counties in the following states: Michigan, Vermont, Massachusetts, New York, New Jersey, Ohio, Kansas and Connecticut. Short-term partnerships were often formed for specific projects of county mapping. The different company names of the Beers included F. W. Beers & Co; Pomeroy and Beers; D. G. Beers & Company; Beers, Ellis and Soule; J. B. Beers & Company.

County atlases cover much of the Northeast and Midwest whereas the South (apart from Florida, and the mountain states) has few, if any, county maps. The greatest concentration is in Pennsylvania, New York, Illinois and Iowa, where some counties would have five or more editions of an atlas produced over three decades. The timing of the coverage was like a tidal wave that swept west. In the 1860s, coverage was restricted to New York and Pennsylvania; by the 1870s, county atlases reached the Midwest states; by the 1890s, the Midwest and upper Midwest; and in the first two decades of the twentieth century, the western plain states were also covered by county atlases.

The standard format was a map of each township in the county, giving detailed landownership information. The maps of the township gave detailed data of who owned land, transport networks, and

53 Title page of Everts, Baskin and Stewart's *Combination Atlas Map of McHenry County, Illinois* (Chicago, 1872).

the spatial location of manufacturing, churches and schools. Additional material included a map of the state, maps of individual towns, sometimes a brief history, and lists of companies. Companies and individuals would often pay for the prominent display of their property or company. The atlases were part map, part historical memorial, part yellow pages.

Let us look at two examples in some detail. *The Combination Atlas Map of McHenry County, Illinois* was published in 1872 by Everts, Baskin and Stewart.[4] Illinois was a state well covered by county atlases and Everts, Baskin and Stewart was an important and prolific producer of these atlases. On the title page of one atlas (illus. 53), the county is linked to the wider community through design. A globe represents the world, there is a US map, then the open book shows a map of the county on one page and townships on the other. The assembled artifacts of dividers, right-angle and theodolite represent the science and practice of survey and mapping: world, nation, county and township all linked in a discourse of mathematical observation and cartographic representation. The atlas has a key in English

54 *Sectional Map of Illinois* explaining the range and township rectangular survey, from *Combination Atlas Map of McHenry County.*

and German with symbols representing farmhouses, schoolhouses, churches, mills, blacksmiths, cemeteries, roads, railroads, proposed rails, quarries, lime kilns, orchards, timber, swamps and creeks. At the beginning of the atlas, there is a map of Illinois explaining the range and township rectangular survey (illus. 54) and a map of McHenry County. A picture of the county courthouse in Woodstock illustrates a central point in the civic life of the county. A business directory provides a range of services to the atlas user. Then there are the maps of each township at 2 inches to 1 mile and some town maps at scale of 1 inch to 500 feet. Pictures of farms are found throughout the atlas. At the end there is a patrons' directory that gives information on individuals. Not only are their location and property noted but after their name is their township, section, date of settlement, nativity, post office address and a description of their business. The county atlas was a detailed inventory of the local subscribing population. For close-knit communities, absence from the atlas could have been a source of shame and regret, while inclusion was the sign of a civic obligation faithfully discharged.

The *Atlas of Kane County, Illinois* was produced by D. W. Ensign in 1892. Opposite the title page is a huge engraving of Kane County Court House in all its neo-Romanesque splendour. This first image of the atlas is a symbol of social order. The first map is a map of the United States that fills up an entire double spread. Longitude is given from both Washington and Greenwich. The national map precedes the map of Illinois, which depicts counties, railroads and towns. There is then a detailed discussion of the government land survey with a map of the principal meridians and baselines used by the GLO.

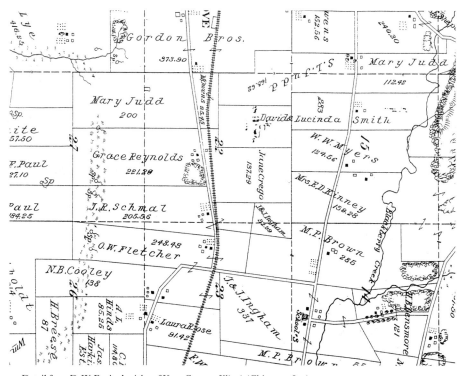

55 Detail from D. W. Ensign's *Atlas of Kane County, Illinois* (Chicago, 1892).

A map of Kane County shows the fifteen townships; each is then shown separately, with township and range numbering very evident at the top of the page and ownership names clearly marked. For example, on p. 59, the owners of Sugar Grove Township are clearly shown along with an estimate of their acreage (illus. 54). After the maps comes a three-page list of patrons of the map; real estate companies and merchants predominate although there are some farmers.

As a subscriber, the first thing you would probably do is to check your own name. Did they include it? Did they get the spelling right? However, read in order, the atlas contextualizes individual landowners in a wider system; their location in a township is placed within the county, the state and the nation. Read from the beginning, the atlases frame the individuals in a wider setting. In the *Atlas of DeKalb County, Indiana,* for example, the framing maps include a map of the entire county with the township and range system clearly marked, a map of Indiana with the township and range system, a railroad map of the United States, and a map of the world.[5] The atlas pulls together the individual farmers and landowners and local business establishments in a wider context of world, nation, the national land survey, the state, the county and the township. In few other cartographies are the links drawn so vividly between the individual reader and the wider world.

The State Atlas

Before the Civil War, only three state atlases were produced – South Carolina, New York (discussed in Chapter 5) and Maine – all in the 1820s. From 1866 to 1890, more than 20 state atlases were produced. The cartographic explosion after the Civil War included state as well as county atlases. As with the county atlas, behind this growth lay developments in printing technology which had reduced the cost and the emergence of a map-publishing industry that was able to produce, distribute and market atlases and maps, as well as discover and increase market demand.

Legislators were keen to see their state represented in bound textual form because they believed it showed the sophistication and development of the state. Although state atlases may have had the blessing of state legislatures, they were privately produced rather than subsidized by the state.[6] Libraries, schools and some private individuals were willing to pay either directly or by subscription to see their state represented in an atlas. The development of state atlases in the last third of the nineteenth century is an early example of state boosterism.

The state atlases developed as the same time as county atlases. The connection is not just temporal. Some of the state atlases are little more than county maps bound together. *The Official State Atlas of Nebraska*, for example, published by the well-known county atlas publishers Everts and Kirk in 1885, consists of little more than a large-scale map of the state and then a series of county maps. Everts and Kirk responded to the low population of Nebraska by producing a state atlas on a subscription basis. Like the county atlases, this atlas has illustrations of businesses and farms and a list of patrons. Among the subscribers were F. J. Wehling, a native of Germany who settled in Madison County in 1880 and was involved in real estate, loans and insurance. Also assisting in the publication was an E. A. Lyon, who had purchased a 160-acre spread in 1871 at Township 35 south, and Range 2 west; the estimated value of the property was $20 per acre and included mules, cattle, horses and hogs.

As with county atlases, there were specialist publishers. Alfred Andreas extended his business to state atlases by producing *The Illustrated Historical State Atlas of Minnesota* in 1874, sold on subscription for $15. This was to be the first of a series. In 1875, he produced the *Illustrated Historical Atlas of Iowa*, again sold on subscription for $15; more than 22,000 copies of this atlas were sold but large production costs made it a financial liability and Andreas was forced to reorganize his company under the name of Baskin, Forster and Company. This company produced *The Illustrated Historical Atlas of the State of Indiana* in 1876. The atlas was not a success and Andreas shifted his attention to straightforward historical works, such as the three-volume *History of Chicago* published between 1884 and 1886.

Henry Francis Walling (1825–1888) was a major publisher of state atlases. From 1865 to 1885, Walling was involved in the compilation of a large number of atlases including those for Ohio (1868), Wisconsin (1876), Illinois (1870, with Robert Allen Campbell), Massachusetts (1871, with Ormando Willis Gray), Pennsylvania (1872, again with Ormando Willis Gray) and New Hampshire (1877, with Charles Henry Hitchcock). The state atlases that Walling was involved in were more than just a collection of county maps. Many of them included some of the earliest and best thematic maps. The *State of Illinois Atlas* had maps of presidential elections, geology, climate and railroads. The *Atlas of the State of Michigan* had state maps that showed contours, railroads, geology, isotherms, congressional districts and state representative districts. The *Atlas of Massachusetts* included thematic maps and discussions of topography, history, railways, geology, climatology, the census and school districts. Walling's state atlases provide a very sophisticated carto-graphic representation of data.

The state atlases also acted as a kind of yellow pages. The last pages of the Michigan atlas are taken up with business cards by county and type. Thus in Detroit we find

Samuel T. Dietz
Counsellor at Law
68 Setz Block

Businesses are grouped by city and type. Some of the categories have stood the test of time, such as attorneys, but the category of wagon maker no longer seems appropriate. In the Michigan atlas, there is a prescient section on car manufacturers, which includes the Detroit Manufacturing Company and Pullman Palace Cars.

State atlases were connected to the economic promotion of the state. Their prefaces are rich in boosterist rhetoric. The *Atlas of the State of Illinois*, published by Warner and Higgins in Philadelphia in 1870, notes:

As an agricultural state Illinois stands without equal . . . The number and character of the splendid edifices which have been erected for court-houses, humane institutions, seminaries of learning and churches and the other public works which adorn the State bespeak at once the enterprise, intelligence and moral worth of the people.[7]

The state atlases also helped in the economic promotion of the state by providing a business geographical information system. The *Atlas of Michigan*, for example, had a gazetteer that listed for each place the post office, railroad station, telegraph station and nearest river landing, as well as population. In effect, it was a mapping of economic space and economic opportunities. It was noted in the preface that 'a country which has been explored and its attractive features intelligibly represented on a good map would far more rapidly become settled.'

The state atlases framed local places. The order of the maps contextualized the state into the wider nation and broader world. The *Atlas of the State of Illinois* begins with a double-hemispheric map of the world, then a map of the United States covering two pages, a series of US regional maps, and then a map of Illinois, thematic maps of the state and a series of county maps. On page 1 – between the phrases 'State of Illinois' and 'General Atlas' – is the phrase 'Combined Town County State National'. The *Official Topographical Atlas of Massachusetts* (1871) has a map of the United States, followed by a map of New England, then a map of the state, county maps and city maps. The framing of the state is explicitly recognized in the preface: 'Maps of New England and the United States are added to show the connection of Massachusetts with the surrounding States and with the Union.'

A National Atlas

Nations and states are represented in maps and atlases. The national atlas is a relatively recent phenomenon. There are early proto-examples, such as Christopher Saxton's 1579 atlas of England, but national atlases as we know them today are in effect a twentieth-century manifestation of the links between national identity, social sciences and geographic representation. The United States provides a rare example of a nineteenth-century national atlas.[8]

One of the earliest national atlases was produced in the United States – the 1874 *Statistical Atlas of the United States*. Based on the data from the 1870 census, this atlas combined two of the three elements identified by Benedict Anderson as important ingredients of national identity (map, census and museum).

The national community of the United States, as in other countries, was – and continues to be – represented and embodied in a national census. The first census was undertaken in 1790 to count the population, an important element in the establishment of congressional districts in each state. The census has been held every ten years since 1790 and now includes a range of information on the population. It is a sort of human inventory that lists and classifies people. The type of information collected and the way it is represented and used is indicative of broader social and political concerns. An analysis of the unfolding categories of the census reveals a history of social concerns and political obsessions.[9]

In the early censuses there were few maps. In fact, not a single map was used until the 1850 census, which had a crude map of drainage basins. The 1860 census only used six maps. In the first volume of the *Report of the 1870 Census*, however, twelve demographic maps were used. These maps and the 1874 *Statistical Atlas of the United States* were the brainchild of Francis Walker (1840–1897).

Walker was born after the age of the polymath but before the age of narrow intellectual specialization. Born into a patrician New England family, a Boston Brahmin, Walker held political and academic posts and wrote and lectured on a range of issues of contemporary concern. He was a public servant and intellectual and began his public career after serving in the Civil War. In January 1869, Walker was appointed chief of the Bureau of Statistics and made the superintendent of the 1870 census.

Walker was a social commentator – we would now call him a social scientist – with an interest in statistics and maps. The statistical analysis of social data was a recurring motif in Walker's work. He introduced a series of maps into the census of 1870. Because of political wrangling in an office dominated by political patronage he left the Bureau and the census. President Grant appointed him Commissioner of Indian Affairs and in 1873, he was appointed to a professorship at Yale. Together with other Yale faculty, he lobbied for a much more sophisticated illustration of census data. The secretary of the interior wrote to Congress of the importance of

graphically illustrating the three quarto volumes of the ninth census of the United States, by a series of maps exhibiting to the eye the varying intensity of settlement over the area of the country, the distribution of among the several states and sections of the foreign population, and of the principal elements thereof, of the location of great manufacturing and mining industries, the range of cultivation for each of the staple productions of agriculture, the prevalence of particular forms of disease, and other facts of material and social importance.[10]

Congress appropriated \$30,000 for the atlas in March 1873 and Walker took leave from Yale to complete it; it was published in 1874. Almost 5,000 copies of the *Atlas* were printed and sent to public libraries, colleges and learned societies to 'inform public opinion and advance political education'.

The *Statistical Atlas* is one of the earliest attempts to present census data in map form. It is full of maps but is especially strong in social data, including health, immigration, religion, ethnicity, economic trends, and population distribution and density (illus. 56). The *Statistical Atlas* contains 60 plates, sixteen of them are geometric illustrations. The maps and diagrams are discussed in some detail by Walker in his introduction, where he provides a section on how to read them, drawing attention to understanding the intensity of shading, the distinction between absolute and relative proportions, and the need to see the diagrams together to make connections.

There are three parts. Part 1 looks at physical features of the United States and includes sections on river systems, woodlands, temperature, coalfields and isobars. Part 2 covers population, social and industrial statistics, and these include maps of black population, foreign born, illiteracy and religious affiliation. Many maps in the *Atlas* depict the foreign-born population. Walker produced maps of

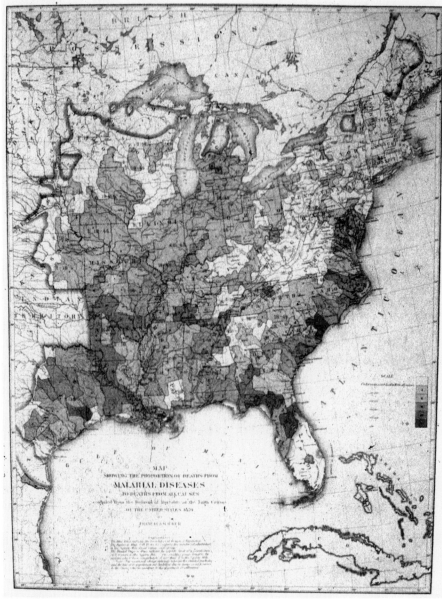

56 Map of the distribution of deaths from malaria, from Francis Walker's *Statistical Atlas of the United States* (New York, 1874).

both the absolute and the relative proportions of different national groups on a carefully graded scale. The resultant maps allow us to see the distribution of nationalities across the country east of the 100th meridian. The Irish are concentrated in the North and North-East while the German presence is particularly pronounced in the upper Midwest. Part 3 was concerned with vital statistics and comprises gender, age, sex, birth rate and a whole series on mortality and afflictions including blindness, deafness and insanity. There is a focus on social difference and a concern with abnormality and illness. Illustration 56 shows the distribution of deaths from malaria – just one of the many morbidity maps in the atlas. Walker was writing at a time when social science, social control and social surveillance were emerging together as important discourse of a nation experiencing rapid urbanization and large-scale immigration. The sense of searching for the locations and causes of social disorder (very broadly defined) lies at the very heart of Walker's statistical rendering of the nation.

Although called a national atlas, many of the social data maps show only the country east of the 99th meridian. This is the ultimate in East Coast bias. There is a section of Pacific maps that shows the western littoral but contains only ten maps, all on one page, which show population, including ethnic maps with Chinese population, illiteracy and wheat. Obviously, this is an insignificant area for Walker and he makes no mention of this bias in his introduction.

Even from a distance of over one hundred years, the atlas is an incredibly sophisticated display of social statistics. This census was the first to introduce the practice of identifying the centre of population. In a section entitled 'The Progress of the Nation 1790–1870', Walker notes that there has been speculation in the press about the centre of the national population. He defines it as 'the point at which equilibrium would be reached were the country taken as a plane surface and each individual exerting the same pressure'. Walker identified the centre and it has been depicted in subsequent censuses with its steady westward progression reflecting westward expansionism and settlement (illus. 57).

Walker, social difference and western expansion

The *Statistical Atlas* is an excellent example of the cartographic presentation of national social statistics. Throughout the nineteenth century, there had been a growing use of national thematic maps. Before the development of sophisticated statistical techniques, maps and graphical displays provided a useful and revealing way of

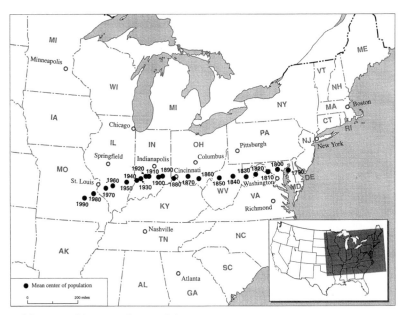

57 Movement of the centre of US population, 1790–1990.

presenting data and possible causal connections. Before the emergence of multivariate and regression analysis, the cartographic representation of data was an important method of displaying and analyzing information. From the 1820s onward there had been increasing sophistication in the display of population data. In France in 1830, Frère de Montizon displayed population data as a series of dots. The next year, A. D. Angeville showed population density as a series of tonal shades – a choropleth map. In 1837, Henry David Harness published maps of Ireland showing population density through tonal shading, cities were represented in their population size by graduated circles and traffic flows were represented in lines of varying thickness to show differing amounts of traffic. The cartographic innovations of the early nineteenth century, including dot maps, choropleth, isopleth and dasymetric maps, all bear witness to the growing use of maps to represent statistical information. The map became a statistical method and a device often employed in the analysis of crime and disease. One of the most famous maps and one that exemplifies the explanatory possibilities of careful mapping was Dr John Snow's 1855 map of deaths from cholera in London. The map showed the distribution around a water pump in Broad Street. Snow called for the pump to be removed and deaths ceased – the local source of a deadly disease had been identified.

Underlying these mapping exercises and cartographic innovations was a desire for greater knowledge of society, a knowledge tied to social power and observation. Mapping became not just an inventory but one way to search for connections and identify sources of disorder, especially crime and disease. The language of statistics is full of social connotations – control population, mean and deviation. Mapping became not only observation but also a surveillance of the sources of disorder in society.

Walker wrote on a variety of issues, including educational reform, monetary policies and economic issues. He argued that wage rates were based more on productivity than on a fixed pool of capital. He also held a range of posts, which included Professor at Yale (1873–81) and President of MIT (1881–97). He was actively involved in various professional associations: he was Vice-President of the National Academy of Science (1891–7), President of the American Economic Association (1885–92) and President of the American Statistical Association (1882–97).

Two themes dominate his census and atlas work: deviations from the norm and the westward sweep of population in the United States. Walker, like many other social commentators, was concerned with the growing disorder in society. The census allowed not only a crude population count but also an enumeration of the 'other'. As superintendent of the 1870 census, he added tables on school attendance, illiteracy, pauperism and crime; among the social categories he included were the blind, deaf, dumb, insane and idiotic. The 1874 *Atlas* also has a section entitled 'The Relations of Race and Nationality to Mortality', written by Walker, where he draws attention to 'the deficiency of foreign children'. Deaths from various causes are disaggregated by age and sex. He also has a map on the 'afflicted classes' – the blind, deaf mutes, insane idiots – all disaggregated by age, sex, race and nationality. By identifying the dependent, the delinquent and the disabled, Walker revealed sources of difference, sites of disorder. As a social observer of the nineteenth century, he had an enduring concern with social order/disorder, control and surveillance.

Walker also had an interest in the westward spread of population. In one of his books he wrote that 'the continuous progress for the westward extension of population . . . the geographical process of our natural growth is among the marvels of the human race'.[11]

Walker left the Bureau of Statistics in 1871 when President Grant appointed him Commissioner of Indian Affairs. He brought his usual clarity as well as his interest in social control and westward growth to the post. He wrote a number of articles for *The North American*

Review and *The International Review* which, along with excerpts from his annual reports, were later turned into a book, *The Indian Question*, published in 1874 by James R. Osgood of Boston. The Indian question according to Walker is 'What shall be done with the Indian as an obstacle to the national progress. What shall be done with him when, and so far as, he ceases to oppose or obstruct the extension of railways and settlements.'[12] Walker draws a distinction between the 'Eastern philanthropist unaffected by the presence of savage reprisals and western settlers unable to see the larger picture'. Because of white incursion, 'thousands of our citizens now living within reach of first murderous attacks of Indian war'. Walker's solution was to buy off hostile Native Americans; even if it cost $3 million, he argued, this is still less than a war would cost. Where Native Americans no longer posed a threat he proposed spending money in training them. Walker supported the reservation system and argued that it should be made the general and permanent policy of the government. However, the present system had too many reservations, land was too valuable and more should go for white settlement. Reservations should be consolidated into two large reservations, and this would enable the government to tighten up on white incursions. 'The eagerness of the average American citizen of the Territories for getting upon Indian land amounts to a passion.'[13] Keep the Native Americans on the reservations but spend money on education and training so they may become 'self-improving'. Walker's book is a pragmatic, clearly argued case for the consolidation of reservations.

Walker retired as Commissioner of Indian Affairs after only two years and became a professor at Yale. He was Professor of Political Economy and History, a post he held until becoming President of MIT in 1881. He did, however, become superintendent of the 1880 census. This time he could do a better job. The 1870 census, the source for the impressive 1874 *Statistical Atlas*, was paradoxically one of the most inaccurate. It was the last undertaken by US marshals who were political appointees, rather than skilled workers. The populations of Indianapolis and Philadelphia were counted twice in the final reckoning. Returns were particularly unreliable in the South. The 1870 census was the first census after the Civil War and there was a huge non-compliance in the South against the counting exercise of a 'Northern' federal power. It has been estimated that 1.2 million Southerners were missed in 1870. For the 1880 census, five times as many local enumerators were employed and the US Census Office had direct control over hiring. Walker argued the case for a professional census; however, only in 1902 was the Census Office made a permanent federal agency. The 1880 census produced 22 quarto volumes that provided the basis for another atlas, the 1883 *Scribner's Statistical Atlas of the United States*, produced by Fletcher W. Hewes and Henry Gannett (chief geographer of the USGS) and published by a private company. The success of the 1874 *Atlas* meant that a private company felt comfortable about such a publishing venture. The book is dedicated to Francis Walker and carries on the tradition of his *Statistical Atlas*. It is a very impressive volume full of facts, graphical displays and maps. There are 150 plates covering physical geography, political history, progress, rank of cities (a great diagram), ethnic immigration, mortality, education, religion, occupations, finance and commerce. One of the co-authors was Henry Gannett (1846–1914) who, after graduating from Harvard, went to work as a topographer on the Hayden Survey. In 1882, he became chief geographer of the USGS under Powell, a post he held until his death. He worked on the tenth, eleventh and twelfth censuses and introduced enumeration districts. As a member of the Cosmos Club, he aided in the formation of the National Geographic Society in 1888 and helped to found the professional organization of the Association of American Geographers. Gannett was also the author of the 1898 *Statistical Atlas of the United States* published by the Government Printing Office in Washington. The data came from the eleventh census of 1890. The atlas, obviously inspired by Walker, is another large book whose mission is as much statistical as cartographic. There are only 69 pages of text but 409 illustrations. There are two broad categories: social and economic. On pp. 3–272 are listed social statistics including population, ethnicity, interstate migration, gender, race, nativity, sex, age, conjugal condition, occupation, illiteracy, education, religion, mortality, and dependent and delinquent populations. Economic data are covered in pp. 274–409 and include information on agricultural yield and manufacturing production.

Walker's atlas of 1874 was the first national atlas which prompted the compilation of other atlases based on census data. Walker's legacy continued into the twentieth century when the census started to use maps and diagrams in their tables on a regular basis, and the centre of population became a standard measure. The social statistics collected by Walker would become an important part of the population count. While government-funded national atlases fell out of favour in the twentieth century – the National Atlas of 1970 was the only government-produced atlas of the twentieth century – private publishers would continue to use the cartographic innovations and statistical diagrams first used by Walker in his atlas of 1874.

There was also another legacy. As noted, a recurring concern of Walker was the westward spread of population. He introduced the centre of population and mapped its westward progression. Walker also educated the public on how to read this novel measure, a measure that has been used in all subsequent censuses. One of the maps in the 1874 *Atlas* is a map of population distribution and density. Walker was keen to show how the density of population varied across the surface of the nation. In the section 'Progress of the Nation 1790–1870', Walker uses the term 'frontier line' and has a table showing its extent, length and area from 1790 to 1870. Walker drew the frontier line when density fell below two inhabitants per square mile. The term frontier became part of the census language; it was also used in commercial atlases. *Scribner's Atlas* began to use the term. Westward expansion was given a solid statistical basis, an empirical line of demarcation. The frontier entered the national discourse. It was with this formal definition in mind that the superintendent of the 1890 census declared that although a frontier line could be shown – and indeed was shown in 1890 census reports – the spread of population and the increasing density of population meant that the frontier was officially closed. A young ambitious historian took this declaration as the basis for a thesis first presented at a history conference at the Chicago Art Institute in 1893. Frederick Jackson Turner, as one of the youngest and least distinguished historians, gave his paper last after four other presenters. The title of his paper was 'The Significance of the Frontier in American History'.

And the rest is history. To be more accurate, national history. In his concern with statistical techniques, Walker gave a measure to the frontier that allowed its closure to be officially noted, which provided Turner with a thesis that has dominated US historiography, political thought, public rhetoric and the national imagination for over a hundred years. A national atlas provided the basis for a national history.

12 Locating the National Economy

> … showing locations of towns, railroads, giving population by
> towns and counties, designating post money order and telegraph
> offices, with the number of banks in each place.[1]

For the first three-quarters of the nineteenth century, Philadelphia was
the principal site of map production. City plans, wall maps, county
atlases and state atlases were produced there. Small family firms and a
few large companies dominated a craft process. In the last quarter of
the century, however, Chicago became the major centre for map
production. This shift also marked a change in the form of production
and the type of maps produced. Chicago and mapmaking meant the
steady rise of Rand McNally to undisputed dominance of map production in the United States. A craft industry was replaced by a corporate
giant. Maps with the names of individual cartographers and engravers
were replaced by anonymous employees of 'company' maps. But there
was also a more subtle change. The depiction of relative space became
just as important as the presentation of absolute space. The new railway
age had collapsed space and time. A new economic space was being
created, a space in which accessibility and relative location were becoming more important than the absolute measures of latitude and longitude. If the maps of the first half of the nineteenth century were
concerned to show absolute location, the maps of the second half were
more concerned with the representation of relative space. The national
landscape of business–economic space, the space of a capitalist economy was represented in a variety of maps and atlases. The new business
and world atlases, especially those of Rand McNally, played an important role in the locating of a national economy, by which I mean the
depiction of economic opportunities, the rendering of the new relative
space of an extended railway network and the representation of an
increasingly global economy. The business atlas both recorded and
helped to define a national economic space, while the world atlas
located the US economy and society in a wider comparative framework.

Rand McNally

William Rand was born in Quincy, MA in 1828. He was apprenticed to his brother's printing business in Boston but, like many a young man of the time, the lure of easy money and adventure made him leave for the California gold rush in September 1849. He ended up in Los Angeles, where he co-founded the city's first paper, the *LA Star*, with John Lewis and Jon McElroy. In 1856 after a return East and a spell in Boston, we find him in Chicago. In June 1856, he opened a printer's office above a bookstore at 148 Lake Street.

Andrew McNally was born in Armagh in Northern Ireland. He was a printer who emigrated to New York City in 1857 and a year later moved to Chicago. He was hired by Rand at a salary of $9 a week. Eventually they joined forces in a partnership in 1868, in which each held 45 per cent of assets. Their first joint publication was the *Annual Report of the President and Directors of the Chicago, Rock Island and Pacific Railroad*.

Much of the business of Rand McNally was connected to the railways, the rise of Rand McNally being intimately tied to the rise of the railways. There were only 31,286 miles of rail in operation or under construction in 1861 but, by 1871, this had increased to 60,292 and by the end of the century the total mileage was a staggering 186,809 miles, giving the United States the largest railway system in the world. Chicago was the major hub of this huge and expanding rail network. Eleven railroads met in Chicago and even as early as 1870 a train was leaving the city every fifteen minutes. Rand McNally began by publishing a large number of rail reports and expanded into tickets, maps and guidebooks for the railway companies (illus. 58). Rand McNally's publishing fortune was tied to the railways both as a source of business and as a method of cheap distribution.

The company suffered an early though very temporary setback from the destruction of its office in the great fire of 1871. They salvaged two of the printing machines and moved to new premises in 108 Randolph Street and were back at work two days after the fire.

Rand McNally's first map appeared in the 1872 issue of *The Railway Guide*. The guide was an annotated railway timetable with a write-up of each town giving population and general information for the travelling public. The next year marked a major turning point in the firm's expansion. In 1873, it published its first railway map of the United States, produced its first machine-coloured maps and became incorporated with a capitalization of $200,000. The firm kept expanding and in 1874 moved to 14–16 Madison Street. The success of Rand McNally lay in

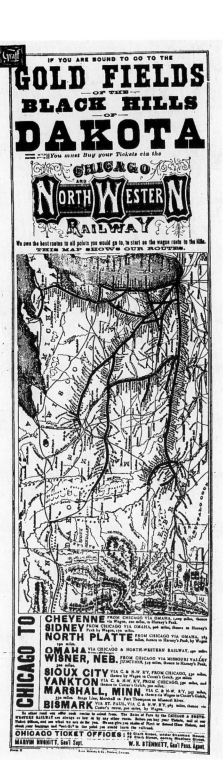

58 Map of the
'Gold Fields of the
Black Hills of
Dakota' published
by Rand McNally
for the Chicago &
North Western
Railway Company
(1876).

its cheap production methods – which reduced costs and enlarged the market – and its efficient distribution and marketing methods.

Maps and atlases were an important part of the company's business success. In 1875, it produced the first pocket maps, eventually putting out a series of 52 state pocket maps. In 1876, the wall map Rand McNally produced to celebrate the US centennial – taking ten compilers and engravers two years to produce and costing $20,000 – started the company's wall and sheet map production. Its large wall map, the *New Railroad and County Map of the USA*, graced many a company office wall.

Rand McNally was not alone in introducing cheaper map production methods. There were three major changes in map production in the nineteenth century. Pulp paper was substituted for the more expensive and harder-wearing rag paper, steam-powered presses replaced the weaker and slower hand presses and lithography replaced engraving. From the sixteenth to the nineteenth century, map production was done by copper engraving. Copper plates were inscribed with a sharp pointed tool. The image was inscribed in reverse and the plate was then inked and wiped clean, leaving the ink remaining on the inscribed lines. The plate was then pressed onto paper and the image emerged. Engraving had reached a fine art but it was slow and expensive. The relative softness of copper plates, which enabled the finely drawn images, reduced the number of times the plates could be used. At most only a few thousand impressions were possible and in some cases only a few hundred. With the invention of lithography in Europe in 1796, printing became possible on a larger, cheaper scale. The lithographic process was a chemical rather than a mechanical process that involved the ink drawing of an image (in reverse) onto a plate that was then pressed onto paper. Lithography was introduced into the United States in the 1820s and by the 1850s was used by most map publishers, although Colton and Mitchell still used the engraving method.

Rand McNally differed from its competitors by using a different method called 'cerography', wax engraving or relief line engraving. The process was invented by Sidney Morse, the son of Jedidiah. The process involved engraving lines and symbols onto a wax layer covering a metal plate. The plate was then electrotyped, transferring the lines and symbols from the wax onto the plate. Morse's first example of what he called cerography was a map of Connecticut for the *New York Observer* on 29 June 1839. He published his *Cerographic Atlas of the US* in 1842–5 with Samuel Breese (illus. 59). The process was most fully developed by Rand McNally and was a crucial element in its success. The process

59 Map of Iowa, from Sidney Morse and Samuel Breese's *Cerographic Atlas of the US* (New York, 1842—5).

allowed longer plate life and thus more maps for less money, the plates were easy to correct and update and both type and graphics could be produced on the same plate. Between 1870 and 1930, Rand McNally maps were produced by this cheap and efficient method. The result was a decrease in production costs, which led to a fall in retail prices. Tanner's *Map of the US* produced in 1829 cost $8, while Rand McNally's *General Map of the US* of 1900 cost only $1.50. The cost of atlases also plummeted. Carey's *General Atlas* of 1814 cost $15, while Rand McNally's 1891 *New Indexed Atlas of the World* cost $10. When we factor in the increase in wages, the fall in real terms is marked. Cynthia Peters has calculated map costs as an average of monthly non-farm wages. She shows that whereas Colton's 1853 $1.50 map of Illinois constituted 7 per cent of the average monthly wage, Rand McNally's 35 cent railroad map of Illinois of 1891 cost only 1 per cent.[2] In real and absolute terms the cost of maps and atlases plummeted.

Other map publishers were also making production changes to

reduce costs. There was intense competition from Alfred Andreas, George Cram, Warner and Beers. By the end of the century, however, Rand McNally was the largest mass producer of maps and atlases in the entire country. Part of its success lay in innovative marketing. The company advertised heavily in journals. Each publication was used to advertise other map products. Rand McNally sent complimentary atlases to local newspapers and cultivated direct sales from railway companies. The central location of Chicago helped their nationwide distribution. Rand McNally also sold atlases to newspapers, which would then sell them as incentive to subscribers. Atlases were used to boost newspaper subscriptions. A newspaper would send a Rand McNally atlas free of charge and postpaid on each renewal or for each new subscription. Sample copies were displayed at the local newspaper office. Rand McNally also farmed out atlas distribution to newspapers or subsidiaries, which then sold them either whole or in parts under the imprint of the newspaper.

Printing was big business. In Chicago, printing firms had the second largest payroll in the city, amounting to $9 million in 1899. There was conflict between capital and labour. The companies wanted to keep costs down, especially labour costs; the workers organized to improve conditions and obtain higher wages. The National Typographical Union and the Chicago Typographical Union no. 16 was formed in 1852. The union was a persistent adversary of Rand McNally over pay and working conditions, especially the length of the workday. The union wanted it reduced from ten hours to eight hours. Rand McNally represented the printing employers in the discussions held in the late 1880s. There was a series of strikes throughout the 1880s and 1890s and after a big strike in 1903, Rand McNally sought to relocate their operations away from union power and printing plants were located in rural (non-union) areas of the country. One was constructed in Ossining, NY in 1908.

Despite labour problems, the company continued to grow. It employed 240 people in 1880 and reinvested much of its profits in railway companies. By 1900, company sales had topped $1 million. At the turn of the century, the company had grown to six divisions: tickets, railroad printing, map publications, bank publications, trade books and educational books. Profits had continued to grow from the date of incorporation. From 1877 to 1913, the firm's sales increased from just under $0.5 million to $2 million. In 1899, Rand retired and transferred shares to the existing shareholders. The firm remained in the hands of the McNally family until a recent corporate take-over.[3] In 1952, the company moved its headquarters from Chicago to Skokie, IL.

The Rand McNally *Business Atlas*

The company produced a variety of atlases. One of its earliest and still-continuing series is its business atlases. These atlases have been published every year since 1876 and were a vital part in the construction of a national economy. Rand McNally's first *Business Atlas*, published under the title of *Business Atlas of the Mississippi Valley and Pacific Slopes* in 1876, contains state maps, presented alphabetically, showing counties, railroads and towns. The coverage is restricted to states in the Midwest and West. The state maps have a double longitude system with Greenwich at the top of the page and Washington at the bottom. The maps are simple black-and-white with colouring used for county and state borders. It is a slim volume, only 77 pages. The text consists of a list of railroads in each state. The largest section of the atlas is the index, which for each place (towns and villages, as well as counties, islands, rivers) gives location according to a grid of letters that run north–south and a grid of numbers that run east–west on the state maps. Chicago is located on D 16. The atlas situates places throughout the country with a standard locational fixing. This atlas is a great example of repackaging existing material.

By 1885, the atlas had grown enormously, becoming a hefty volume of 509 pages. In this atlas, the first map is a world map on a Mercator projection centred on the United States, with the double longitude system of Greenwich at the top and Washington at the bottom. At the beginning there is a general index of railroads with the name of express companies. State maps show counties, railroads, towns and rivers (illus. 60). For each entry the large index gives county seat, location on the map using the number and letter system, railway connections, population, money order post offices, telegraph station and mail address. This is a depiction of the national economic space, a space that has been collapsed by the railroad system, the telegraph and the ability to make financial transactions. Each place is being fixed and recorded in this changing relative space of finance, transport and communications accessibility. The 1890 *Business Atlas* notes that:

the Special features of this edition are locating the branch or particular division of railroad upon which each station is situated; the nearest mailing point of all local places designating money order post offices and telegraph stations, naming the express company doing business at the point where the several companies have offices.[4]

The 1900 version advertises itself as *Business Atlas and Shippers' Guide* and not only shows the entire railroad system but also provides a table

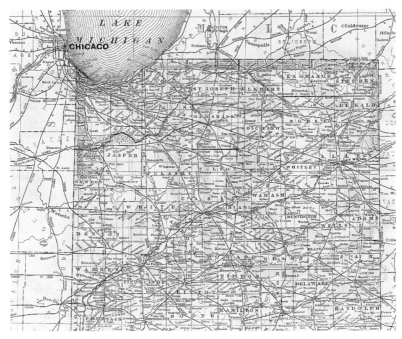

60 Detail from the map of Indiana in Rand, McNally & Co. *Business Atlas and Shippers' Guide* (Chicago, 1885).

of statistics on 165 US cities and includes population, value added, number of hands employed. This table reflects the increasing urbanization of the US population and economy. Cities are now emerging as major production points and important markets for a range of goods and services. This atlas also has maps of all countries. The US economy is now being presented in an international context; both national and international economic space is now being presented.

An examination of the business atlases over the short period from 1877 to 1900 highlights a number of themes. First, the business atlas developed a widening national and international coverage. This trend reflected the growth of the national market and the further development of a global economy. Second, the atlas presented absolute space through standard maps but also developed an increasingly sophisticated system of recording relative space through the index, which grew from a simple locational identifier of letter and number into a complicated set of symbols that recorded access to rail, road, postal and telegraph communications. The atlases are an early example of a geographical information system devised for business use. The business atlas mapped and recorded the changes in the relative space of a rapid space-time transformation brought about by the railroads and telegraphy.

Fast forward almost 100 years. The 1995 edition of the business atlas is now entitled the *Rand McNally Commercial Atlas and Marketing Guide* and advertised as 'the first place to look for up-to-date business planning data'. It is a large, heavy book with 572 large pages. The introduction claims that it brings together the most current economic and geographic information and rightly asserts that it is the oldest annually published reference atlas in existence. The atlas provides data for more than 128,000 places. There are maps of metropolitan areas and detailed maps of localities and neighbourhoods. The range of information covers economic data on retailing and manufacturing and transport data on airlines and highways as well as railways. Transportation has become more sophisticated and contemporary entries give access to airports but the basic system has remained the same. For each county, the index includes data on towns, companies, banks and post offices, and the information in the general index includes population growth, as well as airline and railroad connections. The *Business Atlas* has become more sophisticated over time. The range and depth of information has increased. The intent, however, has remained the same. The atlas locates a place in the national space economy. Places are compared, located, measured, connected with every other place. To the coordinates of latitude and longitude, the atlas provides the coordinates of relative economic space of market strength and space–time connectivity. The *Business Atlas* has mapped the space–time compression of an advanced capitalist economy.

Rand McNally World Atlases

Rand McNally was also a prolific publisher of world atlases. Between 1880 and 1917, the company produced almost 30 different atlases. Most were one-volume atlases produced in a convenient format at a cheap price (around $2 each). They were published under a variety of names, including *Standard Atlas, Family Atlas of the US, Indexed Atlas of the World, Library Atlas, Pocket Atlas, Universal Atlas, Dollar Atlas, Imperial Atlas of the World, New General Atlas of the World, International World Atlas, Pictorial Atlas of the World, Pocket World Atlas, Premier World Atlas, Rand McNally Unrivalled Atlas of the World,* and *Everybody's New Census Atlas of the World.*

The atlases were distributed by various means, either sold directly or marketed by other publishing firms and newspapers. Rand McNally would use its *Standard Atlas* as a template and then modify it according to the customer. Thus *The Republic Advocate's Universal*

Atlas of the World (1900), prepared and published especially for *The Republic Advocate* of Wellsborough, PA, had a distinct Pennsylvanian focus. The first illustration is of the Pennsylvania Capitol Building in Harrisburg followed by photographs of Philadelphia. The atlas also has a gazetteer of Pennsylvania. Sometimes the modifications were slight. *The Cosmopolitan Atlas of the World* had as an opening illustration the headquarters of the magazine in New York State. Often the modifications were restricted to the title page. *The Chicago Chronicle's Unrivalled Atlas of the World* (1899), *The Post Express Pictorial Atlas of the World*, published for *The Post Express* of Rochester, NY in 1900, and *The New Household Atlas of the World* (1885), produced exclusively for *The Chicago Weekly News*, were essentially Rand McNally's *Standard Atlas* unchanged except for the title. Through these different outlets, Rand McNally atlases percolated throughout the country. They were given away and when sold they were comparatively cheap. Rand McNally atlases were the most important source of cartographic information on the outside world to the US reading public. What view did they present?

The standard format was a map of the world, centred on the United States, a list of US possessions, maps of each US state (one to each page which necessitated a variable scale), then maps of other regions and countries of the world. Some of the atlases also had a written commentary, photographs and tables. Let us consider two examples. The 1890 *Rand McNally Standard Atlas of the World* has on its front page flags of the different nations. The international element evokes less a sense of connection and a more an interest in national differences. On an inside page, figures show the area and population of different countries. It is a view of the world seen through a prism of nationalism and like the Mercator projection world map appearing in all the atlases, centred on the United States. Pages are assigned to individual countries and individual US states. This atlas, like many late nineteenth-century atlases, is visually rich with a variety of illustrations, including maps, figures, engravings and even portraits of US presidents. Rand McNally also produced maps in its combined *Encyclopaedia and Atlas of the World*. The 1899 version had nearly 200 engravings and 80 full-page coloured maps.

Advertising was subtle in its location but strident in its message. The last three pages of the 1890 *Standard Atlas of the World* are taken up with adverts for office desks, railroads and real estate brokers. 'Have You Money? And Do You Want to Increase Your Wealth?' asks the headline and goes on to answer:

To capitalists we can offer you first-class investment in the city of Vancouver. Timberlands for the lumberman, Coal and iron properties for the miner, Fish for the Fisherman to say nothing of our Gold and Silver Mines which will probably be rich when developed.

The atlases reflected the racial assumptions of the time. The 1901 *Universal Atlas of the World*, for example, had a written section on the world's people; an insert showed the heads of the following types, in ascending order from Orang-utan, Malayan, Ethiopian, Native American, Mongolian and then a Caucasian. The atlases were produced at a time when assumptions of racial superiority/inferiority were standard beliefs.

Rand McNally was not alone in the imperial tinge to its atlases. World atlases were produced by a variety of companies. *Grant's Bankers' and Brokers' Railroad Atlas* was published in 1887 and its preface remarked that the atlas was 'carefully prepared to fill the wants of banks, bankers, brokers, railroad officials and such as may desire a work which shows, in the simplest manner, the true location of all railroads, giving all Towns, whether on the road or not'.[5] In this atlas the world is presented on pp. 264–5 on a Mercator projection centred on the western hemisphere. In the margins there are statistics showing for the major countries their wealth, national debt, money circulation, the size of armies and navies, and the length of railroads and telegraph lines. Economic and military strengths of the different countries are compared and contrasted. At the end of the atlas, pp. 293–324, there is a section on 'Valuable facts', which is a motley collection including a list of the chief battles of 1812, the mean annual temperature of state capitals, the population of cities around the world, the number of 'deaf and dumb' in various countries and national statistics on commerce, wealth, debt, expenditures and revenues.

The period from 1880 to 1914 is sometimes referred to as the age of imperialism. There was increasing competition for overseas markets and colonial holdings. It was a time of scrambling for Africa by European powers. The US appropriated territory in the Pacific and took effective control of a number of countries in Central America. The 'imperial' in the title of the Rand McNally atlas was not incidental and neither was the depiction of US territories and holdings. The atlas was produced at a time when the United States saw itself as a world power eager to compete with Britain, France and Germany in the international arena. Illustration 61 is taken from the 1898 *Rand McNally New Imperial Atlas*, a series that lasted from 1896 to 1918. The individual countries are compared with one another in graphics, sometimes called 'cartograms', which compare the national debts of many countries. Each country is represented by three circles that reflect the size of the debt, the population and the debt per head. Note how the United States is one of the larger countries in terms of population but has a relatively small per capita debt, only $1,423. These cartograms use a simple design to express complex data and demonstrate the growing elegance and sophistication in atlas design.

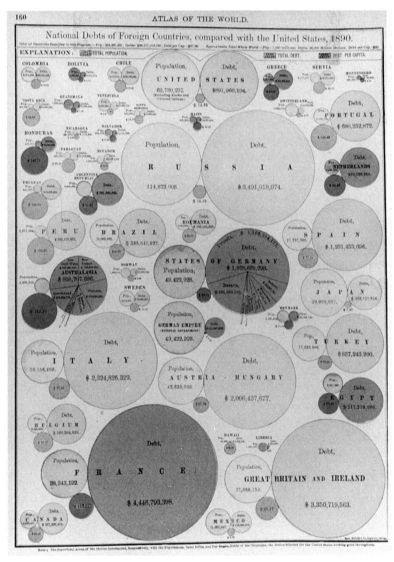

61 Populations and 'National Debts of Foreign Countries compared with the United States, 1890', from the *Rand McNally New Imperial Atlas* (Chicago, 1898).

The international comparisons were often explicit. *The New Pictorial Atlas of the World* (1898), a series that started in 1896, notes in the introduction,

the Atlas includes not only the very latest changes and corrections, together with their minutest details, occurring in the United States, but also the most recent political developments, as well as geographical discoveries and explorations, which have taken place in every quarter of the globe . . . most interesting review of the World's Peoples, their origin, historical and ethnological development, as well as the political status and relative importance of the countries they inhabit . . . these charts exhibit in an attractive form the area, population, agricultural and mineral products, together with the commercial and financial status of nations, as the maps show the geographical and topographical details of countries, affording an unequaled means of intelligent comparison between the United States and foreign nations.

This atlas has a lot of comparative statistics on imports and exports of countries in the world, railway mileage of countries, national debt and population. The atlas thus gives a sense of a nation within an international context. The comparative statistics, the ethnological writings and the sense of national rivalry and competition all give shape and substance to a US national identity in an age of increasing international rivalry. The atlases of Rand McNally gave Americans a sense of their nation and a sense of the world – a world of increasing competition and rivalry.

The atlases of Rand McNally depicted a new world to an increasing number of people in the United States. In the last quarter of the nineteenth century, there was a growing amount of attention to the depiction of economic space and the global economy. In the business atlases of Rand McNally and others, the maps of individual states of the Union represented both absolute and relative location, with particular emphasis on accessibility to railroads, telegraphs and money flows. These atlases depicted and helped embody the creation of a national economy. The world atlases were produced in the age of imperialism when the relative space of international comparisons and contrasts was very important. Maps and diagrams of national population and area, railroad mileage and manufactures, military power, and expenditures and revenue became an accepted cartographic device. The world atlases located the United States in a world polity and a global economy.

13 A Postcolonial Postscript

> The geographical positions are therefore rarely determined absolutely, or even relatively, with certainty, and new surveys are constantly making slight changes necessary.[1]

This book has studied examples of geographic representation and connected them to imperial claims, state formation and national identity. In the United States, Native Americans have featured significantly on early maps and, even into the late nineteenth century, the cartographic depiction and demarcation of the Native-American presence was an important element in maps.

One important theme stressed in this book is the notion that mapping was a collaborative activity. It is important to emphasize this point since a common myth is of the Europeans coming to North America and mapping the wilderness, with little input from the indigenous people. I have sought to show that Native Americans were an important element in geographic understanding and cartographic representation. The Block Map was based on local knowledge and subsequent maps drew upon a rich vein of indigenous knowledge. Illustration 62, a detail from John Mitchell's 1755 map, shows that information was based on 'Accounts of the Indians and our People'. While exploring in the Colorado River. John Wesley Powell noted:

It is curious to observe the knowledge of our Indians. There is not a trail but what they know: every gulch and every rock seems familiar. I have prided myself on being able to grasp and retain in my mind the topography of a country: but these Indians put me to shame. My knowledge is only general, embracing the more important features of a region that remains as a map on my mind; but theirs is particular. They know every rock and every ledge, every gulch and canyon, and just where to wind among them to find a pass; and their knowledge is unerring.[2]

I have concentrated on cartographic presences; more work needs to be done on exclusions. Illustration 63 is another detail from John Mitchell's 1755 map of North America. The Nauchees, it is noted, on

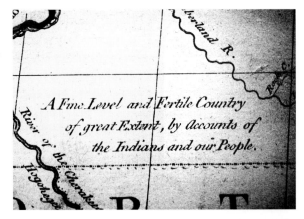

62 Detail of the continental interior, from John Mitchell's *Map of North America* (London, 1755) (illus. 10).

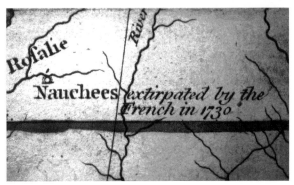

63 Detail, from Mitchell's *Map of North America* (illus. 10).

the map 'were extirpated by the French'. Such frankness is unusual, no doubt a function of the recency of the events and the context, as an English mapmaker was keen to highlight the activities of the pernicious French. Maps tell us about silences as much as utterances, but their identification is much more difficult. In only a few cases are the erasures so vividly described as in the Mitchell map. And yet maps are full of silences and erasures. Events, stories and peoples are ignored and forgotten as much as depicted and remembered.

I began this book by looking at a European map of part of North America: the Block Map (see illus. 1–3), a result of Dutch/Native-American collaboration, was an act of territorial appropriation. Let me end, in a circle of narrative symmetry with a postcolonial twist, with a 'Native-American' map, a result of native/non-native collaboration that is an act of territorial reappropriation. I began the book with a story of maps and the loss of Native-American land. I will end this book with a tale of maps and the reclaiming of this land.

Illustration 64 is a map of contemporary Oneida land claims in central New York. The map is a property claim, an historical claim to

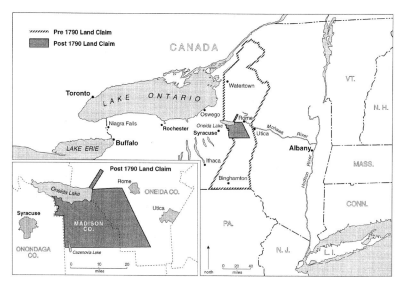

64 A contemporary map of pre- and post-1790 Oneida land claims in central New York State.

right a wrong. The Oneidas are one of the members of the Iroquois, also known as the League of the Iroquois, the Six Nations and the Haudenosaunee (People of the Longhouse). The others are the Mohawk, Senecas, Cayugas, Tuscaroras and Onondagans. By about 1500, these tribes joined together in a League that united them in a powerful alliance. The Tuscarora joined the alliance only in 1712 after being pushed out of their land in North Carolina by the European settlers. The Iroquois were an important factor in the geopolitics of the region, often playing off the French and English to maintain their position and identity. On the eve of the American Revolution, the Iroquois still had most of their land in the central New York area; the Oneidas had almost 6 million acres. In the War, the Oneidas openly supported the revolutionaries and at the Treaty of Fort Stanwix (1784) the Oneidas were given security over their land. This security was reconfirmed by the Canandaigua Treaty of 1794.

Over the next century, however, the land base was destroyed. Treaties with the state of New York took away Oneida land, a process fuelled by bribery and corruption, as well as corrosive factionalism within the Oneida community. The land base of the Oneidas shrunk to 32 acres and part of the Oneida tribe relocated to Ontario and Wisconsin. There are now approximately 16,000 Oneidas; 11,000 in Wisconsin, almost 3,800 in Thames, Ontario and only about 1,100 in New York.

The Iroquois, including the Oneidas, have been disputing the loss of land for 200 years. In recent years, however, the claims have made some headway in the courts. The Oneida claim is founded on the fact that New York State actually broke federal law; to be precise they broke the Indian Trade and Intercourse Acts of 1790 and 1793. The 1790 Act prohibited the purchase of land not authorized by the federal government and the 1793 Act required federal approval, in the form of a commissioner. New York State violated these laws in their land grab. No federal commissioner was present at the 1795 Oneida–New York State treaty or at 24 of the subsequent 26 treaties made after 1798.

In 1970, the Oneidas filed a claim in federal court against two New York counties, challenging the legality of the 100,000 acre transfer from the Oneidas to New York State in 1795. The US District Court dismissed the case but the Supreme Court agreed to hear the case in 1973. In January 1974, the Court upheld the right of the Oneidas to pursue their claim through the federal courts and remanded it back to the lower federal courts. In 1977, a court ruled the 1795 transaction was illegal and void and ordered the two counties to pay damages. A later decision in 1985 (again by the Supreme Court), in a five to four decision, allowed the Oneidas to claim damages from Oneida and Madison County for unlawful seizure of Native-American ancestral land. This decision gave strength to the Oneidas who then filed suit for almost six million acres. Illus. 64 shows the smaller post-1790 land claim which has been endorsed by the federal courts and the much larger pre-1790 claim which was submitted to New York State in 1991. Disputes within the Oneida community and especially between the leadership of the three separate communities has meant a divided house. The lack of consensus has hampered negotiations with the State of New York.

The post-1790 claim amounts to almost 275,000 acres. Because of gambling revenues, the Oneida Nation now owns a highly profitable casino as well as a hotel complex, golf course and gas stations; the Oneidas have started to buy up land in this claim in the open market. At the end of 1997, almost 5,000 acres had already been acquired.

The larger pre-1790 claim is interesting. It is, in effect, an attempt to reclaim all the land lost since the American Revolution. There are no formal documents which allow the Oneidas to lay claim to this territory. The justification for the exact demarcation of this claim is taken from a map made by the American anthropologist Lewis Henry Morgan (1818–1891).[3] He was born near Aurora, NY and as a young man had a fascination with the Iroquois and their social organization. He even fashioned a club organized along what he imagined were traditional Iroquois lines. He had some success as a lawyer and politician in the New York legislature but maintained his interest in the Iroquois, meeting chiefs and making friends with Eli Parker, a Seneca chief who became a general in the Civil War. Morgan's great work – *The League of the Ho-de-no-sau-nee* – was published in 1851. In the book, Parker published a map which outlined tribal boundaries but Morgan never went into details about how the boundaries on this map were determined. The map is the basis for the Oneida claim of almost 6 million acres. In other words, a map drawn by an anthropologist – derived from what may be fieldwork, linguistic analysis and conversations with Iroquois chiefs – forms the basis for the Oneida land claim.

Illustration 64 is an act of territorial reappropriation and historical remembrance.

Maps can also be used to reclaim and remember.

References

Introduction

1 Mark Monmonier, *How to Lie with Maps* (Chicago, 1991), p. 1.
2 J. R. Short, *Imagined Country* (London, 1991).
3 J. B. Harley, *Maps and The Columbian Encounter* (Milwaukee, 1990), p. 1.
4 Recent books that look at maps as systems of communication include J. S. Keates, *Understanding Maps*, 2nd edn (London, 1996), and A. M. MacEachren, *How Maps Work* (New York and London, 1995).
5 L. Bagrow, *History of Cartography* (London, 1964); G. Crone, *Maps and Their Makers* [1953] (London, 1963); L. Brown, *The Story of Maps* (Boston, 1949).
6 Crone, *Maps and Their Makers*, p. xi.
7 J. N. Wilford, *The Mapmakers: The Story of the Great Pioneers in Cartography from Antiquity to the Space Age* (New York, 1981), p. x.
8 There is now significant research that highlights the connection between maps and embedded interests, cartography and the politics of knowledge. A standard reference is the projected six-volume *History of Cartography*, edited by J. B. Harley and David Woodward (Chicago, 1987–).
9 One example of his later work is J. B. Harley, 'The Power of Places', *Cartographica*, 26 (1989), pp. 1–20 (reprinted with modifications as 'Deconstructing the Map', in T. J. Barnes and J. S. Duncan, eds, *Writing Worlds: Discourse, Text and Metaphor in the Representation of Landscape* (London, 1992), pp. 231–47. For critiques, see Barbara Belyea, 'Images of Power: Derrida, Foucault, Harley', *Cartographica*, 29 (1992), pp. 1–9, and Denis Wood, 'The Fine Line between Mapping and Mapmaking', *Cartographica*, 30 (1993), pp. 50–60.
10 Some of the interesting new work includes Tom Conley, *The Self-Made Map: Cartographic Writing in Early Modern France* (Minneapolis, 1996); Walter Mignolo, *The Dark Side of the Renaissance* (Ann Arbor, 1995); Barbara Mundy, *Mapping New Spain* (Chicago, 1996); and Winichakul Thongchai, *Siam Mapped: A History of the Geo-Body of a Nation* (Honolulu, 1994). See also the three essays by Edney, Jacob and Smith in *Imago Mundi*, 48 (1996), pp. 185–203.
11 There are a number of books that deal with the general picture, including David Buisseret, ed., *From Sea Charts to Satellite Images: Interpreting North America through Maps* (Chicago, 1990), and Seymour Schwartz and Ralph Ehrenberg, *The Mapping of America* (New York, 1980).
12 See the useful study on Webster by H. G. Unger, *Noah Webster: The Life and Times of an American Patriot* (New York, 1999).
13 Benedict Anderson, *Imagined Communities* (London, 1983).
14 Benedict Anderson, *Imagined Communities*, rev. edn (London, 1991).
15 Among the vast and growing literature, see G. Balakrishna, ed., *Mapping the Nation* (London, 1996); H. Bhabha, ed., *Nation and Narration* (London, 1990); G. Eley and R. Suny, eds, *Becoming National* (Oxford, 1996).
16 D. Cosgrove and S. Daniels, eds, The *Iconography of Landscape* (Cambridge, 1988); J. R. Short, *Imagined Country* (London, 1991).
17 Lyn Spillman, *Nation and Commemoration* (Cambridge, 1997), p. 14.
18 Fast forward a hundred years, and ritual and symbol had been mobilized once again. Now,

regional differences and state rivalries were less of an issue. Both events praised political liberties and economic prosperity. The fundamental belief in the march of progress had weakened over of the century; cultural diversity was celebrated rather than ignored. Indigenous peoples were given a more central role; in Australia, this occurred mainly as a result of Aboriginal protest at the concept and practice of the celebrations. The countries differed. The importance of the founding moment was still important in the United States, but the sense of international recognition that marked both nineteenth-century celebrations was less apparent there. Now a superpower, it had less need for international recognition. This remained a critical aim of the Australian bicentennial, even more critical as the country sought to forge a post-British, post-Commonwealth, post–Anglo-Celtic premise (see Spillman, *Nation and Commemoration*).

19 The connection between national identities and the discourse of geography is considered by a number of authors; see, for example, D. Hooson, ed., *Geography and National Identity* (Oxford, 1994); A. Paasi, *Territories, Boundaries and Consciousness* (Chichester, 1996).

1 *'The Seeking Out and Discovery of Courses, Havens, Countries, and Places'*

1 Quoted in E. B. O'Callaghan, *History of New Netherland*, vol. 1 (New York, 1868), p. 70.

2 Drenthe was only a territory and did not send a delegation to the States General.

3 P. Kennedy, *The Rise and Fall of the Great Powers: Economic Change and Military Conflict from 1500 to 2000* (New York, 1987).

4 Kennedy, *Rise and Fall of the Great Powers*, p. 48. Kennedy goes on to note that 'At the center of the Spanish decline, therefore, was the failure to recognize the importance of preserving the economic underpinnings of a powerful military machine' (p. 50).

5 This idea is developed at length in Simon Schama, *The Embarrassment of Riches* (London, 1987).

6 *A Plan of the English Commerce* (1728), p. 192.

7 Hudson was soon back at work. He returned to sea the next month. In April 1610, he set sail for a newly formed English company searching for a passage to the East Indies. He arrived at the bay that now bears his name in August and spent the next three months surveying its eastern shore. The ship was stuck frozen by early November, and food was rationed. The crew mutinied over the rations, and on 22 June 1611 the mutineers put Hudson, his young son and seven infirm crew members in a small boat and cast them adrift. They were never seen again. His name lives on in the Hudson Strait, Hudson River and Hudson Bay.

8 Quoted in O'Callaghan, *History of New Netherland*, p. 70.

9 Quoted in J. Sullivan, ed., *History of New York State 1523–1927*, vol. 1 (New York, 1927), p. 116.

10 Sullivan, *History of New York State*, p. 116.

11 The map was found in a case in the Royal Archives in The Hague by J. R. Brodhead, who signed himself 'Agent of the State of New York'. Brodhead had been charged with obtaining copies of documents in foreign archives relating to the history of the state of New York. There was no mark on it to ascertain its exact date, but it was found along with a document dated 1616, which has led to the map often being dated in some libraries, such at the State Library of New York, as 1616. The map found in the case is probably a copy of Block's original map.

12 When Charles V of France asked the King of Aragon for a copy of the latest world map, he was given the atlas produced by Abraham Cresques, who was the cartographer to the King. His son Jafuda carried on the family trade after Abraham died in 1387. But religious intolerance was sweeping through Spain, and Jafuda had to renounce his Jewishness and become a Christian in 1391 with a new name, Jaime Ribes. He still did not feel safe and took up an invitation from Henry of Portugal to instruct the Portuguese in the making of charts. By such movements the knowledge of mapmaking was diffused, and dominant mapmaking centres waxed and waned.

13 See the interesting article by David Woodward, 'Reality, Symbolism, Time and Space in Medieval World Maps', *Annals of Association of American Geographers*, 75 (1985), pp. 510–21.

14 Orienting maps in different directions can be revealing. In Blaeu's *Grand Atlas* of 1662, the

map of the New England shore, based on Block's map, is shown with west at the top and gives a good feeling of the view of the coast encountered by sailors from Europe. Centuries later, Donald Meinig produced a map of north-eastern America also with west at the top to illustrate his narrative on the implantations by north-west Europeans; see D. W. Meinig, *The Shaping of America*, vol. 1 (New Haven, 1986), fig. 5, p. 34.

15 Compass roses were practical devices, but as the seventeenth century progressed they were often added to maps simply as artistic flourishes. By the latter half of the century, they had become a standard if anachronistic element in many maps.

16 The problem was solved by Mercator. In his world map of 1569, entitled *New and Improved Description of the Lands of the World, amended and intended for use of Navigators*, he used a map projection that now bears his name in which the ratio between latitude and longitude remains constant. This involved increasing the value of latitude toward the poles. The map thus exaggerates the size of the polar regions but has the tremendous practical value of representing the world such that a navigator could use a straight line to plot a course.

17 We know this from the names used to describe features. In the case of May's maps, the names were used as they were in the original. The names used by Champlain were translated into Dutch. See I.N.P. Stokes, *The Iconography of Manhattan Island, 1498–1909* (New York, 1915–28), esp. vol. 2, chap. 3.

18 R. Putnam, *Early Sea Charts* (New York, 1983).

19 J. B. Harley, 'New England Cartography and the Native Americans', in E. W. Baker, E. A. Churchill and R. D'Abate, eds, *American Beginnings: Exploration, Culture and Cartography in the Land of Norumbega* (Lincoln and London, 1994); L. De Vorsey, 'Amerindian Contributions to the Mapping of North America: A Preliminary View', *Imago Mundi*, 30 (1978), pp. 71–8; G. Malcom Lewis, ed., *Cartographic Encounters: Perspectives on Native American Mapmaking and Map Use* (Chicago, 1998).

20 Quoted in J. F. Jameson, ed., *Narratives of New Netherland, 1609–1664* [1909] (New York, 1990), pp. 23–4.

2 *Representing the New Netherlands*

1 Svetlana Alpers has drawn attention to the connection between knowledge and decoration in the Dutch Republic, showing that mapping and picturing were based on common notions of knowledge and the shared goal of creating assemblages of the world. Painting in northern Europe, unlike the more rhetorical use of persuasion in southern Europe, was more concerned with graphical description; art involved mapping, and the map was an art form. In a later essay, she looks at the work of Vermeer, especially his picture *Art of Painting*, to develop her theme: S. Alpers, *The Art of Describing: Dutch Art in the Seventeenth Century* (Chicago, 1983); 'The Mapping Impulse in Dutch Art', in D. Woodward, ed., *Art and Cartography* (Chicago, 1987), pp. 51–96.

2 I am grateful to Stephanie Abbot Roper, who, in 1996, sent me her unpublished paper on how seventeenth-century Dutch maps reinforced European hegemony. I have drawn on some of her ideas.

3 There are a few copies of Blaeu's great atlas. More accessible is the reprint: John Goss, *Blaeu's The Grand Atlas of the 17th-Century World* (New York, 1991).

4 This map appeared in de Laet's book, *New World*; it was first published in 1625. A 1630 Dutch edition contained a map that was used by the Blaeus to construct their map of the area. De Laet described the inhabitants of the New World thus:
They are like most barbarians suspicious and fearful, although greedy of revenge; they are fickle, but if humanly treated, hospitable and ready to perform a service; they ask only a small remuneration for what they do, and will make very long journeys in a short time with greater fidelity than could be justly expected from such a barbarous people. Nor it is to be doubted that by associating with Christians they could be imbued with civilized manners and with religion, especially if there should be planted among them colonies of well ordered people, who would employ their services without violence or abuse, and in return accustom them to the true God and habits of civilized life.
Quoted in J. F. Jameson, ed., *Narratives of New Netherland* (New York, 1909), p. 58.

5 According to Stokes, this map was probably reduced from a large map by Blaeu that was

probably lost on *Princess*, a Dutch ship lost at sea in September 1647 that had 'very exact Maps' on board. See I.N.P. Stokes, *The Iconography of Manhattan Island*, vol. 1 (New York, 1916).

6 T. Campbell, 'New Light on the Jansson-Visscher Maps of New England', *Map Collectors' Circle*, 24 (1965), pp. 3–44.

7 Details of land sales are available in Appendix A of S. W. Dunn, *The Mohicans and Their Land* 1609–1730 (Fleischmanns, NY, 1994).

8 I have drawn heavily on the enlightening and entertaining introduction by Thomas O'Donnell, in Adriaen van der Donck, *A Description of The New Netherlands* (Syracuse, 1968).

9 O'Donnell, 'Introduction', in van der Donck, *A Description*, p. xxi.

10 *Ibid.*, pp. 71–2.

11 *Ibid.*, pp. 97–8.

12 It is paradoxical that van der Donck's triumphalist document would be ignored so quickly. His book written in Dutch soon disappeared from the canon of increasingly and then entirely English-language works. His book was only translated into English in 1841 and still remains a little known and rarely read classic of 'American' literature.

3 Imperial Claims

1 J. B. Harley, *Maps and The Columbian Encounter* (Milwaukee, 1990), p. 2.

2 In his journal, de Champlain provides detailed descriptions. At one point in 1609, he describes a battle with the Iroquois:
I rested my musket against my cheek, and aimed directly at one of the three chiefs. With the same shot, two fell to the ground; and one of their men was so wounded that he died some time after ... The Iroquois were greatly astonished that two men had so quickly killed, although they were equipped with armour woven from cotton thread and with wood which was proof against their arrows. This causes great alarm among them. As I was loading again, one of my companions fired a shot from the woods, which astonished them anew to such a degree that, seeing their chiefs dead, they lost courage and took to flight, abandoning their camp and fort, and fleeing into the woods, whither I pursued them, killing still more of them. Our savages also killed several of them, and took ten to twelve prisoners. The remainder escaped with the wounded. Fifteen or sixteen were wounded on our side with arrow shots; but they were soon healed. After gaining the victory, our men amused themselves by taking a great quantity of Indian corn and some meal from their enemies, also their armour, which they had left behind that they might run better. After feasting sumptuously, dancing and singing, we returned three hours after with the prisoners. The spot where this attack took place is Lake Champlain
(S. de Champlain, *Voyages of Samuel de Champlain*, 1604–1618 [New York, 1907], p. 23).

3 Delisle's advancement is apparent in his maps. His self-descriptions over the years are illuminating. In 1700, he is simply *Géographe*, by 1702 his title is *Géographe de L'Academie des Sciences* and by 1718, he is *Premier Géographe du Roi*.

4 See David Buisseret, ed., *Monarchs, Ministers and Maps: The Emergence of Cartography as a Tool of Government in Early Modern Europe* (Chicago, 1992).

5 I am very grateful to Professor Martha Houle, a specialist in French literature at the College of William and Mary, Williamsburg, VA for helpful commentary on the terms.

6 The name eventually changed to the Board of Trade. Although the Privy Council was nominally in charge, the Lords Commissioners were the main supervisory body of the North American colonies; their main function was to make them profitable for the mother country. One of their more illustrious members was the philosopher John Locke.

7 A facsimile copy and interesting commentary are available in W. P. Cumming and H. Wallis, *A Map of the British Empire in America by Henry Popple* (Lympne Castle, Kent, 1972).

8 *Memorial of the English and French Commissioners concerning the limits of Nova Scotia or Acadia* (1755), vol. 1, p. 277.

9 John Mitchell, *The Contest in America between Great Britain and France* [London, 1757] (reprint 1965), p. vi. The original text uses 'f' for 's' in most instances. I have changed this in the quotes from 'f' to 's' to aid understanding.

10 If the French then in North America are joined by the Indians, instead of being opposed by them, as they have hitherto been, it will make a very great difference in there situation of our affairs there. Add to this; the French have now joined their two colonies of Canada and Louisiana together, and can at any time muster up all their own force, as well as that of their allies, at any one place they think proper, which they never could before. It is this that has made them become so powerful in North America all of a sudden, before any one seems to have suspected it, or would believe it. This makes it high time and highly necessary for us, to look out for some safe and secure Barrier for our colonies, against the inroads and invasions of both the French and the Indians (Mitchell, *Contest in America*, p. 213).

11 There was intense contemporary debate regarding whether Britain should accept the division. Many argued that France, by giving up Canada for the rich islands of Martinique and Guadeloupe, was getting the better deal. The role that this Canada-vs-Guadeloupe debate played in the American Revolution is considered by Theodore Draper, in *A Struggle for Power* (New York, 1996), esp. pp. 1–71.

12 In 1764, Holland proposed to his employers, the Lords Commissioners for Trade and Plantations, a general survey of North America east of the Mississippi. It was to be a major scientific undertaking involving the construction of a geodesic and geographic co-ordinate system. Although it never came to pass as envisaged by Holland, he was involved in estimates of longitude as well as descriptions of the territory's economic geography. His project was part of the scientific movement in mapping and geography. He also wrote papers for the Royal Society.

13 We are fortunate in having access to Montresor's methods through his journals. See G. D. Scull, ed., *The Montresor Journals*, Collections of the New York Historical Society for the Year 1881 (New York, 1882).

14 These atlases, including Thomas Jefferys's 1776 *American Atlas* and William Faden's 1777 *North American Atlas*, are discussed at some length in terms of internal and external power in J. B. Harley, 'Power and Legitimation in the English Geographical Atlases of the Eighteenth Century', in John A. Wolter and Ronald E. Grim, eds, *Images of the World: The Atlas through History* (Washington, DC, 1997), pp. 161–204.

15 One authority refers to it as the 'culminating achievement of maps of New York'; see W. P. Cumming, *British Maps of Colonial America* (Chicago, 1974), p. 23.

16 A copy of the memorial is available in E. B. O'Callaghan, *Documentary History of New York* (Albany, 1851), vol. 4, pp. 661–75.

4 Representing the New State

1 D. Ellis *et al.*, *A History of the State of New York* (Ithaca, NY, 1967), p. 79.

2 The victors get to write history and designate good and bad acts. The action at Cherry Valley was designated a massacre and led to a fearful reputation for Brant and the Iroquois, especially the Senecas and Mohawks. Their reputation persists. In Philadelphia, just a block away from Independence Hall, sits the Greek Revival Second Bank, which is now a portrait gallery. It contains portraits of members of the Continental Congress, signers of the Declaration of Independence and various Revolutionary worthies. There is a 1797 portrait in oils of Joseph Brant by Charles Wilson Peale. Underneath is a notice that tells the viewer 'Brant's Mohawk warriors had terrorized the New York-Pennsylvania frontier during the Revolution ...' Brant is viewed from the side of the victors, and his actions are described as acts of terror.

3 Quoted in William W. Campbell, *The Border Warfare of New York During the Revolution or, The Annals of Tyron County* (New York, 1849), pp. 154–62.

4 Quoted in F. W. Halsey, *The Old New York Frontier* (New York, 1901), p. 282.

5 J. C. Fitzpatrick, ed., *Writings of George Washington*, vol. 7 (Washington, 1970), p. 65.

6 See J. P. Snyder, 'The Erskine-DeWitt Maps', *Surveying and Mapping*, 39 (1979), pp. 33–48.

7 He was tempted in May 1796 by an offer from Washington to become Surveyor General of the United States; he thought about it a great deal but wrote back in June that after comparing the prospects he was not justified in making a change.

8 The names are deceptive. The new military tract was designated before the old one.

9 The process of land speculation, politics and literary representation in Cooperstown is

given marvellous treatment in Alan Taylor, *William Cooper's Town* (New York, 1995).

10 *New York: A Collection From Harper's Magazine* (New York, 1991), pp. 216–18.

5 *A New Mode of Thinking*

1 J. Morse, *Geography Made Easy* (1784) (Utica, NY, 1819), p. iii.
2 R. M. Rollins, *The Long Journey of Noah Webster* (Philadelphia, 1980), p. 37.
3 P. G. Adams, 'Benjamin Franklin and the Travel-Writing Tradition', in J. Lemay, ed., *The Oldest Revolutionary: Essays on Benjamin Franklin* (Philadelphia, 1976).
4 W. Guthrie, *A New System of Geography*, 11th edn (London, 1788), p. 7.
5 *Ibid.*, p. 6.
6 I have drawn extensively on the small but detailed pamphlet by James Green, 'Mathew Carey: Publisher and Patriot' (Philadelphia, 1985).
7 See J. Tebbel, *A History of Book Publishing in the United States*, vol. 1, *The Creation of An Industry* 1639–1865 (New York and London, 1972).
8 Weems went on to sell more books, but he is perhaps best known for his biography of George Washington, which came out in 1800 as *The Life and Memorable Actions of George Washington*. The book eulogizes Washington as a model of patriotism and virtue. The cherry-tree story was first told by Weems. The book was enormously successful; it sold 50,000 copies and went through 25 editions. It fixed, early on, the mythic character of the Father of the Nation, a rendition that has persisted down the years in the popular imagination. Washington represented, for many, the virtues of honesty, courage, honor and love of country. Weems knew his market and wrote what the people wanted to read and feel. At a crucial time in the history of the Republic, he presented the new nation's first 'authentic' hero.
9 W. Clarkin, *Mathew Carey: A Bibliography of His Publications* (New York, 1984).
10 E. Rink, *Technical America. A Checklist of Technical Publications Printed before* 1831 (Millwood, NY, 1981).
11 The standard work is R. D. Arner, *Dobson's Encyclopaedia: The Publisher, Text and Publication of America's First Britannica, 1789–1803* (Philadelphia, 1991).

6 *The Father of American Geography*

1 J. Morse, *The present situation of other nations of the world, contrasted with our own* (Boston, 1795), p. 11.
2 For material on Morse, see these two biographies: R. J. Moss, *The Life of Jedidiah Morse: A Station of Peculiar Exposure* (Knoxville, 1995); J. W. Phillips, *Jedidiah Morse and New England Congregationalism* (New Brunswick, NJ, 1983).
3 My reading of the book is based on the twentieth edition published in 1819 by William Williams of Utica, NY.
4 J. Morse, *Geography Made Easy* (Utica, NY, 1819), p. iii.
5 *Ibid.*, p. 66.
6 *Ibid.*, p. 113.
7 *Ibid.*, p. 212.
8 *Ibid.*, pp. 214–17.
9 J. Morse, *American Geography* (Elizabethtown, 1789), p. v.
10 *Ibid.*, p. vii.
11 J. Freeman, *Remarks on The American Universal Geography* (Boston, 1793), p. 5.
12 J. Morse, *The American Universal Geography* (Boston, 1793), vol. 1, p. 551.
13 J. Morse, *In a Sermon exhibiting the Present Dangers and consequent Duties of the Citizens of the United States* (Charlestown, 1799), p. 15.
14 *Ibid.*, p. 16.
15 J. Morse, *A Report to The Secretary of War of The United States on Indian Affairs* (New Haven, 1822), p. 11.
16 *Ibid.*, p. 21.
17 *Ibid.*, p. 21.
18 *Ibid.*, p. 66.
19 *Ibid.*, Appendix, p. 2.

7 *A Sensible Foreigner*

1 J. Melish, *Geographical Description of the USA: with the contiguous British and Spanish possessions intended as an accompaniment to his map of these countries* (Philadelphia, 1816), p. 4.
2 There is very little written on Melish. A rare example is M. E. Wolfgang, 'John Melish: An Early American Demographer', *Pennsylvania Magazine*, 82 (1958), pp. 65–81.
3 J. Melish, *Travels in the United States of America in the Years 1806 & 1807, and 1809, 1810 and 1811* (Philadelphia, 1812), pp. ix–x.
4 *Ibid.*, p. 31.
5 *Ibid.*, p. 276.
6 'Review of Melish's Travels', *Port Folio* (February 1813), p. 23.
7 A. E. Bergh, ed., *The Writings of Thomas Jefferson* (Washington, DC, 1907), vol. 13, pp. 206–13.
8 Melish, *Travels in the United States*, p. 439.
9 J. Melish, *Information and Advice to Emigrants to the United States* (Philadelphia, 1819), p. i.
10 J. Melish, *Traveller's Directory Through The United States of America* (Philadelphia, 1816), pp. 34, 38.
11 Bergh, *Writings of Thomas Jefferson*, vol. 14, pp. 219–21.
12 This map and its various editions are discussed more fully in W. W. Ristow, 'John Melish and His Map of the United States', *Library of Congress Quarterly Journal of Current Acquisitions*, 19 (1961), pp. 1, 159–78.
13 Bergh, *Writings of Thomas Jefferson*, vol. 14.
14 Melish, *Geographical Description*, p. 4.
15 I have drawn heavily on R. R. John, *Spreading the News: The American Postal System from Franklin to Morse* (Cambridge, MA, 1995).
16 The information on the Scots Thistle Club is taken from their records, which are kept at the Balch Institute for Ethnic Studies, Philadelphia (ref. M92-19, three boxes, 1806–95).
17 J. Melish, *Views On Political Economy* (Philadelphia, 1822), p. 27.

8 *Mapmaking in Philadelphia*

1 S. A. Mitchell, *Accompaniment to Mitchell's Reference and Distance Map of The United States* (Philadelphia, 1835), p. 5.
2 J. M. Moak, *Philadelphia Mapmakers* (Philadelphia, 1976).
3 H. S. Tanner, *Memoir of The Recent Surveys, Observations and Internal Improvements in The United States*, 'List of Maps & Supplement' (Philadelphia, 1829), p. 6.
4 The slave population of 1820 is noted: Virginia had 425,153; South Carolina, 256,457; New York, 10,088; and New Hampshire, 0. In terms of urbanization, the states with the biggest cities were New York with 166,000 and Philadelphia with 151,871, while North Carolina had Raleigh with 6250. In terms of manufacturing, Pennsylvania had 60,215, New York, 60,038 and Mississippi, 650.
5 Tanner, *Memoir of The Recent Surveys*, pp. 4–6.
6 H. S. Tanner, *A Geographical and Statistical Account of the Epidemic Cholera from its Commencement in India to its Entrance Into the United States* (Philadelphia, 1832), p. iii.
7 Mitchell, *Accompaniment to Mitchell's Reference*, p. 5.

9 *Inscribing the National Landscape*

1 J. S. Wilson, *Annual Report of the General Land Office* (Washington, DC, 1868), p. 12.
2 *Ibid.*, p. 15.
3 *Ibid.*, p. 111.
4 *Ibid.* (1880), p. 31.
5 *Ibid.* (1867), p. 10.
6 *Ibid.* (1866), pp. 9–10.
7 *Ibid.* (1868), p. 12.
8 The role of the locators in one state, Montana, is described by Jonathan Raban in his evocative book, *Badland: An American Romance* (New York, 1996).

1 Instructions issued by Brigadier-General Humphreys, Chief of Military Engineers to Lieutenant George Wheeler, in a letter dated 23 March 1871. Cited in G. Wheeler, *United States Geographical Surveys West of the One Hundred Meridian*, vol. 1, *Geographical Report* (Washington, DC, 1889), p. 31.

2 A national survey of these state surveys is contained in A. A. Socolow, *The State Geological Surveys* (Grand Forks, ND, 1988).

3 D. D. Owen, *Report of a Geological Survey of Wisconsin, Iowa and Minnesota* (Philadelphia, 1852).

4 *Ibid.*, p. 185.

5 *Ibid.*, pp. xxii–xxiii.

6 *Ibid.*, p. xxiv.

7 *Ibid.*, p. xxiv.

8 King gained much of his experience in J. D. Whitney's State Geological Survey of California (1860–1870). The highest point of land in the 48 coterminous states is aptly named after the leader of this bellwether survey.

9 Wheeler, *Report Upon United States Geographical Surveys*, vol. 1, p. 762.

10 *Ibid.*, vol. 1, p. 34

11 *Ibid.*, vol. 1, p. 173.

12 *Ibid.*, vol. 1, p. 223.

13 G. Wheeler, *Topographical Atlas* (New York, 1874).

14 F. Hayden, 'The Wonders of the West', *Scribner's*, lll (1872), pp. 388–96.

15 *The Yellowstone National Park* (New York, 1876). Described by Prof. F. Hayden (geologist-in-charge of US Government exploring expeditions) and illustrated by Thomas Moran (artist to the 1871 expedition).

16 Hayden, *Yellowstone National Park*, pp. 1, 4, 28.

17 F. V. Hayden, *Geological and Geographical Atlas of Colorado* (Washington, DC, 1877).

18 F. Hayden, *The Great West* (Philadelphia, 1880).

19 *Ibid.*, p. 209.

20 J. W. Powell, *The Exploration of the Colorado River and Its Canyons* (New York, 1895), p. 119.

21 I have drawn heavily on the work of Debora Ridge and especially her paper 'Science and Art Meet in the Parlor: The Role of Popular Magazine Illustration in the Pictorial Record of the "Great Surveys"' (presented at a conference of the American Philosophical Society entitled 'Surveying the Record: North American Scientific Exploration to 1900', 14–16 March 1997, Benjamin Franklin Hall, Philadelphia).

22 J. Prescott, ed., *The Unspoiled West: The Western Landscape as Seen by its Greatest Photographers* (New York, 1995).

23 *Exploration of the Colorado River of the West and Its Tributaries* (Washington, 1875).

24 Ron Tyler, 'Illustrated Government Publications Relating to the American West' (paper presented at a conference of the American Philosophical Society entitled 'Surveying the Record: North American Scientific Exploration to 1900', 14–16 March 1997, Benjamin Franklin Hall, Philadelphia).

25 See B. Latour, *Laboratory Life: The Social Construction of Scientific Facts* (Beverly Hills, CA, 1979); M. Lynch and S. Woolgar, eds, *Representation in Scientific Practice* (Cambridge, MA, 1990); M. Serres, *Conversation on Science, Culture and Time* (Ann Arbor, 1995).

26 Powell also wanted the abolition of the General Land Office as well as the Wheeler and Hayden surveys. His plan to place the surveying of the public domain in federal hands was defeated by the Western representatives in Congress.

11 *Constructing the National Community*

1 H. F. Walling, *Atlas of the State of Michigan* (Detroit, 1873), p. 2.

2 See the section on Robert Pearsall Smith in W. W. Ristow, *American Maps and Mapmakers* (Detroit, 1985), pp. 339–54.

3 A. T. Andreas, *An Historical Atlas of Lee County Iowa* (Chicago, 1874).

4 Louis H. Everts was a prolific publisher of county atlases. Born in 1836 in New York, he moved in 1851 to Illinois, where his father was a farmer. He formed a partnership with

Thomas Thompson soon after the ending of the Civil War; together, they produced a number of county atlases in Illinois and Iowa. Other atlases were produced under the names of Everts (Fairfield, Licking and Medina counties in Ohio), Everts and Kirk (Nebraska), Everts and Stewart (county atlases in Pennsylvania, Michigan and New Jersey), Everts, Ensign and Everts (Broome, Cortland, Genesee and Yates counties in New York), and Everts, Baskin and Stewart (county atlases in Illinois and Wisconsin). Most of these atlases were produced in the 1870s. Others produced by Everts include *Official State Atlas of Kansas* (1887) and *New Century Atlas of Counties of New York* (1911).

5 *Atlas of DeKalb County, Indiana* (Chicago, 1880).
6 One exception was Hayden's *Geological and Geographical Atlas of Colorado*. Published by the Department of the Interior in 1877, it is more concerned with topographic mapping and geological sections than with individual counties. It is interesting, however, to compare the quality of this atlas, an expensive, beautiful work underwritten by the federal government, with the more prosaic and utilitarian state atlases produced by private companies in a competitive market.
7 *Atlas of the State of Illinois* (Philadelphia, 1870), p. 1.
8 Another example is Finland. The *Atlas of Finland*, sponsored by the Finnish Geographical Society, was first published in 1799.
9 A good example is the different ethnic/racial classifications used in the census and how they have varied over time. I discussed this more fully in Chapter 15 of my 1996 book, *The Urban Order* (Cambridge, MA, and Oxford).
10 Quoted in US Census Office, *Statistical Atlas of the United States*, compiled by Francis A. Walker (New York, 1874).
11 F. Walker, *The Making of the Nation 1783–1817* (New York, 1899), p. 264.
12 F. Walker, *The Indian Question* (Boston, 1874) p. 17.
13 *Ibid.*, p. 76.

12 *Locating the National Economy*

1 A. A. Grant, *Grant's Bankers' and Brokers' Railroad Atlas* (New York, 1887), p. iv.
2 C. H. Peters, 'Rand MacNally and Company–Printers, Publishers, Cartographers: A Study in Nineteenth-Century Mass Marketing', Master's Paper, Graduate Library School, University of Chicago, 1981.
3 Successive presidents of the company have been Andrew McNally (1900–1933); Andrew McNally II (1933–48); Andrew McNally III (1948–74); and Andrew McNally IV (1974–97).
4 Rand McNally, *Business Atlas* (Chicago, 1890), p. 3.
5 Grant, *Grant's Bankers' and Brokers' Railroad Atlas*.

13 *A Postcolonial Postscript*

1 Lieutenant Gouverneur K. Warren in a letter to Captain Humphreys, 1 March 1857. One reader of this mansucript objected to the modernist assumption of this quote. Sometimes, irony is lost on the more dull-witted.
2 John Wesley Powell, *The Exploration of the Colorado River and its Canyons*, reprint of 1895 edn (New York, 1961), pp. 299–300.
3 Morgan was a major influence in the development of anthropology, especially social anthropology and the study of the role of kinship systems in social structure. Lévi Strauss described him as a genius. Morgan also influenced Marx and Engels. In his extended essay – *The Origin of The Family, Private Property and The State* (1884) – Engels described Morgan's *Ancient Society* (1877) as one of the 'epoch-making works of our time'. Engels even subtitled his work *In The Light of the Researches of Lewis H. Morgan*. Morgan's developmental model of savagery-to-barbarism-to-civilization echoed Marx and Engels's evolutionary model of society. Engels, and indeed Marx, saw his work as a compelling example of historical materialism.

Select Bibliography

Arner, R., *Dobson's Encyclopedia: The Publisher, Text and Publication of America's First Britannic 1789–1803* (Philadelphia, 1991)

Barbour, V., *Capitalism in Amsterdam in the Seventeenth Century*, The Johns Hopkins University Studies in Historical and Political Science Series 67, no. 1 (Baltimore, 1950)

Bartlett, R. A., *Great Surveys of the American West* (Norman, 1962)

Black, J., *Maps and History: Constructing Images of the Past* (New Haven, 1997)

——, *Maps and Politics* (London, 1997; reprint Chicago, 1998)

Bridge, R., 'The Oneida Land Claims: A Struggle for Native American Sovereignty', MA Thesis, Syracuse University, 1997

Brown, R. H., 'The American Geographies of Jedidiah Morse', *Annals of Association of American Geographers*, 31 (1941), pp. 145–217

Cazier, L., *Surveys and Surveyors of the Public Domain, 1785–1975* (Washington, DC, 1976)

Chazanof, W., *Joseph Ellicott and the Holland Land Company: The Opening of Western New York* (Syracuse, 1970)

Cohen, P. E., and R. T. Augustyn, *Manhattan in Maps, 1527–1995* (New York, 1997)

Conzen, M., ed., *Chicago Mapmakers: Essays on the Rise of the City's Map Trade* (Chicago, 1984)

Conzen, M. P., 'The All-American County Atlas: Styles of Commercial Landownership Mapping and American Culture', in J. A. Wolter and R. E. Grim, eds, *Images of the World: The Atlas Through History* (Washington, DC, 1997), pp. 331–65

——, 'The County Landownership Map in America: Its Commercial Development and Social Transformation 1814–1939', *Imago Mundi*, 36 (1984), pp. 9–31

——, 'North American County Maps and Atlases', in D. Busisseret, ed., *From Sea Charts to Satellite Images: Interpreting North American History Through Maps* (Chicago, 1990), pp. 18–21

Cosgrove, D., ed., *Mappings* (London, 1999)

Cumming, William P., *British Maps of Colonial America* (Chicago, 1974)

Donck, A van der, *A Description of the New Netherlands* (first Dutch edn 1656; first English edn 1841; Syracuse, 1968)

Dunn, S. W., *The Mohicans and Their Land 1609–1730* (Fleischmanns, NY, 1994)

East, W. G., 'An Eighteenth-Century Geographer: William Guthrie of Brechin', *Scottish Geographical Magazine*, 72 (1956), pp. 32–7

Edney, M., 'Politics, Science and Government Mapping Policy in the United States, 1800–1925', *American Cartographer*, 13 (1986), pp. 295–306

Flick, A. C., ed., *History of the State of New York*, vol. 1: *Wigwam and Bouwerie* (New York, 1933)

Gannett, H., *Statistical Atlas of the United States* (Washington, DC, 1898)

Gates, P. W., *History of Public Land Law Development* (Washington, DC, 1968)

Geyl, P., *The Netherlands in the Seventeenth Century* (New York, 1961)

Goetzmann, W. H., *Army Exploration in the American West 1803–1863* (New Haven, 1959)

——, *Exploration and Empire: The Explorer and the Scientist in the Winning of the West* (New York, 1966)

Goss, J., *Blaeu's The Grand Atlas of the 17th-Century World* (New York, 1991)

Graymont, B., *The Iroquois in the American Revolution* (Syracuse, 1972)

Green, J., *Mathew Carey: Publisher and Patriot* (Philadelphia, 1985)

Grim, R., 'Maps of the Township and Range System', in D. Buisseret, ed., *From Sea Charts to Satellite Images: Interpreting North American History Through Maps* (Chicago, 1990), pp. 89–110

Halsey, Francis W., *The Old New York Frontier* (New York, 1901)

Harley, J. B., 'New England Cartography and the Native American', in E. Baker *et al.*, eds, *American Beginnings* (Lincoln, 1994), pp. 287–314

——, and David Woodward, eds, *History of Cartography* (Chicago, 1987–)

——, B. B. Petchenik and L. W. Towner, *Mapping the American Revolutionary War* (Chicago, 1978)

Hauptman, L. M., *Conspiracy of Interests: Iroquois Dispossession and The Rise of New York State* (Syracuse, 1998)

——, *The Iroquois Indians and the Rise of the Empire State* (Syracuse, 1999)

——, *The Iroquois Struggle for Survival: World War ll to Red Power* (Syracuse, 1986)

Heidt, W., Jr, *Simeon DeWitt* (Ithaca, NY, 1968)

Hewes, F. W., and H. Gannett, *Scribner's Statistical; Atlas of the United States* (New York, 1883)

Jameson, J. F., ed., *Narratives of New Netherland, 1609–1664* (New York, 1909; facsimile reprint Bowie, MD, 1990)

Jennings, Francis, ed., *The History and Culture of Iroquois Diplomacy* (Syracuse, 1985)

Johnson, H. B., *Order upon the Land: The US Rectangular Survey and the Upper Mississippi Country* (New York, 1976)

——, 'Toward a National Landscape', in M. P. Conzen, ed., *The Making of the National Landscape* (New York and London, 1994), pp. 127–45

Kammen, Michael, *Colonial New York* (New York, 1975)

Karrow, R. W., Jr, 'George M. Wheeler and the Geographical Surveys West of the 100th Meridian, 1869–1879', in D. P. Koepp, ed., *Exploration and Mapping of the American West* (Chicago, 1986), pp. 121–58

Keates, J. S., *Understanding Maps*, 2nd edn (London, 1996)

Kelsay, I. T., *Joseph Brant 1743–1807: Man of Two Worlds* (Syracuse, 1984)

Keys, Alice M., *Cadwallader Colden: A Representative Eighteenth Century Official* (New York, 1967)

King, G., *Mapping Reality: An Exploration of Cultural Cartographies* (New York, 1996)

Klooster, W., *The Dutch in The Americas* (Providence, 1997)

Lewis, G. M., ed., *Cartographic Encounters: Perspectives on Native-American Mapmaking and Map Use* (Chicago, 1998)

MacEachren, A. M., *How Maps Work* (New York and London, 1995)

Mano, J. M., 'History in the Mapping: Simeon DeWitt's Legacy in New York State Cartography', *Proceedings of the Middle States Division of the Association of American Geographers* (1990), pp. 27–34

——, 'The Iroquois and New York State: Two Centuries of Broken Treaties and Map Lies', *Middle States Geographer*, 26 (1993), pp. 35–40

Martin, G. J., "The Emergence and Development of Geographic Thought in New England', *Economic Geography* (1998 [extra issue]), pp. 1–13

Merwick, D., *Possessing Albany: 1630–1710: The Dutch and English Experiences* (Cambridge, 1990)

Middleton, R., *Colonial America* (Oxford and Cambridge, MA, 1996)

Mitchell, John, *The Contest in America between Great Britain and France* (London, 1757; reprint 1965)

Moak, J. M., *Philadelphia Mapmakers* (Philadelphia, 1976)

Monmonier, M., *Drawing the Line: Tales of Maps and Cartocontroversy* (New York, 1995)

——, *How to Lie with Maps* (Chicago, 1991)

——, 'The Rise of the National Atlas', in J. A. Wolter and R. E. Grim, eds, *Images of The World: The Atlas Through History* (Washington, DC, 1997), pp. 369–99

Morgan, L. H., *League of the Iroquois* (originally published New York, 1851 as *League of the Ho-de-no-sau-nee or Iroquois*) (New York, 1962)

Morse, J. K., *Jedidiah Morse: A Champion of New England Orthodoxy* (New York, 1939)

Moss, R. J., *The Life of Jedidiah Morse: A Station of Peculiar Exposure* (Knoxville, TN, 1995)

Munroe, J. P., *How to Lie with Maps* (Chicago, 1991)

——, *A Life of Francis Amasa Walker* (New York, 1923)

Norton, T. E., *The Fur Trade in Colonial New York* (Madison, 1974)

O'Callaghan, E. B., *Documentary History of the State of New York*, 4 vols (Albany, 1850–51)

——, *Documents Relative to the Colonial History of the State of New York*, 15 vols (Albany, 1853–87)

——, *History of New Netherland; or New York under the Dutch*, 2 vols (New York, 1848)

Pattison, W., *Beginnings of the American Rectangular System, 1784–1800*, Department of Geography Research Paper 50 (Chicago, 1957)

Peters, C. H., 'Rand MacNally and Company – Printers, Publishers, Cartographers: A Study in Nineteenth-Century Mass Marketing', Master's Paper, University of Chicago, 1981

Phillips, J. W., *Jedidiah Morse and New England Congregationalism* (New Brunswick, NJ, 1983)

Powell, J. W., *The Exploration of the Colorado River and Its Canyons* (first published 1895 as *Canyons of the Colorado*) (New York, 1961)

Price, E. T., *Dividing the Land: Early American Beginnings of Our Private Property Mosaic* (Chicago, 1995)

Price, J. L., *Holland and the Dutch Republic in the Seventeenth Century* (Oxford, 1994)

Rand McNally Business Atlas (Chicago and Skokie, IL, 1877–)

Regin, D., *Traders, Artists, Burghers: A Cultural History of Amsterdam in the 17th Century* (Amsterdam, 1976)

Reinhartz, D., *The Cartographer and the Literati: Herman Moll and His Intellectual Circle* (Lampeter, 1997)

Rink, O. A., *Holland on the Hudson: An Economic and Social History of Dutch New York* (Ithaca, NY, and London, 1986)

Ristow, W. W., *American Maps and Mapmakers: Commercial Cartography in the Nineteenth Century* (Detroit, 1985)

——, 'John Melish and His Map of the United States', *Library of Congress Quarterly Journal of Current Acquisitions*, 19 (1961), pp. 159–78

Rohrborough, M. J., *The Land Office Business* (1968; Belmont, DC, 1990)

Schama, S., *The Embarrassment of Riches* (London, 1987)

Schein, R., 'A Historical Geography of Central New York: Patterns and Processes of Colonization on the New Military Tract 1782–1820', PhD diss., Syracuse University, 1989

Schmidt, B., 'Mapping and Empire: Cartographic and Colonial Rivalry in Seventeenth Century Dutch and English America', *William and Mary Quarterly*, 54 (1997), pp. 549–78

Schubert, F. N., 'A Tale of Two Cartographers: Emory, Warren and Their Maps of the Trans-Mississippi West', in D. P. Koepp, ed., *Exploration and Mapping of the American West* (Chicago, 1986), pp. 51–60

Schwartz, Seymour I., and Ralph E. Ehrenberg, *The Mapping of America* (New York, 1980)

Shattuck, G., *The Oneida Land Claims: A Legal History* (Syracuse, 1991)

Snow, Dean, *The Iroquois* (Oxford and Cambridge, MA, 1994)

Snyder, C. M., *Red and White on the New York Frontier* (Harrison, NY, 1978)

Snyder, J. P., 'The Erskine-DeWitt Maps', *Surveying and Mapping*, 39 (1979), pp. 33–48

Sprague, W. B., *The Life of Jedidiah Morse D.D.* (New York, 1874)

Stegner, W., *Beyond the Hundredth Meridian: John Wesley Powell and the Second Opening of the West* (Boston, 1953)

Stephenson, R., *Land Ownership Maps: A Checklist of Nineteenth Century United States County Maps in the Library of Congress* (Washington, DC, 1967)

Stewart, L. O., *Public Land Surveys: History, Instructions, Methods* (Ames, IA, 1935)

Stokes, I.N.P., *The Iconography of Manhattan Island, 1498–1909*, 6 vols (New York, 1915–1929)

Sullivan, J., ed., *History of New York State 1523–1927*, vol. 1 (New York, 1927)

Taylor, A., *William Cooper's Town* (New York, 1995)

Tebbel, J., *A History of Book Publishing in the United States*, vol. 1: *The Creation of an Industry 1639–1865* (New York and London, 1972)

Thompson, J. H., ed., *Geography of New York State* (Syracuse, 1966)

Thrower, N.J.W., 'The County Atlas of the United States', *Surveying and Mapping*, 21 (1961), pp. 365–73

Trelease, A. W., *Indian Affairs in Colonial New York* (Ithaca, NY, 1960)

Turnbull, D., *Maps Are Territories* (Chicago, 1993)

Van der Zee, H., and B. van der Zee, *A Sweet and Alien Land* (New York, 1978)

Vecsey, C., and W. A. Starna, eds, *Iroquois Land Claims* (Syracuse, 1988)

Walker, Francis A., compiler, *Statistical Atlas of the United States* (New York, 1874)

Wheat, C. I., *Mapping the Transmississippi West*, 6 vols (San Francisco, 1960)

White, C. A., *A History of the Rectangular Survey System* (Washington, DC, 1983)

Wilson, C. W., *The Dutch Republic and the Civilization of the Seventeenth Century* (London, 1968)

Wolfgang, M. E., 'John Melish: An Early American Demographer', *The Pennsylvania Magazine*, 82 (1958), pp. 65–81

Wood, D., *The Power of Maps* (London, 1993)

Woodward, D., *The All-American Map* (Chicago, 1977)

Wyckoff, W., *The Developer's Frontier: The Making of the Western New York Landscape* (New Haven, 1988)

Zandvliet, K., *Mapping for Money: Maps, Plans and Topographic Paintings and Their Role in Dutch Overseas Expansion During the 16th and 17th Centuries* (Amsterdam, 1998)

Index